The Semiotics of Banknotes and Coins

Bloomsbury Advances in Semiotics

Series Editor: Gregory Paschalidis

Formerly Continuum Advances in Semiotics.

Bloomsbury Advances in Semiotics publishes original works applying semiotic approaches to linguistics and non-verbal productions, social institutions and discourses, embodied cognition and communication, and the new virtual realities of the digital age. It covers topics such as socio-semiotics, evolutionary semiotics, game theory, cultural and literary studies, human-computer interactions, and the challenging new dimensions of human networking afforded by social websites.

Titles published in the series:

The Semiotics of the COVID-19 Pandemic, Sebastián Moreno Barreneche
Semiotics with a Conscience, Marcel Danesi
Developing a Neo-Peircean Approach to Signs, Tony Jappy
The Social Semiotics of Populism, Sebastián Moreno Barreneche
Systemic Semiotics, Piotr Sadowski
The Semiotics of Architecture in Video Games, Gabriele Aroni
Semiotics of the Christian Imagination, Domenico Pietropaolo

Computational Semiotics, Jean-Guy Meunier
Cognitive Semiotics, Per Aage Brandt
The Semiotics of Caesar Augustus, Elina Pyy
The Social Semiotics of Tattoos, Chris William Martin
The Semiotics of X, Jamin Pelkey
The Semiotics of Light and Shadows, Piotr Sadowski
Music as Multimodal Discourse, edited by Lyndon C. S. Way and Simon McKerrell
Peirce's Twenty-Eight Classes of Signs and the Philosophy of Representation, Tony Jappy
The Semiotics of Emoji, Marcel Danesi
Semiotics and Pragmatics of Stage Improvisation, Domenico Pietropaolo
Critical Semiotics, Gary Genosko
The Languages of Humor, edited by Arie Sover
Semiotics of Happiness, Ashley Frawley
Warning Signs, Marcel Danesi
Semiotics of Religion, Robert A. Yelle
Computable Bodies, Josh Berson
The Semiotics of Clowns and Clowning, Paul Bouissac
The Semiotics of Che Guevara, Maria-Carolina Cambre
The Visual Language of Comics, Neil Cohn
The Language of War Monuments, David Machin and Gill Abousnnouga
A Buddhist Theory of Semiotics, Fabio Rambelli
Introduction to Peircean Visual Semiotics, Tony Jappy

The Semiotics of Banknotes and Coins

Reading Contemporary Currency Design

Sebastián Moreno Barreneche

BLOOMSBURY ACADEMIC
LONDON • NEW YORK • OXFORD • NEW DELHI • SYDNEY

BLOOMSBURY ACADEMIC
Bloomsbury Publishing Plc, 50 Bedford Square, London, WC1B 3DP, UK
Bloomsbury Publishing Inc, 1359 Broadway, New York, NY 10018, USA
Bloomsbury Publishing Ireland, 29 Earlsfort Terrace, Dublin 2, D02 AY28, Ireland

BLOOMSBURY, BLOOMSBURY ACADEMIC and the Diana logo are trademarks of Bloomsbury Publishing Plc

First published in Great Britain 2025

Cover design: Jade Barnett
Cover image © Peter Dazeley/Getty Images

A catalogue record for this book is available from the British Library.

A catalog record for this book is available from the Library of Congress.

ISBN: HB: 978-1-3504-5136-0
ePDF: 978-1-3504-5137-7
eBook: 978-1-3504-5138-4

Series: Bloomsbury Advances in Semiotics

Typeset by Newgen KnowledgeWorks Pvt. Ltd., Chennai, India

For product safety related questions contact productsafety@bloomsbury.com.

To find out more about our authors and books visit www.bloomsbury.com and sign up for our newsletters.

Contents

Figures

Tables

Preface

In September 2024, I spent one week in Warsaw, Poland, attending the 16th World Congress of Semiotics. During that week, I did not hold in my hands any banknote or coin of the *złoty*, Poland's official and national currency. To exchange currency and pay for my purchases, I used a digital app. Even if I had not had such an app, I could probably have survived the entire week paying with plastic cards. That is, my week would have been either way cashless.

While walking around Warsaw, I ended up in the building of the Polish Security Printing Works – Polska Wytwórnia Papierów Wartościowych (PWPW) – the entity responsible for printing the banknotes of the *złoty* on behalf of the National Bank of Poland. At the time of my visit, the security fence surrounding the building displayed panels presenting the PWPW's work over the years, including the design of the *złoty* banknotes. This is how I encountered the beautiful designs used in the five banknotes of the Polish currency currently circulating in the country.

This anecdote illustrates one of the causes why I felt that writing this book could be an interesting contribution to the social sciences and the humanities. We live in a historical moment in which banknotes and coins, the two material objects that compose the official currencies of almost every country around the world, are tending to circulate less and less, and even disappear. Because of this change, the space that banknotes and coins provide for people to encounter social discourses about the nation and the state is also being lost. Sooner than later, the material objects that we usually carry with us to pay for the things we consume might not be used anymore. At least, not in the form we have used them for the past several decades. Once these two technologies are abandoned – as many technologies were throughout history – something else will disappear with them, something located beyond the mere economic function that banknotes and coins have and that relates to issues of culture, discourse and identity.

To begin approaching the subject matter of this book, I invite you to get your wallet and take out the banknotes and coins that you store there. This will only be possible if you store any banknotes and coins in your wallet at all, and not only plastic cards, as is becoming more and more frequent throughout the world. Besides, the availability of banknotes and coins in your wallet will probably depend on the country you live in – while in some countries cash is still broadly required and used for economic transactions, in others the cashless option is almost ubiquitous.

In case you could find any banknotes and coins in your wallet, look at them for a minute. Have you ever looked at them like this? Do you recognize the images you are looking at? If you see the portrait of a person, do you know who he or she is? Do you have an idea why he or she might have been chosen to adorn a piece of the currency you are holding? Do you agree that this person is relevant enough in your country's cultural memory as to be included in the design of the banknote or coin you are looking at? If what you see is an animal, have you seen it directly while living in the country? Would you agree that this animal is typical of your country? If what you see is a landscape, a building, a monument or an archaeological site, do you know it? Have you been there? Does it play a relevant role in the narratives of your country? Moreover, how does the banknote or coin you are holding include information about the state producing it? Does it include the full name of the country that issued it? Can you recognize the symbols referring to the state included in the design? Can you remember the design elements included in other banknotes and coins of the same currency system? If so, can you remember if there is any relation between the front and the back sides of each piece? Finally, is there anything that you are seeing for the first time in the banknote or coin you are looking at now? (Apologies to readers based in countries where the euro is used, since only a few of these questions are relevant in this case.)

What you have just done is what we will do in this book. In what follows, we will focus on a very reduced portion of the social world: the banknotes and coins that are currently used in a selection of countries. In our attempt to understand how these material and tangible objects produced and regulated by states produce specific effects of sense thanks to the intervention of discourse, we will use semiotics as the main theoretical and analytical perspective.

In what follows, we will work with banknotes and coins, two objects that belong to the economic domain of life. However, we will not approach them with an interest in their economic nature of function, which certainly can be an object of interest for semioticians given that money and currency are sign systems. Neither will we deal with sociological, political or philosophical approaches to money and currency, which are also of interest for the social sciences and humanities and which scholars from these disciplines have already studied. Our interest is set in the imprint that discourses of the nation and the state leave in currency design.

The research programme guiding this book is relatively straightforward and simple: we will use the imagery we found on banknotes and coins as the entry point to access the semiospheres within which they were produced. In doing so, we aim at shedding light on how banknotes and coins are culturally and discourse-shaped material objects that function as carriers of meaning and sense. By studying visual texts, we aim at understanding the functioning of culture and, with it, of discourse. To achieve this goal, we propose specific analyses of sets of banknotes and coins and use visual and cultural semiotics to do so.

I cannot remember when, how or why my interest in currency iconography and design awoke. It might be related to the circulation of currency that I was exposed to as a child growing up in Uruguay, where both the Uruguayan peso and the US dollar were used – and still are. Perhaps this coexistence of two currency systems provided me with a point of comparison between different designs, unlike what occurs in countries where only the local currency circulates.

Family trips to neighbouring countries such as Argentina and Brazil might also have awakened my interest for the topic. These trips exposed me to the diversity of currencies and, particularly, currency design. As children, we normally take many things of the world we inhabit for granted and we only discover that they are not a given when we experience the world outside the environments that are familiar to us. Realizing that the Uruguayan peso was only valid within the Uruguayan territory (and perhaps some border regions), that neighbouring countries had other currencies that could be exchanged for the peso, and that the value of a product could be mathematically 'translated' from one currency to another were major discoveries for me.

As a child, I could also probably easily realize how the banknotes and coins I saw in countries other than the one I lived in usually showed a visual consistency and unicity that allowed me to identify them as part of a single visual system, even though this happened without my being conscious of the systemic nature that is common to find in a country's currency thanks to the conventions that are constitutive of the discursive genre. As we shall see throughout the book, design elements such as shapes, colour, typeface, positioning of design elements in the space delimited by the frame, and repetition of signs, all serve to produce a sense effect linked to the visual unicity of a series.

In my previous two books, I used semiotics to study populism and the Covid-19 pandemic. To work with these two major phenomena of our day and age, it was necessary to construct the object of study and to propose analyses that could inform and sustain my arguments about signification and sense around them.

The nature of this book is different. In a way, it is less ambitious, simpler and more straightforward than the two previous ones.

However, this statement does not mean that the work presented in what follows lacks complexity. Studying currency design using a semiotic perspective requires more than working descriptively with what we see in the units that compose a specific country's corpus – that is, in the banknotes and coins being currently used in that country. To properly grasp the sense they convey, as well as the meanings and discourses they express, it is necessary to *establish relations* with other texts and discourses circulating in that semiosphere. Examples of these other texts are the designs of older banknotes and coins, symbols of the state, or what could have been used instead of what was actually used to provide a banknote or coin with its identity. In this sense, the discursive genre of currency design is not an exception to a major principle governing the practice of semioticians interested in culture and society: value and sense are relational and depend on oppositions with other units of the system.

My work with currency design began in 2022. Since then, I have discussed the ideas presented in the book in a number of academic events, such as the 50th Congress of the Associazione Italiana Studi Semiotici (AISS – Italian Association for Semiotics Studies), which took place in Palermo, Italy, in December 2022; the Fifth International Conference on Semiotics of Culture and Visual Communication, organized by the Cyprus Semiotics Circle in Limassol, Cyprus, in June 2024; the 16th World Congress of Semiotics, organized by the International Association for Semiotic Studies (IASS) in Warsaw, Poland, in September 2024; and one session of the Smart Semiotics webinar, organized by Paul Bouissac in March 2025. Moreover, a handful of papers on the topic were published in journals such as *Cuadernos del CLAEH* (Uruguay), *Estudios Sociales* (Argentina), *E|C* (Italy) and *Inmediaciones de la Comunicación* (Uruguay).

I would like to thank Fernando Andacht, Kristian Bankov, David Blaazer, Alexandre Marcelo Bueno, Paul Cobley, Mariano Dagatti, Maria Giulia Dondero, Tiziana Migliore, Alain Perusset, Heinz Tschachler and Evripides Zantides for their valuable comments after reading parts of the manuscript. As is usually the case, feedback and comments from colleagues not only help ensure that the text is as accurate, clear and reader-friendly as possible but also make the adventure of writing a book less solitary.

1

The Social Relevance of Currency, or Why Study Banknotes and Coins

1.1 The relevance of currency beyond economics

Money and currency are two social institutions that we intuitively tend to locate within the economic domain. This intuition is not inaccurate, since it was due to economic reasons that humans created money and currency as social constructs that facilitate their practices and economic interactions, such as trading, saving and investing. Hence, money and currency are two good examples of the many social arrangements and institutions that originate in the functioning of the social realm. Particularly, they are good examples of institutions grounded on one functioning that is dominant in our day and age: capitalism.

As an economic system, capitalism involves production, consumption, exchange and trade of goods and services at the local, regional and global levels. Social actors – both individual and collective, physical and juridical, public and private – are entangled in these activities and, in doing so, sustain and reproduce the system.

As time passed, humans created technological innovations aimed at simplifying these activities. Usually these innovations involve a change regarding the technologies previously used. Numerous economic institutions that we nowadays take for granted, such as markets, banks, loans, credits, mortgages, stocks, investment funds, bonds, money and currency, among many others, were created at some point of history for the capitalist system to function more efficiently and effectively. These are all technological innovations originating in the economic domain of social life.

Money, monetary forms and monetary elements are innovations of this type, even if they are a constitutive part of how we live our lives and seem as if they were self-evident or given. Nowadays, for almost everything we consume, we are expected to pay money in exchange (unless we make another type of arrangement, which will probably include some type of *relation* between what we receive and what we give in exchange). However, apart from some very exceptional cases, we use money to pay for what we consume. Also, money is what we receive monthly in exchange for our work when engaged in a professional activity. Salaries are an addition of units – dollars, euros and so on – that belong to a specific monetary system and that function as a compensation for our work. This compensation is not anything natural but the result of contingent historical processes that established a code between effort (work) and money as its reward. Other social practices created by humans such as playing lottery or tipping someone providing us with a service also involve money.

Examples like these, among others, evidence a process of *monetization*, which sociologist Viviana Zelizer (2017: 18) defines as 'the increase in the portion of all goods and services bought and sold by means of money'. As a social process linked to the modern and contemporary ages, it involves money being used as a means that mediates social exchanges. It is probably in this sense that historian Carl Wennerlind (2001: 557) sees money as a social relation that mediates interactions between people and that is 'part of an elaborate web of dynamic social structural conditions within which people act and interact'.

Money and currency are two central components of any contemporary economic system. Therefore, they are certainly objects of interest for economists, in their attempts to describe and explain the economic dimension of human life. However, historians, sociologists, geographers, anthropologists and philosophers have also occupied themselves with these social institutions and their effects. Examples of non-economic issues related to money and currency are how the possession of money can express wealth and social status, how we tend to measure the value of things depending on how much we are expected to pay for them – think of luxury brands, characterized by a relationship of mutual determination between price and value – or the instrumentalization of human relations through money, making them more impersonal.

Money and currency are so pervasive in our everyday lives that we usually take them for granted. This means that, while using them, we are not fully aware of their nature as social institutions that were constructed at some point in history and that are sustained through human practice and collective belief. As philosopher John Searle (1995: 22) writes, 'people may use money to buy and sell without thinking about the logical structure of imposed function'.

Moreover, we sometimes forget that the banknotes and coins we take for granted as part of economic practice were not the form currency always had. For many of us, banknotes and coins 'are there', as toilet paper and napkins are, to fulfil a specific function of the many we need to fulfil to successfully operate in our daily lives. We tend to use these material objects without thinking about their nature or the institutions, beliefs and practices sustaining them. When we came into the world, they were already there, and that is why we see them as part of the 'furniture' of the world we inhabit.

However, banknotes and coins were not always part of the everyday lives of individuals. While coins have existed since antiquity, currency in the form of banknotes was only possible after the invention of printing (Weatherford, 1997). Hence, the possibility of a material object depends on specific technological innovations. Currency systems composed of banknotes and coins became the standard form of currency only recently in history, namely when national states in Europe actively implemented strategies to construct their spheres of action, sovereignty and identities *in national terms*, thanks to the establishment of differences with other national states (Hobsbawm, 1991; Gilbert, 1998; Gilbert and Helleiner, 1999; Gimeno-Martínez, 2016). Hence, it was a specific and contingent historical process – the creation of national states in the eighteenth and nineteenth centuries – what gave certain material objects – banknotes and coins – the role and relevance they have today. However, as scholars have shown, these two material objects existed long before the emergence of the national states sustaining them.

Particularly, we do not usually think about the currency we use in our everyday life *in semiotic terms*. In our day and age, currency consists of a selection of two material supports – paper money and a variety of metals – that are not valuable intrinsically but that we use as carriers of economic value, a type of value that is abstract, socially defined and dependent on specific regulations. In this sense, the main purpose of banknotes and coins, which are not intrinsically valuable as material objects, is to *stand for*, *store* and *express* a specific type of value – *economic* value – making it easy and practical to handle.

Throughout the years, the practice of using banknotes and coins as currency stabilized and, in 2025, is still dominant around the world. This is partly the case because we still live in a world composed of nations, which are the basis for the administrative units that we call 'countries'. In standard circumstances, every individual is a citizen of a specific country, and this enables us to have a passport issued by that country, pay taxes there, being economically supported by that country in cases of vulnerability and so on.

However, at the end of the twentieth century, specific trends started developing already that are becoming dominant as time passes. Thanks to technological developments, over the past decades money has become more virtual and less material, responding to a process of technological change that involves a *dematerialization* of money (Gorin, 1989). This process consists in replacing the tangible, offline, material support of money with immaterial, intangible, online options. As anthropologist Jack Weatherford (1997: xii) argued in the late 1990s – that is, when these changes were beginning – 'in the realms of cyberspace, money is now being reinvented as a free-floating force that can appear instantaneously anywhere in the world in any amount'. In 2025, this statement is a good description of how societies and individuals deal with money and monetary transactions.

The process of dematerialization of money is a major change in the nature and essence of money as we know it, which has historically been strongly dependent on its material support, such as commodities, seashells, precious metals and, more recently, banknotes and coins. If throughout history people were used to the possibility of touching and manipulating their wealth through tangible objects that function as a vehicle for it, now their beliefs and standards seem to accept the virtuality of money, for example, as intangible numbers that express credit in a bank account.

The challenges that the Covid-19 pandemic posed to societies throughout the world certainly fostered the passage from the material option to the virtual. During the years of the pandemic, banknotes and coins were regarded as possible vectors of contagion thanks to their material nature because they circulated between different people. Therefore, many organizations began implementing cashless policies, reducing the circulation of banknotes and coins.[1]

As a social institution that mediates interactions between social actors, money can take different forms. As argued above, the practice of carrying banknotes and coins with us might not be common in the future. We live in a historical moment in which cash is receding and might even disappear to be replaced by other types of currencies. Banknotes and coins might soon be a thing of the past, accessible only in museums, archives and flea markets.

The dominant and standard form that money took over the past couple of centuries was that of an *official* and *national* currency, that is, one created, managed and regulated by the state. Contingently, the modern and contemporary currencies that exist around the world are systems composed of two elements: banknotes and coins. While banknotes are used as the material support for the units of the system expressing the higher values, coins are used for the lower ones. As a result, people are less worried when losing a coin.

As mentioned above, the materials that are used for banknotes and coins are not intrinsically valuable. However, this was not always the case. Pieces of paper

Figure 1 Banknotes and coins displayed as decorative objects in *pasticceria* 'Maria Grammatico', in Erice, Italy.
Source: Photograph taken by the author in July 2024.

and metal become banknotes and coins thanks to the design used to make the units recognizable as part of a currency system. In currency systems in which all the banknotes have the same shape and size, the only thing allowing us to differentiate one piece of paper from the rest is its design. Hence, it is the design what makes of a banknote an expression of a specific monetary value.

Focusing on issues linked to their design, banknotes and coins can be valuable independently of their economic value, for example, as an object for decoration. Figure 1 shows the counter of the *pasticceria* 'Maria Grammatico', in the town of Erice, Italy. There, banknotes and coins from around the world are displayed as decorative items, and not as carriers of economic value. The reason for their display is not related at all to economics. Upon encountering these banknotes and coins, customers probably can assume that they were donated by visiting tourists and that they are carriers of low values, even in those cases where the nominal value has four or five digits.

Semioticians belong to the group of researchers with an interest in studying money and currency beyond their standard economic function. One area of their interest is the nature and genesis of monetary signs, for example, in comparison to linguistic signs (Bankov, 2022; Wennerlind, 2001; Rastier, 2005; Coratelli, Galofaro and Montanari, 2015). Either when fulfilling their economic function or when regarded with a focus on their visual dimension – as design objects, pieces of art and so on (Hewitt, 1995; Standish and Dunne, 2000) – banknotes and coins are material objects that circulate in the context of everyday life. Therefore, they carry and reproduce specific cultural contents and worldviews, and in doing so, they convey meaning and produce sense.

This is the case because, even if users might not pay specific attention to the iconography and visual elements used for currency design, banknotes and coins are the object of a type of enunciation that is officially sanctioned. This enunciative praxis produces texts that, as a general principle, highlight elements of the local semiosphere that the entity creating them – that is, the state or, more broadly, a political entity – considers relevant and worthy of being used to design currency. This is why these texts are of interest for semioticians.

Several other features of currency in the form it currently has are of interest for semioticians as well. To begin with, currency design changes over time. Even if these changes are usually motivated by a need for more advanced security measures and to prevent counterfeiting, changes in design are usually dependent on non-economic decisions and hence socially motivated. As an example, shortly after the passing of Queen Elizabeth II and her son's Charles taking over the throne in the UK, arrangements were made to replace her portrait with his in the banknotes and coins of the pound sterling, as well as in those of the Canadian dollar. Changes such as these are not related to economics but motivated by sociocultural – and in this case political – issues. The chapters dedicated to studying currencies from South American countries will illustrate this point with clarity.

Moreover, some currencies circulate in social contexts that are different to those where they were produced. One example is the US dollar, used in several countries as the means of exchange for specific – usually more valuable – goods and services such as property, vehicles and plane tickets. Some countries even use it as the main currency, leaving aside their local currency in favor of the US dollar. While the process of dollarization might be a phenomenon of interest for economists, the circulation of a specific national iconography in contexts other than that of its creation might be of interest for other researchers, such as semioticians.

Thirdly, one of the strongest currencies of the world we live in does not have any direct link to any of the existing national states. The euro was created at dusk of the twentieth century as a *supranational* currency for several countries to use it as its official currency, displacing their own currencies which were national. As we will see in Chapter 12, the euro means an innovation to currencies linked to national states because it depends on the EU, a supranational governmental organization, and is regulated by the European Central Bank – two entities that are not dependent on a specific national state. However, as political entities, they function in the same way as national states and national central banks do when creating national currencies.

As we will see in Chapter 11, the designs created in the 1990s for the euro were influenced by a number of discursive constraints. To begin with, there was an identified need to produce a design that could be recognized as owned by citizens from every state that would be a member of the Union. This principle limited the creative possibilities because it specifically excluded national repertoires – that is, thematic repertoires defined in terms of the nation – and required proposing a supranational iconography, one that could work transversally to every nation member using the euro, as an expression and, at the same time, construction of the project of European integration. Issues of this type are still being discussed in the wake of a new design for the euro, announced in December 2021 and still not completed in 2025.[2]

We can also find several examples of currency design influenced and shaped by discursive disputes and challenges that are relevant in our day and age, such as the representation of minorities, gender balance or the exclusion of historical figures accused of slavery, colonialism and genocide. In 2018, the Bank of Canada introduced a new 10-dollar banknote portraying Viola Desmond, a Black woman and social rights activist. Social discourses such as feminism, postcolonialism and multiculturalism, which became relevant thanks to specific sociocultural and historical conditions and events, can also influence and shape currency design. Again, this is not an issue of economics but related to culture, politics and identity.

Moreover, besides changing throughout time in how they look, currencies are created and can disappear. Creating a new currency requires that the government of a political entity chooses, at a specific moment of time, a series of elements and repertoires to adorn currency. This was already the case in ancient Hellenic *poleis* (Eich, 2022: 22–5) and, more recently, when political entities such as Yugoslavia and the USSR collapsed. Upon their disintegration, countries that were part of them had to create their own national currencies, including coming up with the specific visual designs that would be used. As Tim Unwin and Virginia Hewitt (2001) show, countries drew on different iconographic elements, ranging from nature to national heroes, but usually focusing on the past, which was seen as the time of history where the foundations of the nation should be located, probably to produce a sense effect of continuity beyond the discontinuity that the fallen political entities meant in terms of the national community.

Symmetrically, when a national currency is abandoned and/or replaced by other, a portion of discourse linked to the nation and the state gets lost. This is the case because the iconography that adorned that currency's banknotes and coins, which was a carrier of this type of discourse and imagery, disappears from everyday circulation. In January 2023, when in Croatia the *kuna* was replaced by the euro, a medium for the expression of discursive contents linked to the nation and the state disappeared with its banknotes and coins. This will be the case every time a country joins the Eurozone.

Issues like the ones listed in the previous paragraphs fall beyond the economic domain and tap onto political, cultural and identity issues. Hence, they evidence the social relevance and the value of currency beyond economics and open the door for scholars working in other social sciences and humanities. Even if we intuitively tend to locate money and currency into the domain of economics considering the predominant economic function of these inventions, they are also relevant, valuable and meaningful in other domains of the social realm. Particularly, they are relevant through the lenses of society, culture and discourse. These are the dimensions we will be dealing with in what follows.

1.2 Money and currency as institutional facts

Our interest in this book consists in studying the design of banknotes and coins with a focus on how discourse and culture sustain and influence the selection of iconographic elements used to decorate them. To do so, we shall study the visual dimension of banknotes and coins because it functions as one of the entry points we have if we want to access the domain of discourse. Before doing this, an explanation of the foundations of the social realm seems pertinent, so we can understand how money and currency gained the relevance, value and status they have nowadays.

To refer to banknotes and coins, the words *money*, *currency* and *cash* are usually employed in everyday language, even interchangeably. This challenges the distinction between these three concepts and merges their differential meanings into one broad nebulous. In this section, we will distinguish them with a focus on the social arrangements that make them possible.

For Heinz Tschachler (2010: 10), money is 'anything people can use to buy something else with', what makes of it 'the measure of value', whereas currency is 'the medium of exchange'. The relationship between money and currency is one where the latter is the concrete support of the former.

In what follows, we draw on the following hypothesis: currency is the form that money takes, and banknotes and coins – what we normally refer to using the word *cash* – are two forms that currency can take. This means that the instruments we nowadays use to pay are contingent and historical and neither necessary nor natural. The concept of money is independent of the existence of banknotes and coins. As argued above, these instruments are contingent and result from technological developments and social practice.

Currency, specifically in the form of systems composed of banknotes and coins, is therefore only *one way* that can be used to organize and implement the social institution of money. This is what has become dominant throughout recent history thanks to the segmentation of the world's territories and peoples in units corresponding to national states, which are assumed to be sovereign and self-determined. As a result of this organization, Emily Gilbert and Eric Helleiner (1999: 2) argue that 'it is sometimes assumed that territorially homogenous and exclusive national currencies are a "natural" way of organising money'. Nevertheless, as we shall see, there is nothing natural in it.

Studying the distinction between the Italian nouns *denaro* and *moneta* – terms that respectively correspond to *money* and *currency* in English, to *argent* and *monnaie* in French, to *dinero y moneda* in Spanish or to *Geld* and *Währung* in German – Maria Grazia Turri (2014: 222, my translation) claims that, although the two terms are related and were created by humans for their practical action, they differ in their nature: 'They operate in reality in a convergent mode but with different modalities.' Turri (2014: 223) claims that the English language contributed to making of the two terms synonyms. In her view, the work of nineteenth-century economists and philosophers was one of the causes of this terminological confusion.[3] While economists usually expressed an interest in the functioning of currency, philosophers were above all interested in money (Turri, 2014: 223). The work of Georg Simmel (1978) in *Philosophie des Geldes* (*The Philosophy of Money*) is a good example of the latter.

In the book *The Construction of Social Reality*, philosopher John Searle (1995) proposes a distinction between 'brute' and 'institutional' facts as a means to explain how social reality functions. According to Searle, while brute facts are independent of human agency and opinions, the latter depend on humans and the institutions we create for them to be possible. Both money and currency are examples of institutional facts, that is, of things that exist thanks to human agreement and a shared belief in their being objective facts, independent of our personal opinions.

When explaining the nature of institutional facts, Searle frequently uses the example of money. This is one of the objects that puzzle him at the onset, as evidenced in his main question of inquiry: 'How can there be an objective world of money, property, marriage, governments, elections, football games, cocktail parties and law courts in a world that consists entirely of physical particles in fields of force?' (Searle, 1995: xi–xii). To answer this question, he develops a theory of the ontology of social facts and institutions. Searle (1995: 1) conceives of social facts as 'portions of the real world, objective facts in the world, that are only facts by human agreement', that is, that exist 'only because we believe them to exist'. The author claims that these are 'objective' facts because they are commonly agreed upon and do not depend on an individual's preferences, evaluations or attitudes.

According to Searle's constructivist account, three elements are necessary for institutional facts to exist. These are (1) the assignment of function, (2) collective intentionality and (3) some constitutive rules. Regarding the first of them, Searle (1995: 14) argues that 'functions are never intrinsic to the physics of any phenomenon but are assigned from outside by conscious observers and users', an assignation that depends on their interests. Then, collective intentionality is about sharing beliefs, desires and intentions that are not limited to the individual domain but are common to a group. These lead people to do things for a common project or goal, like a violinist playing his or her part in an orchestra that collectively performs a symphony (Searle, 1995: 24). When people engage in collective behavior, collective intentionality is in action.

Finally, Searle distinguishes between regulative and constitutive rules. While the former regulate pre-existing activities – that is, activities that exist before the rule is set, such as driving on public roads – other types of rules, such as those of sports, are required for activities to exist. For Searle, institutional facts such as money can only exist within systems of constitutive rules, which regulate the practice from the onset. In the end, money is a sign system that we manipulate and exchange because we *know* it carries economic value. This knowledge is dependent on many other assumptions based on constitutive rules.

Money and currency are good examples of things that exist thanks to these three elements. As Searle (1995: 32) writes about money, 'if everybody stops believing it is money, it ceases to function as money, and eventually ceases to be money [...] If everybody always thinks that this sort of thing is money, and they use it as money and treat it as money, then it is money'. Our treasuring of banknotes and coins, that is, of rectangular pieces of paper and circular pieces of metal that are not intrinsically worthy, depends on some social arrangements and beliefs. These make them valuable objects for us. As Gottfried Gabriel (2016: 37, my translation) argues, 'in order for money to fulfil its economic functions, the belief in money is indispensable. The validity of money depends on people recognizing and believing in money. Although belief in money is not a sufficient condition for the functioning of a currency, it is a necessary one'.

Moreover, money and currency depend on confidence and social trust. As Heinz Tschachler (2010: 9) argues, one of the most salient traits of banknotes and coins is their anonymity, contrary to signed cheques (for example), which tie the debt to the person signing them and the credit to the one holding them. Banknotes require people to have confidence in their relationships with one another. As Hans de Heij (2012: 10) claims, 'confidence in banknotes is based entirely on trust in the authenticity of the note and in the organisation behind it, the reason why central banks see it as one of their main tasks to maintain this trust in the paper money, genteel phrased as preserving the integrity of the currency'.

As mentioned above, the term 'money' refers to an abstract system of exchange that needs specific elements to function as those that express and carry economic value, that is, as something (concrete) that stands for something else (abstract). This has led scholars, including semioticians (Bankov, 2022), to argue that the monetary sign is to some extent equivalent to the linguistic sign. For Carl Wennerlind (2001: 560),

> In the same sense that a word has no meaning outside of a language, money cannot be understood outside of a monetized culture. Hence, both are self-contained discursive systems in which the meaning and experience of a symbol must be interpreted by making references to the system within which the symbol operates. There is neither an extra-linguistic nor extra-monetary reality that may aid in the understanding of these symbols.

Different media can be used to store, carry and express economic value. Banknotes and coins are only two of the media used for these purposes – media that thanks to custom and social practice became hegemonic. However, not only other media have been used as currency, but also specific items that are not currency in the traditional sense can become currency in specific contexts. As an example, think of cigarettes, which in specific contexts of high deprivation and limited resources, can be used as a means of exchange in social environments where banknotes and coins do not circulate.

In what follows, we will conceptually conceive of currency as the specific material support for money that humans have created to regulate their economic relationships. In *Politics*, Aristotle (1998: 16) wrote about currency:

> For the purposes of exchange people agreed to give to and take from each other something that was a useful thing in its own right and that was convenient for acquiring the necessities of life: iron or silver or anything else of that sort. At first, its value was determined simply by size and weight, but finally people also put a stamp on it, so as to save themselves the trouble of having to measure it. For the stamp was put on to indicate the amount.

We can see the logic that sustains the currency we use nowadays already in action in the ancient world. After an initial period in which humans exchanged items that were intrinsically valuable and a second moment in which objects embedded with symbolism, such as seashells, were used for trade and exchange purposes, the items used to store and express economic value to facilitate exchanges began being *marked* items – marked with what Aristotle calls 'a stamp'.

This stamp consisted of *a mark of visual nature* that allowed not only a quick identification of the unit within the system but also detaching economic value from the material used for minting the coin. Moreover, the stamp allowed users to distinguish pieces from one currency system from those issued by another *polis* (Eich, 2022). This logic still sustains the banknotes and coins we use nowadays: thanks to the use of a set of visual marks, we can not only identify banknotes as coins as such, but we can also distinguish between the units that compose a given currency system and, besides, between different currency systems. That cognitive process is based on design elements.

Commenting on money in Medieval Europe, Searle distinguishes between three forms that money had: commodity, contract and fiat. Commodity money is intrinsically valuable thanks to the value that is socially attributed to the material support used as currency, such as gold or silver. In some cultures, other items that we nowadays would not consider intrinsically valuable were also used for this purpose.

Something different happens with the two more recent types of money. Contract money refers to a monetary system where bits of paper are 'regarded as valuable because they are promissory notes to pay the bearer in valuable commodities such as gold'. In fact, for a long period, banks – both private and national – were requested to possess amounts of gold that could cover the economic value stored in the pieces of paper they issued. Finally, fiat money is composed of bits of paper that are 'declared to be valuable as money by some official agency such as a government or a central bank' (Searle, 1995: 41–2).

What we see in the progression from commodity to fiat money is a detachment of economic value from the material object storing it. Hence, we encounter a movement towards a major degree of arbitrariness and convention (Bankov, 2022). Nevertheless, the three types of money have in common that a given material support is always involved. This is something that is changing in the process of dematerialization of money we are currently experiencing. According to Searle (1995: 34–5, original emphasis),

> Any sort of substance can be money, but money has to exist in some physical form or other. Money can be bits of metal, slips of paper, wampum, or entries in books. In fact, most of our money in the past couple of decades underwent a revolutionary physical transformation that we did not even notice. Most money is now in the form of magnetic traces on computer disks. It does not matter what the form is as long as it can *function* as money, but money must come in some physical form or other.

Jack Weatherford (1997) identifies three major milestones in the history of money. The first one was the invention of coins in the ancient world, around 700 BC, in Lydia, a kingdom located in the current territory of Türkye. According to the author, 'the invention and dissemination of coins and the accompanying market created a whole new cultural system – the classical civilizations of the Mediterranean' (Weatherford, 1997: xiii). The second milestone began in the Renaissance and led to the creation of the modern capitalist system we currently are part of. This stage originated in Italy and 'created the system of national banks and the paper money that they issued for use in daily commerce' (Weatherford, 1997: xiii). The third milestone was the creation of electronic money and a virtual type of economy, in which the use of a material support for money is not any longer a given.

Although it is the social institution of money what legitimizes currency, the latter must be regulated. Regulation occurs thanks to an authority that defines which pieces of paper are valid as such. According to Searle (1995: 28), in a given spatial context (the Canadian territory), a given material object (banknotes and coins of the Canadian dollar) issued by a specific authority (the Bank of Canada) counts as money. For Emily Gilbert (1998: 76), 'what gives money its authority – what distinguishes a banknote from a piece of paper – is its backing by a trustworthy individual or institution', and this is 'reinforced (but not guaranteed) by its iconography'. We will come back to this issue in the next section.

These issues are related to the confidence and social trust that are necessary for a fiat currency system to be able to function in a society where people do not directly know each other. For Tschachler (2010: 14), 'of particular importance [...] is the question of trust, without which neither the legal tender clause nor the promise to pay the bearer on demand clause on a variety of notes would make much sense'. The current stage was finally achieved thanks to the backing of trustworthy institutions, particularly government institutions linked to national states and supranational political entities such as the EU.

Visual design and, specifically, the iconographic elements used to decorate banknotes and coins are the visual marks allowing us to identify, recognize and accept them as such. These elements provide these bits of paper and metal with their social value thanks to the support of the institutions of money and currency, which we all recognize and accept thanks to our living in a world where they exist as institutions and regulate the functioning of the social life. These institutions are regulated by governmental power linked to a political entity, which is usually the state. However, it can also be a supranational entity such as the European Union.

That governmental power is the social agent with the legitimacy and responsibility of producing banknotes and coins, including making decisions on their appearance. Therefore, as we will see in what follows, a strong relationship can be expected between designing banknotes and coins and discourses revolving around the state and the nation. As Gabriel (2016: 38, my translation) writes, 'money not only functions as a medium for exchanging goods [...] in accordance with its value as currency; it is also, in the form of cash, a medium for direct and indirect political messages intended to strengthen trust in the respective currency'.

1.3 Currency, the state and the nation

Money and currency are institutional facts that depend on intersubjective agreement, common beliefs and social institutions to exist. Moreover, for currency to be valid as a means of payment and exchange within a political entity (usually linked to a territory), it should be regulated by an authority with the power and legitimacy to do it. These institutions are generally the central banks (or banks with a similar function), which are part of the set of bodies that regulate a political entity (usually a state, but also a supranational entity such as the EU, which has the European Central Bank). In this sense, a currency that is tied to an independent political entity can be read as an expression of sovereignty, self-regulation and self-determination (Gilbert and Helleiner, 1999; Eich, 2022). Moreover, a political entity with a strong and stable currency will probably be more powerful than those with weaker or less stable ones.

In the world we live in, and except for the euro, currencies depend on states and, with them, on the nations to which states relate. This is the case because, thanks to how history developed over the past centuries, a vast majority of the existing countries around the world are *national states*, that is, artefacts that tie a political entity to an alleged national identity relating a group of people with a specific territory. In these artefacts, and with some exceptions, the administrative borders of the state are strongly dependent on the imagined boundaries of the nation. As a result, as Eric Helleiner (2003: xi) argues, the form that currency has taken in our age is 'unique to the modern age' and consists of 'territorially homogeneous and exclusive national currencies'.

This is why our approach to currency design in this book will be particularly attentive to discourses revolving around the state, the nation and national identity: one of our specific interests is to explore how specific cultural contents linked to nationhood and statehood shape currency design. Therefore, from a semiotic perspective, we will look at how social discourses leave their imprints and traces in the production of specific texts, usually through the mediation of other discourses. Chapter 2 explains this premise with more detail.

The countries we know, such as France and Germany, are autonomous and sovereign political entities that were created recently in history, even if the peoples called 'the French' and 'the Germans' have occupied the territories of France and Germany for centuries and might have their original roots in ancient times (Smith, 2004). The national states that organize our world are modern inventions and, concretely, a product of the eighteenth, nineteenth and twentieth centuries (Thiesse, 1999; Hobsbawm, 1991). To create them, nation- and state-building strategies were implemented.

A country's flag, its coat of arms, its anthem, its official stamps and seals and its banknotes and coins, among other items, all circulate in everyday contexts and express contents linked to the identity of the state, the nation and the cultural memory of the people (when the people are segmented and distinguished from each other following a national criterion). These objects contribute to the creation, reproduction and transmission of a national type of symbolism (Penrose and Cumming, 2011), that is, a type of symbolism revolving around the idea of the nation as something unique and different from other nations.

Behind these symbols lies a complex organization with agency – with the capacity of doing things – that we usually call 'the state'. However, referring to the state as a single actor when studying agency might be inaccurate, because its agency is generally delegated in various actors located at different levels. That is why Jan Penrose (2011) proposes conceiving the state as *an idea* rather than as a real social actor. Regarding national symbology, although the state is ultimately responsible for national symbols, other agents – graphic designers, special committees, task forces, institutions such as central banks and so on – are involved in the production process as well. Even citizens can be consulted about design elements and have collective agency regarding currency design.

In the specific case of currency design, Penrose (2011: 429) argues that 'non-state actors and institutions are frequently responsible for this key mechanism of official iconographic representation', and that this 'calls for a reassessment of the concept of the state'. Therefore, from a semiotic perspective, rather than of the state as an actor, it seems more accurate to speak of *state effects*, that is, of effects of sense that create a perception – and with it a sense of reality – of something that is the state. Although the state exists as a structure, its dynamics cannot be attributed to only one entity.

As students of nations, nationalism and national identity usually claim, ours is a world composed of nations. This means that states are usually defined and segmented in national terms, and some type of correspondence is established or assumed between a state (Brazil) and the people linked to it, which is normally conceived of in terms of *a nation* or, more precisely, *a collective national identity* (the Brazilians). Particularly, there seems to be a correspondence between the boundaries of both segmentations (the state and the people), since these serve as a criterion to define who is in and who is out in terms of both territory and the imagined community.

This conflation between the national and the statal is only *one* among many other forms of segmenting, ordering and making sense of territory and people. Moreover, it is a contingent and history-dependent method, which is a consequence of the growth of national states over the past centuries. When this 'national turn' happened, humanity witnessed a period in which nations had to be built both politically and symbolically (Hobsbawm, 1991; Thiesse, 1999, 2000; Gimeno-Martínez, 2016; Cerulo, 1995; Hobsbawm and Ranger, 1983), not only to gain their own identity as new national states but also to take distance from the previous political entities they were a part of, such as empires, many of which were multinational.

Throughout history, elements such as signs (and particularly symbols), written texts, music, objects, images, spaces, traditions, food, events, individuals, discourses and specific interpretations of the past were used to construct national states both politically and symbolically. These not only had to be recognized distinctively as linked to a national community – they also had to be meaningful and relevant to the people involved in what Eliseo Verón (1988) calls *conditions of production*, that is, the set of sociohistorical circumstances underpinning a specific discursive production.

National identities are one specific type of social identity (Tajfel, 1982). Hence, they coexist with other identities, segmented using criteria other than nationality and national belonging. Identities do not exist in an essentialist, substantialist or pre-social manner. Social identities are discursive constructions, articulated throughout time at different levels, that serve for the purpose of identification, both internally (Us) and externally (Them). As Michael Billig (1995: 8) argues, 'an identity is to be found in the embodied habits of social life'. As such, identities are constructed intersubjectively, in interaction, based on processes of production, circulation and negotiation of sense.

As a specific type of identity, national identities are configurations of sense that emerge in discourse and are meaningful for our perception of the world thanks to oppositions to other units considered to belong to the same domain but different in the traces that define them. The very concept of a distinctive French identity is meaningful thanks to other units in language (expressing a worldview) linked to national identities that are not French, such as the Belgian identity.

This cognitive and linguistic process involves segmenting a continuum in discrete units, analogously to cutting a sheet of paper to produce specific shapes. Once segmented, these units – the various national identities – are constructed and reinforced in discourse through different strategies. According to Billig (1995: 17), 'if the world of nations is to be reproduced, then nationhood has to be imagined, communicated, believed in, remembered and so on'. Therefore, we are dealing with a phenomenon located in an intersubjective territory of negotiation of sense.

The state is a key player in doing this, although it is not the only one. National symbols and discourses, curricular contents taught at school (in history, literature and geography courses), historical events that a country marks yearly with official holidays and festivities, national heroes immortalized in public monuments and paintings and strategic communication campaigns promoting the country as a destination all help construct the idea of a nation in discourse. They constantly expose citizens to contents that locate them precisely in the continuum of national identities thanks to national identification and belonging.

Currency plays this expressive and constructive role as well. As a social institution, it is created and managed within the frame of the state's sphere of action. Hence, it is linked to official public discourse. Within the complexity of the multilayered state, an actor with agency to do so selects the elements that will form a part of its visual design. Given that (again, with some exceptions) the ultimate enunciator of these texts is a national state, we can expect this type of textual production to be mediated and shaped by discourses of the state and the nation. Just as when enunciating discourse, individuals 'inhabit' language and occupy positions within it (Benveniste, 1966, 1974), so do states when creating texts as part of national discourse.

As we will see in the analytical chapters, the selection of design elements to use in banknotes and coins generally taps onto local encyclopedias that are intertwined with discourses of the nation and the state. Hence, when studying currency design, besides symbols referring to the state (name, shape of the country, symbols that stand for it) and its institutions (the central bank, the government, the ruler), we will usually find design elements that circulate in culture as *distinctive* of the nation sustaining the production of that specific currency. Therefore, to adequately understand the meanings that a country's national currency conveys, a mutually constitutive relationship between currency and the national state can be suggested, as scholars interested in the topic have done (Gilbert and Helleiner, 1999; Tschachler, 2010; Hobsbawm, 1991).

Even if currency is produced and sanctioned on a statal – and hence official – sphere of action, it is a material object that circulates in everyday contexts. Banknotes and coins are part of our daily lives, contrary to other national symbols that we encounter more sporadically, usually in extraordinary circumstances, such as the national anthem or the coat of arms. Banknotes and coins coexist with us daily.

To account for this type of more mundane circulation of national discourse, Michael Billig (1995) introduced the idea of *banal nationalism*. This is a type of nationalism referring to the contact with discourses of the nation that occur in everyday life and non-official contexts. Since the concept was proposed, it has been of great interest for researchers (Palmer, 1998; Edensor, 2002; Skey, 2011; Skey and Antonsich, 2017). According to Billig (1995: 8),

> in the established nations, there is a continual 'flagging', or reminding, of nationhood [...] Nationhood provides a continual background for their political discourses, for cultural products, and even for the structuring of newspapers. In so many little ways, the citizenry are daily reminded of their national place in a world of nations. However, this reminding is so familiar, so continual, that it is not consciously registered as reminding.

Even if we might not be aware of it, several elements circulating in the spaces of sense that we inhabit in our everyday lives remind us that we are citizens of a specific national state. The contact we have with these elements considered national forges senses of national belonging. Therefore, as Javier Gimeno-Martínez (2016: 8) argues, banal nationalism can be described as 'a recurrent reference to the idea of a country that is present in numerous everyday activities; a reference that, despite going unnoticed, reminds the citizen that she or he belongs to the group'. Hence, Billig (1995: 8) proposes that 'the metonymic image of banal nationalism is not a flag which is being consciously waved with fervent passion; it is the flag hanging unnoticed on the public building'.

If the nation, nationhood and national identity are discursively constructed in different instances – some more formal and official, others less so – and in different material supports, studying how the idea of nation appears in everyday instances is a fundamental task to understand the sense and meanings that this discourse can activate in the citizenry. This task is appropriate and relevant for semioticians.

Up to this point, we have introduced a constructivist approach to the nation and national identity. This approach stems from works from the 1980s. Concretely, it has been informed by authors such as Benedict Anderson (1983), Ernest Gellner (1983), Eric Hobsbawm and Terrence Ranger (1983) and Anthony Smith (1991, 2004), among others. These authors believe that a nation is not given but the result of a discursive construction mediated by elements such as symbols, practice, media contents and social discourse. As such, they tend to disregard primordialist accounts of the nation that conceive them as natural entities that have existed since long, independently of human action, in a process of continuous evolution.

For example, Benedict Anderson (1983: 6) conceives of the nation as an imagined political community that is both limited and sovereign. This means that nations are cultural artefacts, that is, the result of a construction process that develops over time that contributes to the idea of the nation being a collective entity (a group of people) with some limits and sovereignty. As Anderson (1983: 4) writes,

> nationality, or, as one might prefer to put it in view of that word's multiple significations, nation-ness, as well as nationalism, are cultural artefacts of a particular kind. To understand them properly we need to consider carefully how they have come into historical being, in what ways their meanings have changed over time, and why, today, they command such profound emotional legitimacy.

Within this constructivist framework, nations *become* such through specific dynamics linked to sense- and meaning-making. In this regard, Anne-Marie Thiesse (2000: 52, my translation) argues that

> the list of elements that a nation worthy of the name must possess is now well established: founding ancestors, a history establishing the nation's continuity through the vicissitudes of history, a gallery of heroes, a language, cultural and historical monuments, places of memory, a typical landscape, folklore, not to mention a few picturesque identifications such as costume, gastronomy, an emblematic animal.

In our analytical work with currency design, we will encounter discourses that are salient and relevant in the public sphere of a country regarding what should be remembered, highlighted and privileged in material objects such as banknotes and coins. Since these discourses are enunciated by the state, analyzing them will allow us to identify the strategies used to construct in discourse a semiosphere segmented in national and statal terms, for example, drawing on institutions of the state, its territory, its national history, flora and fauna and human beings and what they did.

To sum up, we assume as a theoretical premise that, as cultural artefacts, nations and national identity are discursively constructed in different spaces, supports and media and by different social actors. Moreover, we claim that currency functions as a material support, among many others, for the construction of the nation and national identity. Hence, besides storing, expressing and standing for economic value, currency serves to convey – as well as to reproduce – discourses of the nation and national identity.

Finally, banknotes and coins not only serve the purpose of national self-identification (that is, for members of the ingroup) but can also be meaningful for outgroups, such as tourists visiting a country. As Unwin and Hewitt (2001: 1009) argue, banknotes and coins are 'often the very first opportunity [visitors] have to see and feel something of the national identity of a country'. In this sense, they can have a similar function to that of souvenirs, which some people like to collect as signs standing for the identity of nations other than theirs (Edensor, 2002: 113). According to Hans de Heij (2012: 11), in cases like these, currency functions as 'the ambassador of the country and the culture it represents'.

1.4 Currency design, heritage and cultural memory

Until now, we have not discussed how statal and national discourses and contents are brought to life in banknotes and coins using images and design elements that we can recognize and make sense of. To do so, we will introduce the concepts of heritage and cultural memory. Commenting on coinage in ancient Greece, Stephan Eich (2022: 24) writes that

> by minting their own coins, citizens of Athens, Corinth, Delphi, and other city-states were distinguishing themselves from each other but also tying each other together. In an age before the printing press, circulating coins were reproducible symbols that inscribed the polity into social memory. Ancient coins functioned as a medium for the construction of the social and symbolic imaginary of the polis, just as the rise of modern imagined communities would be tied to new technologies of print and mechanical reproduction.

Eich's idea that the polity is linked with social memory is relevant to us. As we shall see in the analytical chapters, the past is a crucial repository when constructing nations and national identity. This is the case because the sense of nationhood in the present requires some type of *narrative continuity with the past*, that is, a projection of the current imagined community into the past, so it can also be projected into the future. Following Billig (1995: 10), 'the reproduction of nation-states depends upon a dialectic of collective remembering and forgetting, and of imagination and unimaginative repetition'.

This reproduction requires creating a national history, which is an official type of public discourse sanctioned by the state. It is the state that reproduces it in various contexts. The official discourse about the common past usually functions as the source for the creation of monuments, cherishing national heroes, choosing dates of national commemoration and celebration, identifying places of memory and deciding what is taught to children in school as part of the mandatory curriculum.[4]

Studying how a social actor constructs the past in the form of its national history implies working with cultural memory, a category that semioticians have used extensively over the past decades. The premise is that culture plays a key role in mediating and shaping how a community remembers and reconstructs its past, as well as what items and elements it recovers from the past to produce sense in the present (Lotman, 1998; Lorusso, 2015; Violi, 2014; Demaria, 2006). According to Patrizia Violi (2014), we should study the semiotic-cultural processes that precede the construction of a group's collective identity because the way in which a community remembers and projects its shared and common past plays a key role in the process of identity construction. As we will see in the analytical chapters, the iconography used to adorn banknotes and coins usually contributes to this end.

Like any other process of identity construction, this process is one of sense attribution based on individual identification with cultural units that are part of the semiosphere with which one nationally identifies. According to Violi (2014: 18, my translation), 'based on the more or less truthful representation we give to our past, we build our present and, above all, our future identity, and on the basis of it, we narrate ourselves and relate to others'.

When approaching it from a sociocultural semiotic perspective, we do not conceive of memory in biological terms – that is, as an individual psychological faculty of storing lived experience. Rather, we approach it as something external to individuals that is shared and constructed intersubjectively, in processes of negotiation of sense. According to Jurij Lotman (1998: 109, my translation), the semiotic aspects of culture develop following some laws that are 'reminiscent of the laws of memory, under which what happened is neither annihilated nor passes into non-existence, but, undergoing selection and complex codification, becomes preserved in order to – under certain conditions – manifest itself again'.

Therefore, for Violi (2014: 27, my translation), 'thinking of memory as something externalized implies [...] assuming the character of symbolic mediation that texts have within a culture and, therefore, the interpretative and productive practices that they determine'. Due to their defining ontology of being located *in the past* – and hence inaccessible through direct experience – past events are stored in and circulate as texts that help construct and update collective memory.

Cultural memory is crucial to understanding the practice of currency design. All national currencies evidence a tendency to use elements belonging to a past segmented in national terms to decorate banknotes and coins. Even the banknotes of the euro, a supranational currency whose design is not meant to display specific national contents, taps on the past for its designs, using the major eras of European history as the creative matrix, as we shall see in Chapter 11.

Studying the iconography used by Eastern European countries to design their newly created national currencies after the collapse of the USSR, Unwin and Hewitt (2001) found that the new designs tended to construct the nation as a shared historical experience and not as a new beginning, which could also be an option considering how history developed. There seems to be a shared assumption of the pertinence of tapping into the past to construct continuity between past, present and future of the national community.

In the analytical chapters, the design elements used to decorate banknotes and coins will function for us as an entry point to the national semiosphere. Once we are in, we must understand the meaning and value attributed to the elements that were used in those designs. Although we will focus on the currency being currently used, in some instances we will also use a diachronic perspective, that is, we will relate current banknotes and coins with past ones. In some cases, this method will allow us to visualize how cultural memory becomes a *national* memory, together with how it is constructed, projected and negotiated in the design of banknotes and coins.

States have different semiotic resources and strategies to construct the idea of a common and shared national past. One of them consists in tapping onto heritage, that is, a set of items and elements that are considered as a collective inheritance from past generations and that we should guard to pass it on to future generations. UNESCO (1972) classifies heritage into two encompassing categories: cultural and natural. Examples of the former are monuments, groups of buildings and sites:

> monuments: architectural works, works of monumental sculpture and painting, elements or structures of an archaeological nature, inscriptions, cave dwellings and combinations of features, which are of outstanding universal value from the point of view of history, art or science;
>
> groups of buildings: groups of separate or connected buildings which, because of their architecture, their homogeneity or their place in the landscape, are of outstanding universal value from the point of view of history, art or science;
>
> sites: works of man or the combined works of nature and man, and areas including archaeological sites which are of outstanding universal value from the historical, aesthetic, ethnological or anthropological point of view. (UNESCO, 1972)

Regarding natural heritage, this is what UNESCO proposes:

> natural features consisting of physical and biological formations or groups of such formations, which are of outstanding universal value from the aesthetic or scientific point of view;
> geological and physiographical formations and precisely delineated areas which constitute the habitat of threatened species of animals and plants of outstanding universal value from the point of view of science or conservation;
> natural sites or precisely delineated natural areas of outstanding universal value from the point of view of science, conservation or natural beauty. (UNESCO, 1972)

Anne-Marie Thiesse (2000) claims that, through the ages, nations transmit a collective and inalienable heritage. For Thiesse (2000: 52, my translation), 'the creation of national identities consists in inventorying this common heritage – in other words, in inventing it'. Heritage, both cultural and natural, will play a central role in the discursive articulation of national discourse as it is found in currency design, namely through the inclusion of items and design elements considered to be distinctively national, such as landscapes, buildings, artworks, practices, fauna, flora and human inventions, among others. As Thiesse (2000: 56) argues, the construction of nations is strongly linked to the idea of a collective material heritage, which is what we will usually find in currency design.

1.5 About this book

In what follows, we use a semiotic perspective to study currency design. This means that we use semiotic theory, concepts, methods and instruments to study currency as a discursive genre. In doing so, our purpose consists of identifying the discursive forces that underpin this enunciative praxis – or act of sign production – by the state.

This option leaves asides issues that are constitutive of currency as a social institution, such as anything related to economics and finance, or the impact that national currencies had in the development of national states. We set the focus on how the iconography used to design banknotes and coins taps on and reproduces social meanings that are considered relevant in the public sphere of the political entities (countries, the EU, etc.) where they are used, and particularly by the state. Moreover, we will try to explain why and how these design elements produce effects of sense linked to the nation, the state and, more broadly, the community defined in political and/or cultural terms.

The countries whose currency we study as of Chapter 4 are the United States, Canada, the UK, Switzerland, Brazil, Uruguay and Argentina. Besides these national currencies, we also study the euro, to include an example of a supranational currency that challenges currency design's traditional and customary national focus. The selection of countries and currencies is certainly arbitrary and is justified not only by the knowledge the author has of them but also due to the diversity of design elements and discursive strategies we encounter when studying them. Therefore, these eight currencies should function as *models* that can inspire similar analyses of other currencies, both current and past. We believe that the analysis of each of the selected currencies will add something new to our project of developing a semiotic approach to currency design, for example, using a different type of design element or preferring a different discursive strategy. Hence, a criterion of pertinence and relevance was used to justify the arbitrary selection of currencies that made it into the book.

In the analytical chapters, we approach currency design with a focus in the present time. Hence, we work with the current units being used in the countries of the selected currencies. This choice excludes currencies that could also function as entry points for discourses about the nation and the state, particularly in

Europe, where many national currencies were abandoned in favour of the euro in the early 2000s. Such an approach is certainly relevant but loses the focus in the present that we embrace here. Moreover, if we studied the eight selected currencies historically, we could probably write one book for each of them. In this sense, hopefully the book can inspire researchers to study other currencies, both being currently used and past ones.

Despite our focus in the present, in the analyses we will consider previous series and designs whenever they can serve us to make sense of the current ones. Let us not forget that, for the type of sociocultural semiotics we draw on here, meaning, sense and value are *relational* phenomena, that is, they depend on relations with other elements. More on this follows in Chapter 2.

As is argued in the two following chapters, we approach banknotes and coins as *texts*. As is customary in sociocultural semiotics, we use this analytical category in a broad sense, that is, one that allows using it to refer to articulations of sense that are not limited to the verbal domain (although banknotes and coins always include some words). Our goal will be to render visible how texts we encounter in currency tap onto pre-existing discourses and social imaginaries of national identity and the state, which circulate in the local semiosphere and, in so doing, function as the material support for the construction of an idea of the nation and national identity. The semiotic examination of eight different currencies should allow us to propose some preliminary conclusions regarding how currency design can be the object of specific semiotic strategies revolving around the collective identity of a nation, as well as the aspects of its cultural memory that those in charge of the state want to bring to the fore as distinctive traits of that collective identity.

Although this book is certainly not the first one interested in the design of banknotes and coins, it is probably the first one tackling them using a declared *semiotic* perspective.[5] We expect that the book can provide useful insights and analytical inputs, produced within a clearly identified semiotic framework, for scholars and researchers of nationalism studies, political science, cultural and political geography, history, discourse analysis and other disciplines in their efforts to approach these issues. For that purpose, we try to be as friendly as possible to readers unfamiliar with semiotics. This means that we prioritize the analysis and try to avoid metalanguage and complex theoretical arguments. However, at the same time, we expect the book will be a valuable contribution to semiotics thanks to the specific case study and the concrete analyses it presents, which are dealt with using a methodological approach that combines visual and cultural semiotics.

Chapter 2 introduces semiotics in a broad manner, with a focus on the visual and cultural branches of the discipline since these are those we will draw upon in the analyses. Then, Chapter 3 is about studying currency design using a semiotic perspective, including an introductory literature review and some methodological considerations. Starting with Chapter 4, we analyze our eight currencies: the US dollar (Chapter 4), the Canadian dollar (Chapter 5), the British pound sterling (Chapter 6), the Swiss franc (Chapter 7), the Brazilian real (Chapter 8), the Uruguayan peso (Chapter 9), the Argentine peso (Chapter 10) and the euro (Chapter 11).

2

Introducing Semiotics

Banknotes and coins can be objects of interest for researchers of history, sociology, political science, social psychology, geography, cultural anthropology and cultural studies, among other disciplines. Depending on their specific interests, each discipline will be keen on exploring certain aspects of currency design.

As argued in Chapter 1, banknotes and coins are material objects that circulate in our everyday environments. Since antiquity, societies have developed the practice of marking these objects to identify them not only as a specific type of social object (that is, currency) but also to relate them to a specific political community, usually the one granting and ensuring its validity as currency. This historical development has a consequence that is relevant for our purposes: we can expect the signs used to mark currency to be somehow influenced or motivated by the need to identify currency units with a specific political entity. Hence, besides signs related to economic value, we shall encounter others that relate to other social discourses.

The approach to currency design we propose is a semiotic one. In what follows, we will be interested in studying how banknotes and coins signify and produce specific effects of sense drawing on pre-existing social discourses and, more specifically, thanks to the mediation and intervention of these discourses. The defining and differential characteristic of the approach we propose is that our analytical perspective draws on theories, concepts, methods and instruments produced within the specific research field called 'semiotics', which is one that developed and gained disciplinary autonomy throughout the twentieth century, and specifically since the 1960s. The purpose of this chapter is to introduce this research field and some of the instruments it has produced that will serve us for our analyses of banknotes and coins.

2.1 Semiotics in a nutshell

Approaching currency design using a semiotic perspective involves doing a specific type of work, which draws on the discipline, science, outlook, research field or analytical perspective called 'semiotics'.[1] Although the semiotics of a given phenomenon – that is, the dimension linked with signs, meaning, signification and sense – can be approached by many disciplines, there is a specific one that grew during the twentieth century and that is usually designed using the noun 'semiotics'. Some of its most notable references are Algirdas J. Greimas, Umberto Eco, Jurij Lotman, Paolo Fabbri, Roman Jakobson, Roland Barthes and Eliseo Verón, among many other scholars.[2]

In terms of its origins, semiotics-as-a-discipline is usually linked to the work of linguist Ferdinand de Saussure (1959) and philosopher Charles S. Peirce (2020), who, independently but closely in time, made of the sign a central analytical category. Since then, semiotics developed throughout the twentieth century in two major schools or traditions following the ideas of these two founding fathers. As a result, it is common to speak of two types of semiotics (Traini, 2006): interpretative, referring to Peircean schools, and structuralist, referring to approaches based on de Saussure's ideas.

Here we conceive of semiotics as a specific domain within the division of scientific labour and research. This domain is characterized by its interest in signification and sense-making, in terms of both structures and processes. These are semiotics' objects of study and are those that define its identity as a research discipline. Given the number of phenomena in which signification and sense-making occur, it is customary to divide general semiotics into two major domains, which are segmented and defined considering both their main scope of interest and their theoretical sources: these are bio- and sociocultural semiotics, stemming respectively from the works of Peirce and de Saussure.

Clearly, the work we propose in this book belongs to the latter, since we are interested in understanding signification and sense-making in the human realm and through artefacts produced by humans, that is, in the webs of signification that constitute culture (Geertz, 1973). We will specifically work with banknotes and coins, which are two specific human-made items that belong to material culture.

As a discipline informed by analysis, sociocultural semiotics works with texts and sets of texts to sustain its hypotheses and conclusions regarding signification, sense- and meaning-making. This is a differential trait of our discipline and helps distinguish it from other sciences, disciplines and approaches which also might have an interest in signification, sense and discourse, such as the philosophy of language, theoretical accounts of discourse and philosophical approaches to culture. As the analytical chapters of the book evidence, our conclusions are informed by thorough work with the design of the banknotes and coins included in the corpus. Following the guiding tenets of sociocultural semiotics, we treat these designs as texts.

In the form it currently has, sociocultural semiotics is influenced by European structuralism, and its premises can be found in the work of F. de Saussure (Lagopoulos and Boklund-Lagopoulou, 2021). In his attempts to relaunch linguistics as a positive science, de Saussure (1959) saw in semiology the discipline – still to be founded at his time – that would encompass linguistics and pertain to the more encompassing discipline of social psychology. In his view, semiology's scope would be to study the life of signs within social life.

Around fifty years after the posthumous publication of de Saussure's book *Cours on General Linguistics*, Roland Barthes (1964) tried to establish the discipline of semiology. He did it focusing on signs, sign systems and signification in domains such as fashion and food, in a disciplinary move that surpassed the focus of signs and sign systems in natural language. Anthropologist Claude Lévi-Strauss (1958) did something similar and became influential as well for the development of European semiotics and, particularly, of sociocultural semiotics (Lorusso, 2015: 22–9).

In de Saussure's lessons, we find some key tenets that are still used by contemporary sociocultural semioticians. One of them is the idea that a sign is composed of two dimensions, which he called 'signifier' and 'signified'. Another is that meaning and value are based not on essential traits of the units of a system but on the differences between them. This involves paying attention to relationships and, particularly, to oppositions, with a focus on the differential traits that serve us to identify and delimit a given unit as one that is different from others.

One of the innovations introduced by de Saussure in his approach to language as a sign system is that of *value*. This notion became one fundamental in sociocultural semiotics and is inspired by economic value. Concretely, de Saussure exemplifies this concept drawing on the exchange value of coins, that is, the relationship coins have to each other and to the objects that can be acquired using them as something that stands for something else, as in language a signifier stands for a signified. According to de Saussure (1959: 115),

> To determine what a five-franc piece is worth one must [. . .] know: (1) that it can be exchanged for a fixed quantity of a different thing, e.g., bread; and (2) that it can be compared with a similar value of the same system, e.g., a one-franc piece, or with coins of another system (a dollar, etc.). In the same way a word can be exchanged for something dissimilar, an idea; besides, it can be compared with something of the same nature, another word.

Here we see how de Saussure draws on money and economic value to explain his conception of the linguistic sign. In the quoted passage, the idea of value, according to which a unit becomes meaningful thanks to relationships to other elements independent of it, originates in an example taken from the domain of currency: the 5 (Swiss?) franc piece.

If a person were to travel for the very first time to, for example, Uruguay, upon getting a banknote of 500 Uruguayan pesos, he or she would need to figure out the value of that piece in terms of what it stands for. From the outset, he or she knows that this printed piece of paper money is worth 500 Uruguayan pesos – that is, 500 units of that currency – and that it can be used for economic transactions in the country he or she is visiting. However, a second step is necessary, linked to what he or she can *actually buy* using that note. Once our visitor is in possession of this practical information, he or she might be more or less keen on keeping the banknote safe depending on its value. This will depend on the economic value the specific note stands for in terms of what it can buy. In this sense, a banknote of 500 Uruguayan pesos has a different value than one of 500 Argentinean pesos, even if both store, express and stand for 500 units of currency. Figuring out the system of value linked to a specific currency in a specific society is a relevant cognitive process that involves perceiving and understanding an arrangement that is abstract, local, context-dependent and relative.

Another possible method to grasp the economic value of 500 Uruguayan pesos would be to relate that amount to other currencies that our visitor knows. In doing this, thanks to a method of currency conversion – a practice of mathematical translation – our visitor would discover that, in 2025, 500 Uruguayan pesos are the equivalent of around 12 US dollars and 11 euro. In either case, a process of translation is involved, where something must be made sense of in terms of something else to which it is equivalent.

Based on this conception of value as something dependent on relations and oppositions, and the premise that signs are composed of two dimensions, structuralist semiotics developed and grew, until reaching its maturity in what we refer to as 'sociocultural semiotics of a discursive matrix', 'discursive sociocultural semiotics' or simply 'sociocultural semiotics'. However, more developments occurred within the discipline until it reached its maturity. One of them was introduced by Louis Hjelmslev (1947), who reformulated de Saussure's signifier/signified dichotomy by a conception of semiosis as a relationship between two *planes*: that of expression and that of content. According to Hjelmslev's account, each of these planes is composed of a substance, a matter – also translated as 'purport' – and a form. What is maintained in this reformulation is the bidimensionality – now in terms of a biplanarity – of semiosis, which distinguishes this general approach to semiosis from other approaches based on triadic conceptions, such as Peirce's.

This reformulation of de Saussure's ideas set the ground for the transition of the conception of semiotics as the science that studies *signs* to one interested in *signification*, with particular attention for texts, discourse and the working of the semiosphere. According to Gianfranco Marrone (2021: 9), 'semiotics does not deal […] with signs, but with signification, which in order to function – to be produced, to circulate, to be received and finally transformed – must make reference to texts, the units of meaning that various societies, historical eras and cultures use in order to communicate their own basic values'.

As we shall argue, the design of banknotes and coins can be approached as a text. Hence, it can be regarded as a signifying material that communicates these 'own basic values' that are relevant in the societies producing them.

As human beings, we encounter sense and signification in almost anything we do. We confront sense and signification daily and from the moment we wake up. As Algirdas J. Greimas (1986: 5) argued, human experience is dependent on signification, and the world can only be said to be human if signification is at play. That is why semioticians interested in understanding the social domain have worked in expanding the discipline for it to be capable of studying almost anything with the capacity of signifying. The following quote by Marrone (2021: 10) is enlightening:

> The everyday is full of signification, meaning insinuates its way into everything, especially into that which is most obvious: our bodies, food, architecture, clothing and so on. We could say that signification is the amniotic fluid in which the human being, the social subject, groups and collectives exist, and that there are many more things that hold meaning for us than there are things.

Based on this theoretical premise, what we have called 'sociocultural semiotics of discursive matrix', 'discursive sociocultural semiotics' or plainly 'sociocultural semiotics' is nowadays an active research field. Semioticians interested in the workings of discourse normally use ideas, concepts and instruments that were proposed by the discipline's masters such as Roland Barthes, Roman Jakobson, Louis Hjelmslev, Jurij Lotman, Algirdas Greimas, Umberto Eco and Eliseo Verón, among others, to study signification and sense-making. Generally, they also establish an interdisciplinary dialogue with other research domains and traditions. In what follows, we also draw on the work of these scholars and establish a dialogue with other social sciences.

To sum up, in what follows, whenever we refer to 'semiotics', we are thinking of what we have described in this section. Even if sociocultural semiotics is still not a unified field as it should be (Moreno Barreneche, 2023a), its practitioners share some common views and, above all, concepts and instruments to approach sense and signification. This distinguishes this approach from others that might also use the noun 'semiotics', even in the form of 'social semiotics' (van Leeuwen, 2005; Hodge and Kress, 1989) to describe what they are interested in studying. Even if these approaches are not incompatible, they have different origins, pillars and theoretical premises. Something similar occurs with other types of discourse analysis, including critical discourse analysis and multimodality studies.

2.2 Text, discourse, semiosphere

In their work, semioticians interested in understanding how human experience is one with sense tend to draw on three crucial concepts that constitute the basic theoretical apparatus of the discipline: text, discourse and semiosphere. The purpose of this section is to introduce them, since they will be useful to understand the approach to currency design we propose in the book.

When faced to the word *text*, one might intuitively think of a delimited piece of written language composed of words and sentences on a specific material support, such as a piece of paper or a computer screen. Poems, letters, short stories, recipes, laws and user's manuals are texts in this reduced, limited and classic sense of the word. In texts like the ones listed above, a specific substance – written words articulated in sentences, which are structures composed of words – is manipulated and articulated to express specific meanings. Since they are embedded in culture, these meanings pre-exist the specific act of enunciation, that is, the articulation that an individual can do of a given substance to convey and communicate those meanings. As an example, to write this book, which is a text in the traditional sense, I use English language to express the contents I want to expose, and therefore choose words, formulate sentences and write and rewrite so that those contents can be as clear as possible.

In writing this book, I am articulating contents that pre-exist using a substance that could have been another one.

What characterizes texts in this restricted and traditional sense is that they usually are clearly delimited and hence can be easily treated as units of analysis. Books, short stories, letters, poems, laws, recipes and user's manuals begin and end. Thus, they can be treated as closed units of analysis. We can identify where they begin and end and propose different approaches to study them as texts.

Based on this defining trait, sociocultural semioticians expended the concept of text to cover other signifying conglomerates that evidence an internal articulation and some degree of closure. As a result, the text becomes *a model*, that is, a lens that – thanks to an analogy based on similar internal structural features – is useful to approach phenomena related to signification and sense. As Marrone (2021: 9) argues, for sociocultural semioticians a text is 'any portion of the world that, through the possession of fixed boundaries and a precise internal articulation, makes itself the carrier of any configuration of meaning'.

Conceptualizing anything with the capacity to signify as a text involves that *anything* can in principle be approached as a text, with the condition that it can signify. If someone is on an island in the Mediterranean looking for a beach and suddenly finds an agglomeration of vehicles disorderedly parked along the road, that agglomeration of vehicles can function as a text because it can be approached as an expression of a content – a beach is nearby – and hence as a text (Marrone, 2021). Therefore, according to Marrone (2021: 9), 'any material present in the world – physical and biological, physiological and corporeal, geographical and social, cultural and historic – can be used (if correctly organised) as a signifying expression used as a vehicle for certain content'.

The main condition for something to be approached as a text is that it has some degree of internal consistency. For Marrone (2021: 9), the text 'should not be understood [...] as a disordered collection of signs, any amalgam of things that stand in for others, but as a fabric of relationships, a web of forms that bind substances and aim to produce, set in motion and justify any unit of meaning'. As we will see in what follows, this is the case with banknotes and coins. When encountering a banknote or a coin, not only do we identify its boundaries as a material object, but we can also identify the internal articulation that allows us to treat it as a text. This articulation is visible in a series of relationships sustaining the design, such as the one of nominal signs with written descriptions, or of elements belonging to a national encyclopaedia with symbols that stand for the (national) financial institution issuing currency.

In this sense, what we consider a text is actually a text thanks to decisions we – observers and analysts – make. It is up to us to postulate that the specific material configuration we are interested in studying complies with some conditions that are necessary for something to be approached as a text. Hence, as Marrone (2021: 15) proposes, 'the text is not a given, a phenomenal fact, but the result of a double construction: first, the socio-cultural configuration, and secondly, the analytic reconfiguration'. It is we semioticians who construct the design of banknotes and coins as texts thanks to a recognition we do of a specific signifying materiality as one that relates to meaning and sense, and hence as one that signifies.

Texts are hence the empirical concretion of sense and meaning, and they are the main working matter that semioticians use for their research. According to the social semiotics put forward by Eliseo Verón (1988), texts are a crystallization of social discourse in specific empirical units. Analysts can work with these specific empirical units to access the domain of social discourse, which is a deeper one accessible only through fragments, that is, texts. For Verón (1988: 124, my translation), semiotics consists of 'conceiving the phenomena of sense as appearing, on the one hand, always in the form of conglomerates of signifying matters; and as referring, on the other hand, to the functioning of the semiotic network conceptualized as a productive system'.

A second analytical category relevant for sociocultural semiotics is that of *discourse*. This category became relevant in the social sciences in the 1970s, and nowadays it is still a relatively problematic concept since it refers to different things in different semiotic – and, more broadly, discursive – accounts. Here we will follow Verón and conceive of discourse as a *productive force* that crystalizes in texts and to which we can gain access through the analysis of texts. As a productive force, discourse is dependent on social context – that is, on the specific ways of living situated in a given time and space – that leaves traces in the texts it produces. According to Verón (1988: 124, my translation), 'the possibility of any analysis of sense rests on the hypothesis that the productive system leaves traces in the products and that the former can be (fragmentarily) reconstructed on the basis of a manipulation of the latter'. We could argue that working with texts and discourse reflects the two planes of semiosis introduced above: that of expression and content, respectively.

This is the type of work that we will do when examining the design of banknotes and coins. By looking at specific texts – the designs of banknotes and coins – we will aim at identifying the discursive forces sustaining them. Practising discourse- and text-based sociocultural semiotics requires considering the relationship that exists between a given social discourse and the various empirical texts it produces, and vice versa. As Marrone (2021: 75) argues, this is a reciprocal relationship because 'there is no discourse without texts that exhibit it empirically, and there are no texts without there being a discourse to develop'. The relationship between currency design and discourses sustaining this practice will be central to the analyses we present in the book.

According to this account of discourse and its crystallization in texts, semioticians can access discourse through the study of the latter. These are material signifying conglomerates that are empirically perceivable, as the designs we encounter in banknotes and coins are. Discourse is hence something that cannot be immediately encountered and that we can only postulate as a productive force departing from textual analysis. This postulate can be based, for example, on our identifying of some regularities in a selection of texts and our relating them to their production, as we do when studying a number of paintings (visual texts) and argue that they belong to the same current style (discourse), such as impressionism, cubism or futurism. When studying specific texts, we start gaining access to the discursive forces sustaining textual production.

In this sense, when we approach currency design as a discursive genre that is culturally codified – that is, anyone could describe what elements a piece of paper or metal should include for it to *be* currency – we postulate the existence of a specific discourse that functions as the matrix to produce the visual texts we encounter in the designs of banknotes and coins. That matrix imposes some restrictions and limitations on the creative possibilities, as we will see in Chapter 3.

Finally, texts and discourse relate to a third key concept of relevance for our purposes: the *semiosphere*. This concept was coined by Jurij Lotman, who drew on the idea of the biosphere from the natural sciences. According to Lotman (2005: 207), a semiosphere is – metaphorically – conceived of as 'a specific sphere, possessing signs, which are assigned to the enclosed space'. For him, only 'within such a space is it possible for communicative processes and the creation of new information to be realized' (Lotman, 2005: 207).

Lotman (2005: 208) believes that 'the semiotic universe may be regarded as the totality of individual texts and isolated languages as they relate to each other. In this case, all structures will look as if they are constructed out of individual bricks'. The concept of the semiosphere works as an analytical category to delimit 'spaces' within which meaning is possible, and these tend to coincide with the various cultural spaces existing in different social contexts. According to Lotman (2005: 208), 'the semiosphere is that same semiotic space, outside of which semiosis itself cannot exist'.

The distinction between an *inside* and an *outside* that is characteristic of the semiosphere leads to some of its defining features. To begin with, there is a boundary between the semiosphere and what constitutes its outside (Volkova Americo, 2017). In Chapter 1, we argued how the artefact of the national state generally tends to conflate the boundaries of the state with those of the nation. This conflation allows us to postulate the existence of a semiosphere that is segmented and defined in national terms, that is, one whose boundaries coincide with those of the nation – or, to be more precise, with the imagined national community. This explains the existence of a French semiosphere as different from a Brazilian semiosphere. Within each of these, some signs and texts are meaningful while others are not.

Moreover, within a given semiosphere, elements are located following a hierarchy. If a semiosphere is topologically organized around a core and a periphery, then the elements that are part of it can occupy positions that are closer to one or the other. When studying currency design, in some cases we will identify discursive struggles between social actors – political parties, social collectives and so on – aiming at positioning some elements belonging to the local encyclopaedia in positions that are closer to the core, as a means of strengthening their sense in terms of discourses about national identity. Here currency design can become a *locus* for ideological disputes, as we shall see in the chapter dedicated to the Argentine peso.

In the third place, dynamics of exchange are possible between the inside and the outside, and external elements might enter the semiosphere and become part of it. For this to occur, these foreign elements need to undergo a process of translation into the semiotic system that defines the semiosphere in question. An evident example of these dynamics is the introduction of words of a natural language into another: in Spanish, the word *tweet* has been normatively translated as *tuit* based on phonetic resemblance. Finally, according to Lotman, a semiosphere is characterized by its internal semiotic irregularity.

With regard to the semiosphere, Marrone (2021: 170) writes that it 'describes culture by recourse to the image of a living being with innumerable organs and functions, facing all the problems a living being faces when trying to adapt to a given environment and the internal changes taking place in this process'. As a result of using this metaphor, the author claims that

> the life of the text is compared to that of a living organism: it is possible only if the text relates with other organisms, in highly conflicting fields where the daily

> fight for survival allows the continuous transformation of languages and cultures. Human culture is no longer understood [...] as a static system originating from the primary modelling system of the world due to linguistic verbalisation; it is, instead, the result of a dynamic interlace between language and world, culture and extra-culture: it is the semiotic act that produces language and, as a repercussion, world and culture, and, as a presupposition, nature. (Marrone, 2021: 170)

For our purposes in this book, the concept of semiosphere will be useful because it serves us to tie discursive and textual production to a sphere of sense that is situated in a specific time and a specific space. Therefore, we can expect the specific form that textual production will take to be dependent on the contingent dynamics that are dominant within that sphere of sense in a given time and space to produce sense and meaning. This means that we can expect the designs of banknotes and coins to be relevant within the semiospheres producing them. Specifically, we can expect currency design to be mediated and shaped by elements that belong to the specific semiosphere producing them, including those related to the nation and the state.

Text, discourse and semiosphere will be three recurrent concepts in our analyses of the designs of banknotes and coins. In a nutshell, our overarching working hypothesis for what follows is that banknotes and coins are pieces of design. These texts are created – enunciated – by the state and are shaped by social discourses relevant to the semiosphere in which the state producing them is embedded. To work with this hypothesis, we will examine visual texts (the designs of currency on paper money and metal) and approach them with a focus on their relationships, as cultural semioticians tend to do. In the next two sections, we introduce visual and cultural semiotics, respectively.

2.3 Visual semiotics

Our working matter in this book are banknotes and coins, two types of material objects that we approach as texts, that is, as signifying materialities – or conglomerates – resulting from an enunciation that expresses meanings located at the discursive level. Even if banknotes and coins contain words, sentences, signatures and numbers in them – all elements belonging to the domain of natural language – they are material objects not only characterized by the visual dimension inherent to them but also defined by it. As we saw in Chapter 1, this has been the case since the creation of coins in the ancient world, around 700

BC. Then, what allowed people to identify coins as such was a stamp that gave both each currency and piece of currency a place within a system. Later in time, when technology made it possible, something similar occurred with banknotes. In both cases, how these material objects look like – that is, how they appear to our eyes – is crucial for their *becoming* or *being* banknotes and coins.

Within general semiotics, a specific strand of research interested in visual texts developed during the last quarter of the twentieth century and is still consolidating. The denomination 'visual semiotics' refers to a field of general semiotics defined by the nature of the type of texts it deals with: images. Visual semiotics is only one manifestation – articulated as a sub-branch of a discipline – of the interest that researchers and scholars working with language and discourse have shown for the visual domain and the type of signification occurring in it (Lagopoulos et al., 2025). Together with visual semiotics, other approaches and accounts exist to semiosis and signification in images, such as multimodal discourse analysis (Kress and van Leeuwen, 2001). Usually researchers from different fields and traditions work under the shared assumption that signification appears in texts – syncretic/multimodal – combining various expressive substances, such as words and images.

Practitioners of visual semiotics study signification and sense in texts where images are the expressive substance – the support of semiosis – as opposed to other substances such as words, odour or sound. Therefore, this is a domain of semiotic research defined by the substance of expression, and the disciplinary purpose is to understand how the form that substance takes relates with the form of content.

The world we live in is heavily composed of images, particularly since societies adopted digital media platforms such as YouTube, Instagram and TikTok. As a result, over the past years, visual semiotics has grown significantly, concomitantly with similar research lines within other disciplines such as communication and media studies, or the field of *Bildwissenschaft* in Germanophone universities (Sachs-Hombach, 2021). Currently, visual semiotics comprises specific research areas defined by theme, such as the semiotics of painting (Corrain, 2004), photography (Basso Fossali and Dondero, 2011; Mangano, 2018), comic strips (Barbieri, 2017), street art (Barreto Bogo, Migliore and Paris, 2025) and data visualization (Manchia, 2020), among many other domains that are generally segmented and defined according to the practices sustaining the specific type of visual creation at its core, either static or animated (Lagopoulos et al., 2025).

As Greimas (1989: 629) proposes, all these domains work with 'planar structures', usually in the form of bidimensional surfaces. Therefore, as Greimas

(1989: 629) writes, 'pictorial, graphic, and photographic representations are [...] grouped together in terms of a common "being present to the world"'. For Marrone (2021: 84), 'the role of semiotics in this context is one of integrating [...] formal and substantial elements, demonstrating how their signification is only realised in precise configurations of meaning that are texts'.

For Greimas (1989: 628), visual semiotics deals with the semiology of images, or, in other words, with how images signify, sketching an epistemology of images (Lagopoulos et al., 2025). According to Greimas (1989: 644), 'the hypothesis governing all of our analysis – in conformity with generally accepted intuitions – consists in considering plastic objects as signifying objects. Thus the problem is not one of proclaiming that the plastic signifier [...] "signifies", but rather of understanding how it signifies and what it signifies'.

What matters to semioticians are the *how* and the *what*. Some theoretical developments in this direction were already advanced by Roland Barthes (1977) in the 1960s. For Barthes, images can be read through the lenses of rhetoric because they signify and, moreover, can be created with communicative purposes, as is the case with advertisement. Here the distinction between abstract compositions, such as the artistic works of Jackson Pollock or Joan Miró, and figurative ones should be mentioned.

While for Marrone (2021: 94) figurativity is 'that level of meaning responsible for human and social perception of the world, primarily in a visual way', Barthes (1977: 35) claimed that a figurative image 'assembles in a common space a number of identifiable (nameable) objects, not merely shapes and colours', as abstract images usually do. Hence, when faced with a figurative image such as an advertisement promoting a product – in the essay 'Rhetoric of Image' Barthes studies a visual ad by the pasta brand Panzani – after leaving aside the words we can encounter, we are left with the 'pure image', which also signifies.

This is the case because, in the image, we can recognize the elements that compose it, just as we can identify the words that compose a sentence and, as Marrone (2021: 85) writes, 'usually, when we look at an image, we neglect its signifying aspect in order to concentrate directly on its signified'. This is precisely what occurs with the design of banknotes and coins: when encountering a historical figure, a landscape or a monument in them, we tend to focus on what is represented, and not on the representation. And we can identify what is represented thanks to the *mimetic* type of representation that is customarily used in this discursive genre.

Explaining the concept of *degrees of figurativity*, Marrone (2021: 93) writes that 'generally speaking, the richer a visual text is in visual traits and details, the more realistic that text is considered. And, conversely, the fewer visual traits a text has, the less realistic it is considered'. Currency design could work in both ways, as long as the elements that make it recognizable as currency are respected and easily identifiable. However, empirical evidence shows that banknotes and coins tend to be designed using a high degree of figurativity, so readers can easily get to the reference of what images used in them are standing for.

The passage from abstraction to figurativity – or vice versa – depends on the traits that are used to create an image. Hence, we can speak of a continuum oscillating between the abstract and the figurative, where the inclusion of more traits can help us identify what we are seeing in an image and, at least in the case of currency design, relate it to elements of the real world. These elements can be historical characters, landscapes, buildings, monuments and animals that we might already know as members of the community, a membership that makes us being familiar with the semiosphere that grew around that community. Given the nature of the discursive genre of currency design, we can expect the images we find in banknotes and coins to be almost iconic, that is, a type of textualization whose semiotic nature is almost invisible or, in other words, 'transparent'.

Our capacity to recognize the elements that compose an image means, on the one hand, that we are capable of identifying discontinuous visual signs as those composing the image and, on the other hand, that we are capable of making sense of why, how and what they signify – that is, we can identify them as potential carriers of meaning. Within the boundaries that are set by the frame that every image has – there are no endless images – these signs usually form a coherent whole and, as Barthes (1977: 35) claimed, 'require a generally cultural knowledge, and refer back to signifieds each of which is global [...], imbued with euphoric values'. Hence, following Barthes's account, we can treat images as texts composed of visual signs, just as sentences are composed of words.

Barthes was also interested in the relationship between image and natural language, a relationship that is to be found in the designs of banknotes and coins as well. As we will see in our analyses, besides the images used to decorate them, banknotes and coins contain a series of words that convey information related to practical economic issues (value, country issuing them, etc.), but also of validity, security and legitimacy, such as signatures, serial numbers and written explanations about the nature of the object we are holding. In many cases, these relationships link linguistic and visual contents, as is the case when the portrait of a historical character is accompanied by a linguistic description containing the name of the character.

Barthes (1977: 39) writes that, in some cases, the written text 'helps to identify purely and simply the elements of the scene and the scene itself', and hence, 'it is a matter of a denoted description of the image'. In cases like this, we can speak of a function – or operation – of *anchorage*. Here the linguistic text and the image are related in a codified way. While such a relationship might not be meaningful when studying a collage created by a cubist artist, it probably will be in non-artistic genres such as currency design. Therefore, when we encounter the word 'Franklin' written in the US$100 banknote, besides recognizing it as a family name thanks to our cultural competence, we can expect it to be present as part of the design in some relation with the portrait we see in the front side of that note.

Barthes claimed that the main function of anchorage is to *fixate* what we see. As he puts it, 'language clearly has a function of elucidation, but this elucidation is selective, a metalanguage applied not to the totality of the iconic message but only to certain of its signs' (1977: 40). In the next chapters, we will see how this occurs in the design of banknotes and coins, specifically when linguistic texts are used to clarify what the images included in banknotes and coins depict.

Barthes also proposed a distinction between an image's literal message (what we recognize we are seeing) and a symbolic one, a distinction abandoned when the concept of semi-symbolism was proposed (Greimas, 1989; Floch, 1985). Barthes's was only a first analytical distinction, because we tend to encounter the two types of messages together. Something similar occurs with Greimas's distinction between figurative and plastic.

Three degrees of intelligibility are in play here. In our case, one is related to identifying what we are seeing in the banknote or the coin of our interest, which consists in a recognition of what a sign is standing for in the design we are working with. Besides, we can work with what Greimas calls 'plastic' dimension, as we explain below. The third one is related to recognizing the discursive genre those visual texts belong to as one that is not only culturally codified (that is, it follows some rules) but also authentic/legitimate (vs. forged/fake) since it is an expression of currency – a social institution backed by the state.

Maria Giulia Dondero (2020: 2) argues that when working with images, we must 'analyze their identifying and distinguishing compositional features, but also to identify all the affinities which may help to understand the images thanks to the relations they establish between one another within social domains such as art, science, politics, and advertising'. This means that practising visual semiotics does not only consist of working with the specific images of our interest: it requires working with other images as well, to identify affinities that might help us make sense of them. As we shall see below, this is precisely how cultural semiotics tends to function.

If we consider the possible articulations of the plane of expression, some visual systems are more articulated and codified than others. As Greimas (1989) proposes, if we take road signs as an example, we can clearly recognize them as pieces of a system of signification in which a clear and univocal conventional code is established between a given image and a specific rule. When we take driving lessons, part of what we must learn is that code, as well as how to act upon it. Hence, when encountering a sign with the shape of a red hexagon and the word 'STOP' in it, we should recognize it as an expression of a specific rule – to fully stop the vehicle – and act accordingly. As we shall see, although currency systems are way less codified than road signs being part of a system, some issues seem to be culturally codified and stabilized.

One of Greimas's innovations in the field of visual semiotics is the introduction of three categories: topological, eidetic and chromatic. He proposed these in his attempt to sketch a semiotics of the plastic arts (*sémiotique plastique*), as opposed to figurative semiotics. For Greimas, the first step to be taken when working with an image consists of identifying its boundaries. While the intelligibility of written texts rests on a reading rule that is coded in culture – in English, we read from left to right and from top to bottom of the page – that of images does not. When we face an image, there is not any pre-established order of reading that we can use to approach the signifying conglomerate in front of us. Hence, Greimas (1989: 638) sees the frame as 'the only sure point of departure' for the analysis. Once we have identified the frame that delimits the image as a text, we can identify its topological grid, that is, the logic that was used to organize the spatial disposition of elements, which is delimited by the frame.

For Greimas (1989: 638), topological categories can be of a diverse nature. Some can be 'rectilinear', based in oppositions between the upper and the lower or the left and the right of the surface used as a support for the image, whereas others are 'curvilinear', that is, dealing with the peripheral–central or the enclosing–enclosed distinctions. These, together with the structures they compose, 'carve that surface up into a grid, starting with that which it is not, namely the frame' (Greimas, 1989: 638). The topological mapping of an image helps us, as Greimas (1989: 639) claims, to conduct a 'segmentation of the whole into discrete parts and the mapping out of the possible trajectories that the various aspects of the reading will follow'.

Greimas stresses that the topological grid is conventional, that is, it depends on a shared code – a sort of presupposed and assumed reading contract – between the creator of the image and who might encounter it and try to make sense of it. As he writes, 'these topological categories, projected upon a surface whose richness and polysemy would otherwise render it indecipherable, bring about its reduction to a reasonable number of pertinent elements necessary for its reading' (1989: 639). This is what occurs with the design of banknotes and coins, as we shall see in what follows.

The *eidetic* and *chromatic* categories refer to forms and colours, respectively. Greimas proposes that, when studying these elements, we should not treat them as self-sufficient. On the contrary, we should approach them in relation to other elements, that is, using a 'relational grasping' (Greimas, 1989: 640). While we will see with some detail how this works in the case of currency design, we can already advance something regarding the case of colour: it is common practice to maintain the choice of the colour of a banknote from a precedent to a new series.

To sum up, as a subfield of general semiotics, visual semiotics aims at studying – describing, explaining, analysing and so on – how images signify. This aim is different from interpreting them, a task that is not pertinent for semiotic research. According to Dondero (2020: 3, original emphasis), when analysing an image or a set of images, semioticians try 'to shed light upon what is *commensurable* among all possible interpretations' since 'what determines the commensurability of interpretations is the discursive organization of the image, which provides reading *constraints*'. This type of work can be done immanently, that is, working only with the image and what it contains, but also establishing relationships with other texts circulating in the semiosphere.

Practising visual semiotics, then, involves doing a type of analysis that, as Greimas (1989: 629) argues, 'implies that the markings covering the surfaces chosen to receive those markings constitute signifying wholes and that collections of these signifying wholes […] in turn constitute signifying systems'. This is what semioticians interested in visual signification have been doing over the past half century (Lagopoulos et al., 2025).

Two final necessary references in this brief introduction to visual semiotics should be made. The first one is to the Groupe μ, whose members – based in Liège, Belgium – worked hard to sketch a visual semiotics, for example, writing a treaty of the visual sign (Groupe μ, 1992). The other is Jean-Marie Floch, who worked closely with Greimas. According to Floch (1990: 5, my translation), 'semiotics looks for the system of relations formed by the invariants of these [textual] productions and these seizures [of meaning] based on the analysis of signs, which are variable […] Signs do not constitute the object of semiotics: they are surface units from which the interplay of underlying meanings should be discovered'.

In his work, which is generally informed by case studies – many of them using corpora composed of images – Floch (1985, 1986, 1990, 1995) proposed some interesting instruments to study visual texts, such as a distinction between *referential* and *mythical* types of relationship between texts and what they depict. In the referential type of textualization, elements are depicted neutrally, 'as they actually are', that is, based on a 'referential illusion' that hides enunciation. Hence, what we see does not add any extra meaning to the thing we know. Conversely, the mythical type of textualization adds other meanings that go beyond a mere visual representation (Floch, 1986).

2.4 Cultural semiotics

One could think that studying the design of banknotes and coins from a visual perspective could be limited to describing their appearance only, that is, listing the elements that compose their designs and explaining how, why and what that specific visual articulation signifies thanks to cultural convention. For example, this could be done studying the discontinuity between the various visual elements we recognize as distinct within the boundaries that are set by the frame and relating them with each other. Following the theoretical framework introduced in the previous section, we could be satisfied with studying issues such as the degree of figurativity of the images we encounter in banknotes and coins, or the topological, eidetic and chromatic dimensions of the designs used to adorn them. This would certainly be relevant and meaningful semiotic work, above all as a contribution to visual semiotics.

However, our purpose in this book goes beyond a mere visual dimension of currency. Our goal is to understand how the design elements used to decorate currency stand for something else, something that is located at the level of social discourse and that, hence, is less concrete and only accessible through a work – always fragmentary – with specific texts. It is because of this goal that the concepts of text, discourse and semiosphere introduced in Section 2.2 will serve us. Approaching currency design from the perspective of visual semiotics would leave us at the textual and discursive levels of semiosis, and we would not have much grasping of other signifying phenomena that are relevant for our research purposes. We want to take a deeper dive into social discursivity and explore what the images selected for currency design might mean – express, connote and so on – within the semiosphere – usually segmented in *national* terms, except for the euro – linked to the political entities creating banknotes and coins.

Up to this point, we have been referring to the scholarly approach we use in the book as 'sociocultural semiotics', and we have also insisted that our working matter will be texts as a means to access the level of discourse. The combination of the adjectives 'social' and 'cultural' in one single adjective – 'sociocultural' – to modify the noun 'semiotics' is not a given but a theoretical proposal: by combining two strands of research that grew separately throughout time but that nowadays are closely related, we propose to conceive of human practice and sense-making as located in the intersection between culture and society, because these two domains are interdependent. In grouping these two domains of semiotic interest, we are also proposing a grouping of social and cultural semiotics, which is actually the case when understanding social and cultural semiotics as two broad subfields of general semiotics, and not linking them to any specific school or tradition.

Umberto Eco (1975: 27) saw culture as a complex semiotic system based on processes of signification and communication. Hence, he proposed that 'to look at the whole of culture *sub specie semiotica* is not to say that culture is only communication and signification', but also that 'it can be understood more thoroughly if it is seen from the semiotic point of view'. This is the case because, according to the author, 'in culture, every entity can become a semiotic phenomenon' and, therefore, 'the laws of signification are the laws of culture' (Eco, 1975: 28).

This theoretical perspective is close to approaches to culture that, in the same years, were emerging in anthropology (Geertz, 1973; Hall, 1966). For these perspectives, studying culture with a focus on meaning, sense and signification means doing semiotics, while doing semiotics means studying culture with an emphasis on meaning, sense and signification. That is the reason why, in Eco's (1975: 28) terms, 'culture can be studied completely under a semiotic profile'. This is a theoretical account of semiosis that underpins contemporary semiotic research, at least in academic circles dominated by structuralist and post-structuralist accounts of discourse and sense.

Even if semiotics studies culture and studying culture means doing semiotics, as the discipline developed as a relatively autonomous one within the social sciences and humanities during the second half of the twentieth century, some researchers felt a need to use the adjective 'cultural' to refer to a specific approach to the functioning of culture and the dynamics that are specific to it.

Currently, the denomination 'cultural semiotics' generally is associated with the work of Jurij Lotman, the Tartu-Moscow school and those following this account of semiosis. As a literary scholar and cultural specialist, Lotman was a champion of drawing on a semiotic perspective to approach culture and its sense-making mechanisms. As Anna Maria Lorusso (2015: 67) argues, he was also the first scholar 'focusing on the systematic cultural circle in which every text is implicated'. According to his conception of culture, 'the analysis of texts is subordinate to the identification of general-scale cultural processing and transmission', what makes of a single text 'a place where many codes intertwine, forming new relationships and structures' (Lorusso, 2015: 67).

Therefore, although not always, speaking of 'cultural semiotics' usually implies some type of work with the semiosphere, not with isolated texts. Moreover, when using this denomination, issues of interest for social semiotics – also called 'sociosemiotics' – such as interactions, practices and situations are not so central. As argued above, here we consider them as a joint research project, because culture and society are two dimensions that permeate human experience. Nevertheless, given the nature of the object of our interest in this book, the social dimension will evidently be less relevant for us than the cultural one. This would be different if our interest was set on currency as a social institution, or on how people make sense of currency design, or how they interact with currency, or with each other using currency.

Anna Maria Lorusso (2010: 5, my translation) conceives of cultural semiotics as a lens, that is, as 'the particular optic that serves to focus on certain specific problems'. For Lorusso, the defining traits of this scholarly account to study cultural phenomena are its generality, its 'ability to create correlations between sets of values and sets of morphological-formal traits' and a functional perspective. Therefore, Lorusso claims that studying culture – including studying a particular culture in a specific moment of history – involves studying not only the output of that culture in the form of texts but also analysing the *relationships that exist between these texts* as elements that are related and that belong to the same semiotic system. In Lorusso's (2010: 7, my translation) words,

> Studying culture […] cannot disregard a general consideration of meaning: in short, it cannot limit itself to and be satisfied with the study of a textual micro-phenomenon, a single behaviour, or a particular spot. The semiotics of culture can only deal with these individual texts if it approaches them using a general perspective, that is, in terms of the series of relationships that these singular objects have with the other objects in the series to which they belong (a textual genre, for example) or with the other series in the system (other languages, other types of behaviour, other social systems).

Since cultural semiotics is a discipline that makes of textual analysis its distinctive analytical method, semioticians interested in sociocultural phenomena are generally particularly attentive to the relationships that exist between texts. Our work with the designs currently used to decorate the banknotes and coins of the selected currencies will frequently lead us to relate design elements with other texts that are part of the same semiosphere where these objects circulate, or even from other semiospheres. Lorusso (2015: 6) argues that semiosis lives 'through relationships and differences' and that the specificity of the semiotic perspective lies 'in its capacity to capture and analyze the network of relationships and differences in which meaning is given'. In the analytical chapters, we will see how this principle is in action when analysing currency design.

Lorusso (2010: 13, my translation) proposes that cultural semiotics 'must be able to define the correlation logics that bind texts and codes within a certain system together, the logics that make a certain text compatible with a certain culture and exclude other texts'. The questions and general research motivation sustaining the work presented in this book reflect the logic that Lorusso identifies as the one that defines the cultural semiotic account. Hence, the 'logics of compatibility' of the texts we analyse should be rendered visible.

In this regard, Lorusso (2010: 13, my translation) argues that cultures are 'complex systems of compatibilities and incompatibilities, sets of sets that, in so far as they collect and unite certain elements, they exclude and distance others'. In the case of currency design, we will see how these complex systems tend to include some elements in the design and exclude others. Moreover, we will see how new designs tend to show some degree of compatibility (in terms of design elements and iconographic content used to decorate them) with the previous designs of the system, both the one they are part of and previous ones.

Moreover, through our attempt to take a deep dive into the semiosphere within which the specific designs of banknotes and coins were created, we will be able to identify the functioning of cultural memory and, specifically, of heritage. We will work with design elements (themes, spaces, historical episodes and events, etc.) that, since they have been chosen by the government to decorate banknotes and coins, we can assume they are valorized in positive terms. Here, 'a positive valorization' is a technical term of semiotics. We can see this valorization in action when some of the design elements are maintained from one series to the following one, and particularly when they are replaced by new ones. Relating the texts that constitute our corpus to other texts belonging to the same semiosphere will allow us to study discursive continuity and discontinuity within that semiosphere.

To sum up, in this book we propose a type of cultural approach to banknotes and coins using a semiotic perspective, methodology and analytical instruments. We will use a limited selection of visual texts that were produced within a specific semiosphere to gain access to the discursive forces producing them and, in doing so, to a portion of the semiosphere. Our assumption is, following Heinz Tschachler (2010: 4), that 'money is more than a commercial convenience; it is also always a document of culture'. When doing this type of textual analysis, we will follow the idea that Gianfranco Marrone (2021: 15) summarizes in the following passage:

> The text is not a material excuse for possible interpretations that integrate the context or that even justify its existence, but the formal dispositive through which meaning articulates and manifests itself, circulating in society and in culture. This is, therefore, the specific object of study for the semiologist, who, through analysis, must attempt to reconstruct its forms and dynamics, its internal articulations and levels of pertinence.

* * *

The purpose of this chapter was to introduce semiotics as a discipline with an object of study, methods and instruments, together with some of its key concepts, plus an introductory explanation of two of its sub-branches – those that we will draw on in what follows. It goes without saying that the introduction of semiotics we propose in this chapter is only a brief characterization, and it is meant just to provide the reader – particularly the one with interest in cultural issues but not necessarily familiar with semiotics – with some theoretical and methodological background to understand what comes up next, and particularly what the specificity of our approach is. Much more could have been said about the discipline, specifically regarding its epistemological and theoretical assumptions, as well as its concepts and analytical instruments. We will introduce some more analytical instruments in Chapter 3 when presenting the method to use when studying the design of banknotes and coins.

3

Studying Currency Design Using Semiotics

In Chapter 1, we argued for the social relevance of currency as a material object that signifies, that is, that functions as a carrier of meanings that are grounded on a deeper level, linked to discourses of the nation and the state. There we also claimed that cultural memory shapes currency design because it mediates how discourses of the national state are brought to life, usually through heritage. Then, in Chapter 2, we introduced semiotics as a discipline with both a specific object of study and historical development. We will study texts of a visual nature with the purpose of gaining access to the meaning-making dynamics of culture. By examining texts, we will be in a position to see how culture functions.

In this chapter, we move closer to the semiotic study of currency design. As already argued, using semiotics to study currency design involves using concepts, methods and instruments produced within the discipline called 'semiotics'. Therefore, to begin with, we propose a general – and selective – mapping of the existing scholarship on currency design with the purpose of identifying and delimiting the (interdisciplinary) research area our work should contribute to (Section 3.1). Then, we begin working with currency design using a semiotic perspective. Since this is what we do in each of the analytical chapters, here we only propose general and introductory remarks (Section 3.2). Finally, we elaborate on the semiotic methodology that we use in the analyses as of Chapter 4 (Section 3.3).

3.1 Scholarship on national currencies and currency design

Money and currency have been objects of interest for scholars from various disciplines. Given their complex nature as institutional facts (see Section 1.2 of Chapter 1), they can be approached from myriad scholarly perspectives, and with a focus on different aspects. Therefore, scholars have studied several dimensions of these two social institutions, depending on their research focus and interests. This section proposes a general overview of the scholarship on these issues, with particular attention to those relating to design. This mapping is not extensive but only intended to show the accumulation of knowledge where our book tries to contribute, as well as some of the sources it draws from.

As we saw in Chapter 1, we can find references to currency already in the works of Aristotle, if not before. Nevertheless, probably the most two well-known scholars interested in money were Karl Marx and Georg Simmel, who dealt with the topic in *Das Kapital* and *Philosophie des Geldes*, respectively. As philosophers, they were interested above all in the societal effects of money, and particularly in the interactions between individuals when using money, under the assumption that money can change social relations.

Other scholars, generally historians and political scientists, have studied the history of money and currency, usually with a focus on how these social institutions changed over time, and particularly as technological developments allowed leaving aside the use of valuable objects to carry economic value (Weatherford, 1997; Davies, 2002; North, 2009; Helleiner, 1998; Spufford, 1988). Others have shown interest in the role of money in the construction of political power (Eich, 2022).

Beyond philosophical and historical accounts, and already closer to a semiotics of money and currency, some have approached these social institutions as semiotic phenomena, that is, with an interest in their nature as sign systems where something stands for economic value, storing, carrying and expressing it (Bankov, 2019, 2022; Wennerlind, 2001; Oakley and Zlatev, 2024). Others have approached currency as a medium, that is, as a material object that serves as the vehicle of contents located at other levels and that, hence, carries social meanings (Zelizer, 2017; Wennerlind, 2001; Dodd, 1994).

Eric Helleiner was a pioneer in studying currencies and their link with the national. In a paper from 1998, 'National Currencies and National Identities', Helleiner claimed that national currencies can foster national identities in a number of ways. In the first paragraph of the paper, Helleiner (1998: 1409) claims that 'in the large and rapidly growing literature on nationalism, currency structures are rarely mentioned as significant', and proposes that 'if we turn to shelves of books on money and currencies, the significance of national currencies to national identities is sometimes acknowledged, but usually just in passing before attention is focused on more economic rules'. Things have changed since then, as evidenced in several publications since the 2000s.

Helleiner's main contributions to the study of currency design are found in two books: *The Making of National Money*, published in 2003, and one co-edited with Emily Gilbert, *Nation-States and Money*, from 1999. In the former, the author explores the historical process of territorialization of currencies, that is, of binding them to specific territories linked to national states. In their introduction, Gilbert and Helleiner (1999: 1) argue how 'examining money from a more interdisciplinary perspective may help to elucidate the significance of national currencies for nation-states as well as the challenges to these monetary structures in our contemporary age'. They advocate for a study of currency and money considering geographical, political, social and cultural aspects, with a specific focus on the historical relationship between money and national states.

Probably, this interest in the topic was triggered by the discussions around introducing a common, supranational currency in the member states of the EU. Moreover, the collapse of political structures such as the USSR and Yugoslavia, which was the source of the emergence of new national currencies, might also have been a cause for this interest.

Interest in currency design and the meanings that banknotes and coins carry have grown since the decade of 1990s, probably thanks to the interest of the research community in cultural studies and cultural approaches within the social sciences, such as cultural geography and cultural anthropology. When scholars began focusing on the social and cultural dimensions of banknote and coin design, they usually approached them through the lens of banal nationalism, a fresh and novel analytical category that Michael Billig introduced in 1995. Given that the main intuition was that currency is a means to express nationhood, these researchers aimed at understanding how national and statal contents could be identified in those designs. However, the analyses tended to focus on banknotes and coins from the past and not on current ones (Gilbert, 1998; Hewitt, 1999; McGinley, 1993). Since then, several studies that are relevant for our purposes in this book have been published.

A good example is Hans de Heij's book *Designing Banknote Identity*, published in 2012 under the auspices of De Nederlandsche Bank, the Netherland's central bank. In the book, de Heij studies what he calls a banknote's 'identity' and its function, claiming that 'a banknote is the ambassador of the country and the culture it represents' and proposing readers a journey through the history of currency design. The author supports his theoretical arguments with multiple examples from around the world and from different eras, making this book a must-read for anyone interested in the subject. Other relevant systematic approaches to currency design are available in German, many of them compiled in the collective volume *Der schöne Schein. Symbolik und Ästhetik von Banknoten*, edited by Stefan Hartmann and Christian Thiel (2016).

Besides, there are a few publications on case studies. In those, theory and specific hypotheses about currency design are presented and sustained. In the book *The Greenback*, Heinz Tschachler (2010) presents various ideas that are relevant for us. While some were mentioned in Chapter 1, others will be discussed in Chapter 4 when studying the US dollar. Although Tschachler does not specifically use a semiotic perspective to study US paper money, his cultural perspective based on an analysis of material culture is a good example of the relevance of studying currency design with a focus on national culture. As he puts it, 'studying forms and objects culturally [...] is the study *through* cultural objects and forms of the values, assumptions, ideas, attitudes, and beliefs of a particular community or society at a given time' (2010: 4).

In a paper from 2001, Tim Unwin and Virginia Hewitt (2001: 1005) studied the images used in Eastern European countries for currency design after the collapse of the Soviet Union. The authors claim that banknotes 'provide an important expression of the cultural and political identities that have helped to shape the nations in the past'. In their comparative work, they study 267 banknotes from seventeen Eastern European countries in the 1990s. In line with Hewitt's previous work (1994, 1995; Hewitt and Keyworh, 1987), the authors emphasize the artistic dimension of banknotes, claiming that

> banknotes are remarkable pieces of art; used daily, they rapidly become tattered and damaged, but like any great artwork they require very considerable skill to design and produce. The fine detail of their engraving, the technical knowledge required for the production of the increasingly sophisticated security measures incorporated into their design, and the complexity and beauty of the imagery contained within them make banknotes as worthy of study in themselves as any other art form. (Unwin and Hewit, 2001: 1007)

Other researchers have also emphasized the artistic nature of banknotes (Monestier, 1982). However, designing banknotes and coins is an enunciative praxis with several constraints, many of them originating in the features that characterize currency design as a *discursive genre* that is culturally codified. According to Turri (2014: 228, my translation), as a social object, currency must meet two conditions: a functional purpose and the marked medium, the latter being 'the inscription that gives it a recognized validity-legality'. According to Turri (2014: 228, my translation),

> Only the distinctive mark allows the item to be accepted as currency and perform the functions assigned to it. The very name of the currency – pound,

> dirham, etc. – is the sign of its identity, its autonomy and its guarantee; so that the currency represents the first widely circulating 'publication', created by human work, in specific places and at specific times.

Another relevant author to study currency design is Jacques Hymans. In his 2004 paper 'The Changing Colour of Money', Hymans works with a database composed of banknotes from fifteen European countries before the introduction of the euro. His findings identify geographical similarity and temporal difference. As he puts it, 'the combination of iconographic similarity across space and iconographic difference across time suggests that European states have indeed been less likely to try to use their control of currency to indoctrinate their publics, and more likely to try to use the values fashionable in pan-European society to enhance the legitimacy of their currency and of themselves' (Hymans, 2004: 6).

Studies such as the ones listed above have been crucial in the quest for identifying the encyclopaedic repertoires frequently used for currency design, which usually consist of past rulers, scientists and artists – including writers, painters, musicians, mathematicians, engineers and philosophers (Unwin and Hewitt, 2001: 1016) – but also nature, landscape and, in a more distant time, allegorical figures usually shaped by discourses and imaginaries of classicism. Regarding the latter, Gilbert (1998: 65) argues that 'despite the innovations of monetary form, classical images maintained a continuity with the representations on metallic currencies which had – obviously – featured classical images since their inception'. The analytical chapters shall illustrate all this.

Finally, in this general mapping of existing scholarship on national currencies and, specifically, on currency design, it is also worth mentioning the work of Jan Penrose (2011), who explored the relationship between the nation, the state and its official products such as banknotes and stamps. Focusing on the process of designing currency, Penrose challenges the assumption that national states use currency design – specifically banknotes – to foster banal nationalism. Moreover, together with Craig Cumming, the authors highlight 'the power of the concept of nation to inspire symbolic representations of a socially constructed community across time and in space' (Penrose and Cumming, 2011: 839). The authors also claim that banknote iconography is 'easily adapted to the service of political posturing, the negotiation of power relations and the shoring up of corporate image and stability' (Penrose and Cumming, 2011: 839).

To sum up, it should be clear that this book is not published in a research void, neither is it proposing a new research object. On the contrary, scholars from various disciplines have already shown interest and studied what is being addressed here. As Gabriel (2016: 19, my translation) claims, 'the visual language of money provides material for different research interests, so that one would like to see a research network on the "political iconography of money" as part of an interdisciplinary and international programme of cultural studies'.

In light of this claim, our purpose in this section is to propose a general and introductory mapping to scholarship and research on banknotes and coins in terms of their design and iconography, as well as in terms of their relationship with discourses of the nation and the state. In the following section, we argue what semiotics' specific contribution to studying currency design can be.

3.2 Semiotics' contribution to studying currency design

As discussed in the previous section, with our work we aim to contribute to a research field that has been active at least since the decade of 1990s. In this section, we justify what our semiotic perspective will add to the existing scholarship on the subject. In doing so, we will be dealing with the specificity of a semiotic approach to currency design.

Studying currency design using a semiotic perspective means conceiving of this object of study as both a product and a practice. Banknotes and coins are material objects that circulate in the social space. When we encounter them, we recognize them thanks to their design. These specific designs are the products. Hence, we can handle them as closed units with an internal articulation that we can study as texts thanks to those features.

However, someone must do something for the designs of banknotes and coins to exist. Creating these designs implies both a competence and a performance, that is, a knowledge or know-how – *savoir-faire*, in French – and a directive that grants the power to legitimately create these designs. There is a difference between the competence and the performance of the legitimate currency designer and those of the counterfeiter. Hence, when comparing an authentic banknote with one counterfeited, even if we cannot identify which is which by looking at them, there is a process of creation sustaining the design that contributes to the legitimacy of the product. Therefore, the product is dependent on the process.

As we saw in Chapter 1, various agents are usually involved in creating the designs of banknotes and coins. In this sense, there is a difference between this type of visual creation and traditional artworks. When agents such as a central bank, a government, committees, a graphic designer and so on get involved in the process of designing currency, they have a specific objective in mind: creating designs that serve the purpose of identifying material objects that store and stand for economic value linked to a specific currency, and that must be recognized as such by the users. Therefore, we are dealing with a *semiotic* practice.

As a semiotic practice, creating designs to decorate banknotes and coins is also an *enunciative praxis*, that is, an act in which an enunciator produces discourse in the form of texts. When examining enunciation in the context of the discursive genre of our interest in this book, some challenges arise. Above all, there is the challenge of the multiple layers of enunciation, which are at least two. On the one hand, there is a *technical* enunciator, or a set of them: while a specific human agent (either an individual or a team) creates the designs, another defines the security features to be included, another one prints them on paper, another one mints them on metal and so on. On the other hand, there is an *institutional* enunciator, which has the final say and responsibility regarding the designs. Ultimately, the institutional enunciator will be responsible for the work of the technical enunciator.

For example, if a contested or polemic historical character is chosen to be used on a banknote or coin, accusations will most probably be directed towards the institutional enunciator, and not the technical enunciator, because it is the former who is conceived of as the enunciator behind the enunciation producing that specific utterance (*enoncé*). However, if the design of a banknote is defective, the blame will probably fall on the technical enunciator.

Since we are interested in accessing discourses about the nation and the state, conceiving of the graphic designer in charge of creating the specific designs as the enunciator of the visual texts of our interest will not bring us far. This would be relevant for a semiotic approach interested in artistic creation, and specifically in how the specific traits that define the style of an artist can be found in his/her visual texts. For us, it seems more appropriate and productive to focus on the institutional sphere of enunciation, that is, the one linked with state actors. This focus also applies to those cases where the designs were created by a specific graphic designer, clearly identified and celebrated in the public sphere, such as the newest designs of the Swiss franc (as discussed in Chapter 7).

The enunciative praxis sustaining currency design is multilayered, negotiated between various actors and, generally, a process extended in time. Since it produces material objects whose identification as currency depends on their visual appearance (Mugnaini, 1994), a series of constraints are in place that limit the creative process. To begin with, since banknotes and coins are *official* texts, they must include a set of visual elements that guarantee their authenticity and institutional validity, such as handwritten signatures, official seals and identification numbers, among others. These elements are included in the designs to express their legitimacy as part of a social institution that is backed by the state and dependent on it. Moreover, multiple security measures need to be included to prevent counterfeiting and to assure authenticity, such as watermarks, security strips and translucid windows.

Design elements like these are important because banknotes and coins are not intrinsically valuable, as were the coins minted in gold and silver used in the past. If we destroy a 200 euro banknote, we are in fact destroying a piece of the fabric that we call 'paper money'. Evidently, we would in principle not want to destroy it because we recognize the value it stores and stands for, which is granted by the social institution relating this piece of fabric to an economic value. It is important to emphasize that we cannot perceive the economic value in the banknote itself, other than when the piece of fabric is *marked as such*, that is, it is contained in the visual traces that allow us to identify the note as one of 200 euro.

If we take this line of thought one step further, we can see currency design as a process of textual creation in which a pole of enunciation – composed of various agents – creates a limited set of texts that are conditioned by a number of issues and regulations. To begin with, the units of a given currency system are generally created in a systemic relationship with each other. This relationship regards not only the organization of the economic values to be included as part of that currency system – that is, the nominal values that banknotes and coins will store, which is already an arbitrary decision – but also the visual elements such as colour, shapes, positioning of elements in the topological grid and elements of the local encyclopaedia used for the designs. As we will see, if there is something that characterizes a family of banknotes, that is the continuity we can identify between the units that compose the visual system.

As a process of graphic design that materializes in visual texts, currency design has certainly an artistic dimension, which requires someone to possess a competence, that is, a know-how or *savoir-faire*. For Unwin and Hewitt (2001: 1007), banknotes are 'remarkable pieces of art' and, as is the case in any artistic activity, creating them requires specific competences and skills. This competence involves manipulating shapes and images within the constraints and limitations imposed both by the format of the material support and social practice, the latter including those practices that are traditional and customary and that allow us to identify the discursive genre.

When considered from a semiotic perspective, currency design is hence a semiotic practice that produces visual texts, which circulate in material objects that we can clearly delimit and include as part of our analytical corpus: banknotes and coins. These two elements are created on different material supports that we call 'paper' and 'metal'. The nature of paper and metal as material supports (physical properties) made of them media that humans consider appropriate (efficient) to create currency even today.

The relationship between materials evidences a hierarchy. Within a currency system, coins are usually used for lower values, whereas banknotes are normally used to store higher values. Moreover, it is common to encounter the ranges of nominal values used in each of the two material supports clearly delimited – for example, it is not usual to find economic values interspersed between coins and banknotes: we encounter nominal values in coins up to a certain value, and banknotes from that value on, until the highest one. Hence, we can identify an ordered growing progression beginning in coins and using metal and finishing in banknotes and using paper money. There is a logic governing the use of materials and the organization of units within the system.

In that growing progression from low/coin to high/banknote, there is a point of discontinuity where the economic values of the currency system pass from one material support to the other. That point of discontinuity is a specific value. In the case of the euro, that passage occurs from the 2 euro coin to the 5 euro note. The system does include neither a 2 euro note nor a 5 euro coin. However, some currency systems do have the same value on a coin and a banknote, although this does not seem to be common practice. Moreover, when a currency loses purchasing power, it is common to see denominations that previously were stored in banknotes created as part of the coin system, which is used for lower values.

The passage of a specific value from a banknote to a coin can be accompanied by visual strategies that contribute to producing a sense effect of continuity. A good example is the Paraguayan guaraní. At some point in history, the 1,000 guaraníes banknote was removed from the system, and a coin was created to store that value. As shown in Figure 2, the portrait of Francisco Solano López, the historical character used in the banknote, was maintained in the coin.

Looking at Figure 2, we can see how in our day and age cash currency is produced using two tangible and material supports that bring a number of physical properties with them that condition, limit and affect the creation of visual texts. Because of the material constitution of each support, when passing from paper to metal the figurative traits of Solano López's portrait change: while

Figure 2 Front side of the banknote and the coin of 1,000 Paraguayan guaraníes.
Source: Banco Central del Paraguay.

paper allows for a technique – printing – where high levels of figurative density – even its highest grade: iconism – can be achieved, minting on metal is a technique that highly conditions and limits figurative density.

Regarding banknotes, even if we call the medium used to create them 'paper money', their matter has not been paper for a long time. Nowadays, banknotes are made of fabrics composed either of cotton and linen, or polymer. For example, the banknotes of the US dollar are printed in a fabric that is made with 75 per cent of cotton and 25 per cent of linen, whereas those of the Canadian dollar use polymer – that is, plastic. Currently, there is a tendency to abandon cotton in favour of polymer.

This migration from one material to the other allows new creative possibilities, such as the inclusion of transparencies and holograms as security measures. These were impossible to include in banknotes using cotton-linen, because these materials simply cannot be translucid or shiny. In some currency systems, when transitioning from the use of cotton-linen to polymer, the designs are maintained, even if some details might change thanks to the new possibilities allowed by the physics of polymer as matter.

The gradual historical replacement of paper with a cotton-based fabric, and more recently with polymer, responds to a fundamental need to ensure the institutional nature of money: its permanence and resistance throughout time. As we saw in Chapter 1, currency is a social institution created as a medium, that is, as something that stands for something else which it stores. Therefore, it is necessary for banknotes and coins to last in time and to be as indestructible as possible, because storing them is a crucial need linked to their institutional function.

These requirements are related to the circulation of banknotes and coins in everyday life. Unlike electronic transactions, which exist in the form of digital information that we manipulate using digital devices, banknotes and coins depend on analogical carriers with a physical materiality. Hence, their value is partially dependent on the integrity of the physical carrier: no one would accept a broken or damaged banknote as a means of payment (especially of high values), and central banks usually provide citizens with instructions regarding what to do with damaged banknotes.

The transition towards polymer makes banknotes more difficult to destroy. Hence, it contributes to their durability in time. Although polymer banknotes can be destructed, this will probably be voluntary rather than accidental, as is the case with older banknotes. Unlike banknotes, which can be destroyed by hand or using scissors, coins are indestructible without the aid of specific tools. This somehow supposes a contradiction in the articulation of the discursive genre of currency in terms of the correspondence between nominal values and materials used to store them: intuitively, it would seem logical that the materials carrying the highest values would be the indestructible ones, because they are the most important to preserve.

Beyond the functional needs linked to their durability in time, banknotes and coins carry an institutional type of discourse of which the state is ultimately responsible as their main enunciator. Hence, there is a high degree of formality in the type of discursive construction that banknotes and coins support. It is therefore to be expected that the state institutions in charge of them will try to maintain their physical integrity as neat and pristine as possible. In this sense, one could read the state of the material support as connoting something about the state responsible for it. A damaged or torn banknote printed in cotton may project an unfavourable image of the state responsible for it, whereas a polymer banknote, thanks to the properties of the material, will be more difficult to damage, hence projecting a neater image of the state.

As media with a physical existence, both banknotes and coins have two sides, and both are designed. In the past, this was not always the case, and only one side of the material used for coinage was marked (de Heij, 2012). As we shall see in the analyses, in the current two-sided designs, it is common to encounter some type of relationship between the design of the front and the reverse, at least in banknotes.

To begin with, there is usually a chromatic relationship: the colour chosen to provide a banknote with its identity within the system is usually the same on both sides. This design choice contributes to a colour-coding that allows a quick identification of the banknotes that are part of the system. This is not usually the case with coins, which are easily confused among each other due to the nature of the material used to create them.

Besides, even if exceptions exist, a *thematic* relationship between the design elements included on the two sides of the banknote is also common. Generally, this thematic relationship is easy to recognize because the design elements included on both sides are known by the citizens of a country to be related, for example, as part of the narratives that constitute the nation's social imaginary. An example of this type of knowledge consists of relating an artist included on the front of a banknote with his or her work included on the reverse, or relating a military character depicted on the front with a historical battle in which he or she was involved, on the reverse.[1]

In a book dedicated to the semiotics of format, Tiziana Migliore and Marion Colas-Blaise (2022: 8) argue that, at the empirical and phenomenal level, format is inherent to any form we encounter. This idea also applies to paper money and metal, the two material supports nowadays used as currency. We rarely think about the format of these substances. If format is defined following Migliore and Colas-Blaise (2022: 13, my translation) as 'the set of extensive measurements of a shape', then format issues are relevant and pertinent when studying banknotes and coins, specifically because they condition the frame for the creation of the visual texts. As argued in Chapter 2, the frame – what delimits the surface of the image and distinguishes it from an 'outside' – is a crucial aspect to conduct any visual analysis.

In the case of banknotes, their format involves cutting the fabric in a rectangular shape that establishes a standard relationship – a ratio – between the length and width of the paper. Even if this relationship varies from one currency system to another, the relationship between a longer and a shorter side is a constant of the genre, and it is so because of custom, not because anything in this ratio relates inherently with the institutional existence of currency. One could think of squared, triangular or circular banknotes, although storing them in the wallets we currently use would be challenging. The rectangular shape chosen for banknotes functions as the frame that Greimas (1989) identifies as the starting point for any visual analysis. While historically the rectangular format has been used horizontally, nowadays many currency systems are using it vertically, as we shall see in the analytical chapters.

The shape of coins is usually circular, or eventually one based on polygons, which help distinguish coins within the system from each other thanks to the form they take. Again, nothing inherent to coins as currency justifies these choices, which are arbitrary, based on custom and probably grounded on functional issues. The nature of the geometrical forms that are delimited by the option for a rectangular and a circular frame conditions the design, just as the size and the dimension of a canvas condition what an artist can paint in it, or the shape of the camera lens conditions what we see in a photograph or a film.

We mentioned that the rectangular format of banknotes allows designing them either horizontally or vertically. While throughout history the common practice was to design banknotes using a horizontal format, we currently see a growth in a preference for vertical use. This shift might be conditioned by the influence that vertical image has in our present time thanks to smart mobile phones. Hence, we can argue that decisions regarding the format to be used for currency design can carry connotations linked to the /classic/ vs. /contemporary/ dichotomy, where horizontal serves to express and connote values such as classicism, tradition and the past, and vertical expresses contemporaneity, innovation and the present/future. Through this lens, we could intuitively expect conservative governments to prefer horizontal designs, and progressive ones to prefer vertical.[2]

As Migliore and Colas-Blaise (2022: 9, my translation) propose, 'format contributes to the constitution of the form and thus imposes itself on the gaze. It contributes to the production of the object in the same way as the material from which it is made does'. Hence, format determines the possibility of semiotic creation within the space provided by the shape and frame of each banknote and coin.

The material used for coinage is much more limited in terms of its physical properties than the one used for banknotes. This material conditioning impacts the design work and possibilities. For example, due to the nature of metal, the use of colour is much more limited on coins than it is on banknotes. Moreover, because of the physical constitution of the material, it is more difficult to achieve a high degree of figurativity in coins, which is a challenge when depicting portraits of individuals in them, as shown in Figure 2. This might explain why, according to Heinz Tschachler (2001: 205), paper money is 'generally much more iconographically loaded than coinage. The large, rectangular shape of paper money affords ample space for expressing all kinds of ideas on a familiar canvas and thus for serving functions beyond the mere economic'.

In Figure 2, we saw two depictions of the same historical character. The difference between the two portraits of the same individual is highly noticeable, as is the iconographical load of the two material supports. In figurative terms, while the portrait included in the banknote can be read as one based on a copy of a photograph due to its highly iconic and even hyper-realistic visual nature, the one on the coin is much more simplistic and has less level of detail. Although it is still an iconic type of image (a copy of a picture that should quickly bring us to the individual that is depicted), our recognition of who that depiction stands for is less direct and more mediated by cultural competence. In terms of interpretative semiotics, the question revolves around how we arrive at identifying what we see as something that relates to what it stands for.

To convey sociocultural contents and signify on the two material substances that societies use as currency in our day and age, designers manipulate the visual dimension and hence draw both on figurative and plastic elements. Some of the concepts of visual semiotics such as those introduced in Chapter 2 can be used to study currency design.

To begin with, there are topological, chromatic and eidetic elements at play. As we saw, these terms refer to the dimensions of position and use of space, colours and shapes, respectively. As an example, there are no colourless currency systems in our day and age, or systems created using black and white only. From the moment that technological developments allowed the use of colour to design banknotes, all currency systems include coloured banknotes.

Moreover, currency systems generally have different colours to distinguish the identity of each of the banknotes that compose it. As we shall see in Chapter 4, until its newest designs, the US dollar was an exception to this rule, since all the banknotes were created using green as the dominant colour. Even if each banknote has its own identity thanks to the economic value it stores and stands for, the design elements it includes and eventually its size and colour function as another resource used to distinguish units within the system.

Besides our interest in banknotes from the perspective of visual semiotics, we have an interest in them from a cultural perspective. As argued before, the iconographic elements – historical characters and events, animals, spaces, landscapes, buildings, practices and so on – included in banknotes and coins as part of the design elements reflect the defining traits of a discursive genre grounded on a need of expressing a semiosphere in national and statal terms. This expression consists of recovering from the collective memory specific cultural contents that can be easily linked with the national state by the addressee of the designs. Hence, as we shall see, the selection of design elements is generally made based on the dynamics of the local encyclopaedia, that is, of the body of shared knowledge that is stored in the semiosphere linked to each specific nation as a space of production and circulation of sense and as a repository of collective memory.

Since the number of banknotes and coins that a currency system has is limited, the actors involved in the pole of enunciation must select a limited number of design elements to be used to express the national semiosphere. This involves leaving aside other elements and, eventually, can lead to debates and arguments about what should be included and what should not. As we will see in what follows, the study of what is left out from an iconographic decision can also shed light on the sense that banknotes and coins produce in terms of what the state chooses to celebrate.

Monica Sassattelli (2021: 199) argues that, besides limited, the selection of design elements is in many cases biased, notably influenced by political or historical circumstances. This can be a source of collective public demands for a more equitable and inclusive integration of a plurality of historical figures and events of a nation's shared past, as we shall see in the analyses.

We will use a semiotic perspective. This will allow us to group the design elements we encounter on currency as part of local encyclopaedic repertoires (groups of signs: people, animals, landscapes, etc.). These are portions of the semiosphere. These local encyclopaedic repertoires can be seen as a means of a strategy to express the identity of both nation and state. We will approach them with a focus on how they signify and are meaningful thanks to their opposition with other possibilities. In doing this, we will also explore the discourses that circulate in the specific semiosphere of our interest in each chapter, so we can make sense of why these repertoires, and not others, might have been prioritized.

Another issue relevant for a semiotic account of currency design is that of the relationship of a sign or text with what it is meant to stand for. Drawing on Peirce's ideas, a common classification of signs is based on the relationship they establish with what they stand for. According to this account, signs can be icons, indexes and symbols. Considering the type of textual creation that characterizes currency design, we will have a special interest in iconic signs, that is, in images that are the result of a textual construction anchored in some kind of resemblance to what they stand for, usually involving traits that ensure a high degree of figurativity.[3]

The idea of iconism has been criticized, most notably by Umberto Eco (1975). To avoid the complex discussion regarding the specific mode of sign production involved in icons, in what follows we will use the term to refer to a mode of sign and textual production in which an evident link between image and factual reality can be recognized, as is usually the case in the genre of currency design.

The word 'usually' as used in the previous sentence is relevant because there are exceptions to the hegemony that iconicity has in the genre of currency design. If we consider the banknote of 1,000 guilder (*gulden*), the Netherlands' national currency before being replaced by the euro, depicted in Figure 3, we see that the depictions of the historical character included in the banknotes is less realistic than the ones we generally encounter. In fact, when looking at this type of depiction, it is less evident to use the word 'portrait' to refer to them.

Figure 3 Front and reverse of the 1972 1,000 guilder banknote.
Source: De Nederlandsche Bank.

Although this type of textual creation is also possible in the genre of currency design, it is definitely not the standard.

The banknote depicted in Figure 3 includes a portrait grounded on a specific historical character: Baruch Spinoza. However, it would be hard to consider this image a portrait, since the basic traits that define a portrait (to begin with, that the visual text should resemble as much as possible the model in a *mimetic* manner) are not respected. If we can recognize Spinoza here, it is above all thanks to cultural competence, and not thanks to the figurative or iconic resemblance of the depiction with the individual that is being depicted. Here, besides the salience of the artist in charge of creating the design, some cultural conventions mediate, allowing us to recognize the figure we see in the banknote as one that was created based on the famous Dutch philosopher. Dynamics like these constitute one of the arguments used to criticize iconism as a closed and fixed sign form and to argue that cultural conventions are always involved in textual creation, even those with higher degrees of figurativity.[4]

Moreover, if we look at the design of the reverse of the 1,000 guilder banknote, we encounter an image that definitely is not grounded on iconism. Instead, we encounter a visual text that is closer to the abstract pole of creation than to the figurative one, as discussed in Chapter 2. As we shall see in the analytical chapters, this type of non-figurative, abstract composition is also exceptional to the genre of currency design, which tends to function based on a high degree of figurative density as close as possible to iconism.

To sum up, it should be now clear what our semiotic perspective will be looking at, and how it differs from previous studies of currency design. As argued before, semiotics is a discipline informed and sustained by textual analyses based on work with empirical corpora. As of Chapter 4, in our efforts to explain how and why the designs of banknotes and coins are meaningful within the semiosphere they originate in, we will work with matters of format, colour, shapes, topology and contents.

3.3 Analytical methodology

This section introduces the methodology that we will use to analyse the selected currencies. As already argued, the banknotes and coins that compose the currency system of a given country do not exist in a void – they are dependent on discourses circulating within the semiosphere. Therefore, our analysis from a semiotic perspective should be capable of relating the textual and the discursive dimensions, that is, the visual manifestation in the form of images with the productive forces those images are grounded on.

Each of the following chapters will begin with an introduction of the currency we will analyse. We will propose some general notes on context such as relevant historical information and current status of the currency, so we can situate our object of study in its sociohistorical context. In this sense, declarations of politicians and texts shared on official websites such as those of central banks will function as paratexts and, as such, as sources for us to find interpretative lenses that can help us understand which discourses sustain textual production.

Then, we will introduce and describe our corpus. Every currency system we analyse in the book consists of a limited set of banknotes and coins, generally amounting to a total of eight to thirteen units. In each chapter, depending on the relevance of their iconography, we will decide if we include coins in the analysis or not. This decision is linked to the criterion of pertinence, which is central to semiotic research. Coins might not be pertinent for our analysis because, whereas the design of banknotes seems to be carefully taken care of, in many cases the design of coins is less relevant for those producing them, and we might encounter coins that only differ in the nominal value and not in the design.

We will study the front and the reverse of the banknotes and coins that constitute the corpus. In looking at them, we will describe the design elements we recognize, and we will try to group them as elements that belong to specific local encyclopaedias. These local encyclopaedias are those of historical characters, events and places, arts, scientific activity, landscape, fauna, flora and so on. Therefore, when presenting the corpus, we will create lists of the design elements we encounter in the banknotes and coins, and we will propose a preliminary segmentation of these elements as a way of ordering what we see.

For reasons of focus, we will leave aside from our study commemorative and special banknotes and coins, which are normally produced to mark specific historical moments and events. Although these banknotes and coins are relevant for the theoretical purposes we have here, they are usually clearly divergent in visual terms from the standard currency system. Hence, their discontinuity with regard to the standard designs is generally clearly visible and justified from the outset, which provides a point to identify their nature as a banknote or coin that is *special*.

After introducing and describing the corpus, we will proceed with the analysis of the units that compose it. We will begin with the visual dimension and then move onto the cultural one. In the first place, we will consider visual issues such as format and layout, paying attention to size, colour, shapes and other semiotic resources that produce an effect of seriality and, with it, of a semiotic system grounded on some shared visual traits. Among other issues, we will look at the chromatic and thematic relation between the two sides of a unit, but also between the units of the system.

Moreover, we will consider the semiotic resources used to express the state and its identity in currency design, such as stamps, signatures and names of institutions and authorities. All these seem to be a constant element of the design of banknotes and coins since they grant the design with its validity, legitimacy, security and the necessary institutional backup. Since each currency system can be related to an institutional enunciator as its creator, we can expect signs of its identity to be present in the designs.

Then, we will delve into the semiosphere of the political entity producing the banknotes and coins of our interest in the chapter, in attempting to make sense of why the elements used to decorate them might have been chosen. We will pay particular attention to the local encyclopaedias (characters, activities, animals, landscapes, events, epochs and episodes, etc.) that were chosen for currency design. Moreover, we will try to render visible the type of cultural memory that the iconography selected to design banknotes and coins activates, as well as the idea of national identity it constructs.

Although we addressed this issue in Chapter 2, it is worth repeating that one of the defining traits of semiotics is its empirical anchorage. Semioticians interested in sociocultural issues analyse texts and try to explain how, why, what and when they signify. Therefore, each analytical chapter will focus on the semiotic study of a specific currency and examine how it serves as the material support for conveying a particular idea of the political entity – nation, and European identity, in the case of the euro – using encyclopaedic contents that belong to cultural memory, which is a type of public and collective memory.

The working method and specific instruments that we will use in our analyses are the standard in sociocultural semiotics based on discourse. Hence, through an examination of the dimension of the expression (the designs we encounter in banknotes and coins), we will argue how specific cultural contents are used to produce specific meanings relevant within the local semiosphere linked to the nation and the state. Hence, looking at the visual discontinuities that we identify within the frame of each banknote and coin, we aim to recognize different images, shapes, colours, conventional signs, elements from the natural world and so on and, in the process, dive deeper into their articulation with local discourses about the nation and the state.

Therefore, to grasp the local semiospheres and why the local encyclopaedias used for currency design might be relevant within them, when possible we will try to draw on discussions and debates revolving around collective identity – and specifically *national* identity – in each of the political entities behind the selected currencies. We will work with products (static, closed) and this should allow us to access processes (dynamic, open). We can only access the latter through the former, according to Verón (1988: 126–7, my translation):

> We always proceed from 'packages' of sensitive matters invested with sense which are *products*; in other words, we always proceed from configurations of sense identified on a material support (linguistic text, image, system of action whose support is the body, etc. …), which are fragments of semiosis. Whatever the material support, what we call a discourse or a discursive set is nothing other than a spatio-temporal configuration of sense.

The specific instruments we will use in our analyses are those commonly used in sociocultural semiotics, and our use of them will depend on the analytical needs we encounter in each chapter. In some cases, we will be interested in the workings of narrativity and how the social discourses that we encounter in banknotes and coins articulate national history in narrative terms. In others, we will have a special interest in the use of isotopies – that is, thematic repetitions – to propose a specific idea of the nation and its institutions. Moreover, in some cases we will be interested in exploring the different types of textual construction a design element can be object of.

While the specific analytical needs will be triggered by what the banknotes and coins we encounter tell us, we will normally delve into the dimension of what Greimas calls 'the deep structures of narrativity'. It is here that the main units of meaning – such as nature/culture, humans/animals, past/present, classicism/modernism and so on – that articulate discourses about the nation are to be found. Moreover, we will identify the axiologization that these units of meaning are invested with within the specific social discourses of the nation, usually in positive terms.

Looking at the deep structures, we will identify major semantic oppositions underlying textual construction in the specific figurative designs we encounter. Generally put, our main interest will be to see how specific semantic units are brought to life in figurative terms, through specific design elements that we can recognize as relating to something we already know. Besides exploring the dimension of the deep structures, we will look at how these are thematized in discourse using figurative elements, such as actors, spaces and specific times of history, but also of allegorical figures, such as personifications of the nation. In each chapter, we will introduce relevant analytical tools and instruments originating in semiotics, always trying to apply them to the specific corpus of our interest there.

4

US Dollar

In this first analytical chapter, we study the US dollar, the official currency of the United States. The US dollar is not only the most traded currency in the world but also one the reader is probably familiar with due to the worldwide salience and visibility it has, not only as a means of economic exchange but also in products of the cultural industry such as movies, series, videoclips and visual art (Tschachler, 2001).

Moreover, the consistency of the design elements used throughout the years in the design of the banknotes that compose this currency system, together with the nature of the overarching social discourses upon which it is designed, shall function for us as a benchmark to study the defining traits of currency design as a normative discursive genre, that is, a discursive genre that is governed by rules and norms, even if these are contingent and not necessary.

As was mentioned in Chapter 3, we will try to use an analytical methodology as consistent as possible across the chapters. We shall begin introducing the currency that we will work with through a brief contextual and historical description (Section 4.1). Then, we present the corpus, which is composed of the most recent designs of banknotes and coins with current validity. In doing this, we also compose a list of the iconographic elements we can recognize in the designs (Section 4.2). Finally, we analyse these elements paying special attention to how they might serve to figurativize social discourses related to the nation and the state (Section 4.3).

In the specific case of the US dollar, our interest will be to study how the strong nation-centric discursive strategy sustaining the design of banknotes and coins is brought to life through specific semiotic strategies and resources. As we shall see, the figurativization of the national state in the banknotes of this currency system is grounded above all on a group of historical characters and a set of buildings that are unmistakably related in the social imaginary and official history with the construction of the nation state sustaining this currency. Hence, as we will argue, these serve as semiotic resources for the display of a discursive strategy revolving in an evident and unquestionable manner to the idea of the US-American nation.

4.1 Context

The US dollar is the most traded currency in the world. According to scholars who have studied its history, the creation of paper currency in the United States dates from 1690, when the Massachusetts Bay Colony – one of the thirteen original colonies – created colonial notes to fund military expeditions (Tschachler, 2010: 8). Hence, its origins can be traced back to the colonial era.[1] In April 1792, the US Congress created the country's coinage system, known as 'Mint Act' or 'Coinage Act', which establishes the coinage system of the United States.

Currently, the authority in charge of regulating the US dollar banknotes is the Federal Reserve Board, known as 'the Fed', which has the functions equivalent to those of central banks in countries where such statal entity exists. The Fed was established in 1913 to fulfil in the United States the functions normally overseen by a country's central bank. US dollar banknotes are physically produced by the US Treasury's Bureau of Engraving and Printing, the entity in charge of printing banknotes centrally, since 1869. Before that year, private banknote companies produced US notes and sent them to the Bureau for sealing, trimming and cutting.[2]

The banknotes that compose the currency system of our interest in this chapter are Federal Reserve Notes, as clearly indicated in their design. As such, they are legal tender, an ontology that is guaranteed by the inclusion of the sentence 'this note is legal tender for all debts, public and private' as part of the design. Contrary to what occurs in other countries, US dollar banknotes never lose their validity, and they can be traded anytime (if they are not mutilated), even if they are not any longer printed and regardless of when they were issued (as long as they were produced after 1861). Differently from what is common in other countries, old banknotes – characterized by designs other than those of the current series – are neither recalled nor withdrawn from daily circulation.

Although the official denomination of the banknotes is 'US dollars', people commonly refer to them as 'bills', 'bucks' or 'greenbacks'. Some even refer to the different units of the system using the first name of the historical figure adorning them, such as 'George' for the $1 or 'Benjamin' for the $100.

According to Heinz Tschachler – a scholar who has extensively studied the US dollar and its circulation in popular and pop culture – it was Salmon P. Chase, secretary of the Treasury under Abraham Lincoln's presidency, who in 1863 requested banknote designs to tap on discourses of the nation. As Tschachler (2010: 15) writes, this request 'transformed neutral pieces of paper into symbols of national cohesiveness at a time when the nation's unity was in jeopardy'.

The US Federal Reserve has announced that new designs will be gradually introduced for the $5, $10, $20, $50 and $100 banknotes. According to the schedule in mid-2025, the introduction of the new $10 banknote shall occur in 2026, that of $50 in 2028, that of $20 in 2030, that of $5 in 2032 and that of $100 in 2034.[3] This evidences how studying currency design involves working with open and changing objects of study, and hence a permanent need to update the work done.

4.2 Banknotes and coins of the US dollar

Our corpus in this chapter consists of thirteen units: seven banknotes and six coins. The banknotes are those corresponding to the nominal values $1, $2, $5, $10, $20, $50 and $100, and coins, to $1 and five decimal fractions: 1, 5, 10, 25 and 50 cents. According to the US Mint, $1 and 50 cent coins are currently produced as collectibles, even if the Federal Reserve might still order them for standard circulation, and hence to be used as legal tender.[4] Figure 4 presents the banknotes, and Figure 5, the coins.

Examining the corpus, we can see that one nominal value – $1 – is duplicated and can be found both on a banknote and a coin. Contrary to the case of the Paraguayan 1,000 guaraníes banknote and coin presented in Chapter 3, in this case we do not encounter a visual relationship between the $1 banknote and coin.

In terms of the nominal segmentation used to create banknotes and coins of the US dollar currency system, we can see a standard segmentation using values commonly found in other currency systems, such as those of 5, 10, 20, 50 and 100. However, it also includes banknotes for lower denominations, such as 1 and 2, which are rarer to find in other systems – think of the euro, whose banknote system begins with the €5 note.

Since the introduction of the current general design matrix, in 1929, all the banknotes of the system have the same size: 6.14 by 2.61 inches (equivalent to 15.6 by 6.6 cm). Therefore, there is no relationship between this aspect of format and value, as we will see in other currency systems, where the size of the banknote storing a value grows as economic value does.

Let us now proceed to identify the design elements we encounter in the visual texts from the corpus. While some of them are common to the seven

Figure 4 The seven banknotes of the US dollar currently in circulation.

Source: US Currency Education Program.

Value	Front	Reverse
1 cent (penny)		
5 cents (nickel)		
10 cents (dime)		
25 cents (quarter)		Various designs, many of them commemorative
50 cents		
$1		

Figure 5 The six coins of the US dollar with current standard circulation.

Source: US Mint.

banknotes that compose the system, others are linked to each unit's identity. Each banknote includes the full name of the country – the political entity – on both sides, stylized in bold, using all-caps and in similar sizes. Signatures, identificatory numbers and official stamps are located on the front side, as is the phrase 'this note is legal tender for all debts, public and private'. The back designs include always the inscription 'In God We Trust', although in different typefaces, sizes and locations. Every coin includes the word 'Liberty' – mandatory according to the Coinage Act of 1792 – and the inscription 'In God We Trust' in the front side. In the back, all the coins include the Latin inscription 'E pluribus unum' and the full name of the country, in all-caps but located in different positions.[5] The only design element common to the thirteen pieces of the system is the inscription 'In God We Trust', which a priori draws on a religious type of discourse.

From the common elements we encounter on banknotes, two are particularly relevant for our purposes. The first one is the seal of the Treasury Department, located at the right side of the banknote and combined with the nominal denomination of the note in words, using all-caps. The second one is the seal of the Federal Reserve Bank, located at the left of the main portrait of each banknote. From the previous series to the current one, the design of the latter changed, but its position in the topological grid was maintained. Figure 6 depicts the seals.

These seals are relevant because, as visual marks, they stand for the institutional dimension of the United States' identity as a national state, which is composed of several institutions. The three marks are designed using a similar model, which consist of a circle with some coded information and inscriptions, similar to the royal seals used in the past. We will come back to them in Section 4.3.

Seal of the Department of the Treasury.

Seal of the Federal Reserve Bank used in the 'old' series, with a letter inside referring to a specific bank.

Seal of the Federal Reserve Bank used in the 'new' series.

Figure 6 The institutional seals included in the US dollar banknotes.
Source: Author's own elaboration based on the images of Figure 4.

Table 1 List of Distinctive Design Elements Identified in the Seven Banknotes of the US Dollar.

Value	Front	Reverse
$1	A portrait of George Washington in the centre, surrounded by an oval frame	Word 'ONE' written using all-caps, located in the centre and between two circles, each of them depicting one side of the Great Seal of the United States
$2	A portrait of Thomas Jefferson in the centre, surrounded by an oval frame	A vignette of John Trumbull's painting of the moment of signing the Declaration of Independence
$5	A portrait of Abraham Lincoln in the centre A depiction of the Great Seal of the United States in the background on the right side of Lincoln's portrait	A depiction of the Lincoln Memorial
$10	A portrait of Alexander Hamilton in the centre The torch of the Statue of Liberty in the background on the left side of Hamilton's portrait The phrase 'WE THE PEOPLE' using a typeface that seems handwritten and in the background at the right of Hamilton's portrait A small, modern icon of the torch of the Statue of Liberty on the right of Hamilton's portrait	A depiction of the US Treasury
$20	A portrait of Andrew Jackson in the centre An eagle in the background, on the left side of Jackson's portrait The inscription 'TWENTY USA, USA TWENTY' in all-caps and with a curvy format in the background on the right of Jackson's portrait A small, modern icon of a coat of arms with an eagle on its top on the right of Jackson's portrait	A depiction of the White House
$50	A portrait of Ulysses S. Grant in the centre Two close-up details of the US flag in the background, both on the left and the right sides of Grant's portrait A small, modern icon of a five-points star at the right of Jackson's portrait	A depiction of the US Capitol
$100	A portrait of Benjamin Franklin in the centre A big golden feather in the background on the right of Franklin's portrait, together with a written text, dated 4 July 1776 A golden inkwell next to Franklin's portrait	A depiction of Independence Hall

Source: Author's own elaboration.

Table 2 List of Distinctive Design Elements Identified in the Six Coins of the US Dollar.

Value	Front	Reverse
1 cent	A profile portrait of Abraham Lincoln	The Union Shield, with the inscription 'ONE CENT' on it
5 cents	A portrait of Thomas Jefferson	An engraving of Monticello House
10 cents	A profile portrait of Franklin D. Roosevelt	An olive branch, a torch and an oak branch
25 cents	A profile portrait of George Washington	Various designs
50 cents	A profile portrait of John F. Kennedy	The Presidential Seal of the United States
$1	A back portrait of Sacagawea carrying her baby	Various designs

Source: Author's own elaboration.

Let us now have a look at the differential design elements included in each banknote and coin. Table 1 lists those in banknotes, and Table 2 does the same with coins. Here, elements referring to the economic value of each piece are left aside.

4.3 Analysis

Our analysis shall begin looking at the visual dimension of banknotes, with a particular interest to identify the design elements that allow us to recognize them as part of a series and, particularly, of the same visual system. When looking at the seven banknotes presented in Figure 4, we can rapidly see that two visual systems are currently coexisting. We will call these two systems 'old' and 'new'. While banknotes of $1 and $2 belong to the former, those of $5, $10, $20, $50 and $100 belong to the latter.

Despite the discontinuity we can identify thanks to how it is evidenced by a number of design elements, we can also recognize some sort of 'family resemblance' between the two systems. This allows us to postulate a discursive continuity between them, one that makes us regard the new designs as an update of the previous one and not one aiming at replacing and/or cancelling it.

The designs of the new system are relatively recent: they were introduced between 2004 and 2013. These banknotes were created gradually to replace those in the old system. This means that the current designs of the $1 and $2 banknotes

Figure 7 The remaining five US dollar banknotes from the old series.
Source: numista.com.

are not dissonant with the dominant visual system – the new – for a specific reason – that is, the discontinuity is not meant to be an act of communication but only a residual remanent of the previous system. In this sense, we could justifiably expect the design of these two banknotes to be updated and brought to the style of the new visual system. However, the authorities have already announced that these two banknotes will not be redesigned.[6]

In terms of its overarching visual identity, the old system contains some visual elements that foster quite neatly a sense effect of a series. Design elements help create this sense effect linked to the unity of the pieces that compose the system. Figure 7 shows the designs of the $5, $10, $20, $50 and $100 banknotes from the old system. Besides these nominal values, at some point in history the series also included banknotes for 500, 1,000, 5,000, and 10,000 dollars. These included the portraits of William McKinley, Grover Cleveland, James Madison and Salmon P. Chase, respectively, and their designs were consistent with the overarching visual system.

The systemic consistency is partially grounded on a series of topological, eidetic and chromatic elements that can be identified using a topological grid as the one presented in Figure 8, based on the design of the current $1

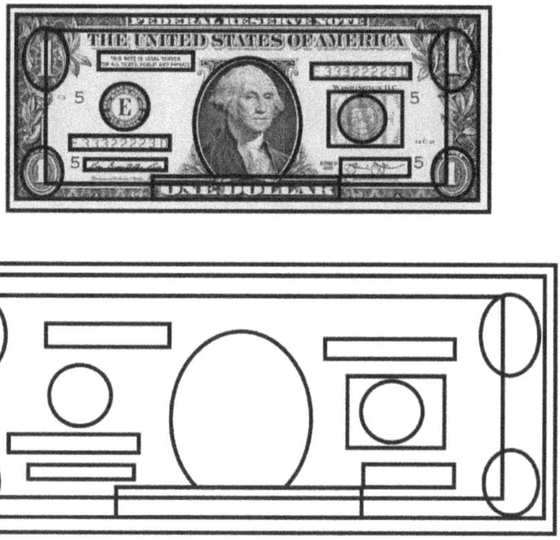

Figure 8 Topological grid of the US dollars from the old series.
Source: Author's own elaboration.

banknote. The seven banknotes of the old system were designed upon this same matrix, which helps to see them as highly related in visual terms.

In topological terms, we can identify a common disposition of elements in the surface that is delimited by the rectangular and horizontal frame, as shown in Figure 8. Perhaps the most salient feature of this visual system is the central oval used to frame the portrait of the historical character. The stamp and security marks located in central spaces both at the left and the right of that oval are also unchanged, contributing to a sense of unity.

However, some of the elements used to design the front side of the series differ from one banknote to the other, such as the portrait of the historical character used in the centre, the position and style of the country's name, the ornaments used for the internal coloured frame and the style of the numbers expressing the nominal value.

Since the oval used to embrace the central figure is a shape, its analysis would belong to the eidetic domain. We do not see any reasonable argument to justify the selection of this shape to highlight the character other than historical practice. However, the curves that define the oval shape somehow rhyme with the curvy forms used to design the Baroque internal frame of each banknote of this series.

These curvy elements, which connote some type of classicism, tradition and a past time (they could easily remind us of the wooden cravings used to decorate European furniture from past centuries and in artistic movements such as the Baroque or *art nouveau*), disappear in the new series (at least in the front designs). In eidetic terms, the curvy forms and design elements used are typically Baroque, a design style that dates from a past age and that contrasts with a classical (and neoclassical) style. As such, the Baroque style used in the old series contrasts with the newest designs, which are much more contemporary in how they look. The new series is first and foremost characterized by straight lines, which replace the curvy shapes from the previous one.

In chromatic terms, the seven banknotes of the old series were created using the same colour: a tone of green. This choice is based on historical practice: if US dollar banknotes are called 'greenbacks', it is because, at some point of history, this colour was used to give this currency its identity. This chromatic decision is the cause for some practices, such as in some Spanish-speaking countries where an informal way of referring to US dollars is using the word *verdes* (greens). The use of the same colour is a visual decision that helps to construct a sense effect of a series, that is, of units that belong to a same system. In this point, the US dollar from the old series constitutes an exception to the genre of currency design, which is usually characterized by a preference to use different colours for each banknote of the system.

The five banknotes of the new series were gradually introduced and set into circulation since the mid-2000s. Since they were created as pieces of the same (new) visual system, they include some common design elements that help to create an effect of seriality. However, the new designs left aside other elements of the previous series, such as the curvy shapes and the exclusive use of green. Regarding the former, the central oval was removed, and the internal coloured frames are now more rectilinear. The visual opposition between curves and lines seems meaningful, because it could function as an expression of the semantic opposition between /classic/ and /contemporary/, /old/ and /new/, and /traditional/ and /modern/. We could claim that the removal of curvy shapes also removed the classical and traditional imprint of the old series. The designs of the new series look much more contemporary and actual than those of the previous one, which have a reminiscence of a past era and, with it, of tradition.

This interpretative hypothesis can be supported by some facts. The designs used for the old series were introduced in 1929, that is, almost one hundred years ago. If we follow Eliseo Verón's (1988) claim that conditions of production leave an imprint in the texts, we can see how design trends and styles from the early twentieth century shaped the design of banknotes. Since the new banknotes were produced in the early years of the twenty-first century, we can expect them to be shaped by design trends from our time. This hypothesis seems confirmed when we look at the new designs, which we might tend to feel closer to the style of our day and age.

Regarding colour, the banknotes of the new series still include green as the dominant colour. However, other colours are used as well. As evidenced in some paratexts, this decision was taken due to a need to strengthen security measures. Beginning in the $5 banknote, each of the banknotes of the new series contains a distinctive colour, albeit used subtly. These are light purple and grey in the $5 note; orange, yellow and red in the $10 note; green and peach in the $20 note; blue and red in the $50 note, and golden in the $100 note.[7]

Despite all these visual changes, the designs of the new series still bear a family resemblance with those from the previous one. This is a sense effect based purely on design elements. To begin with, the new designs maintain the coexistence of a clear-coloured background and a dark-coloured internal frame, which helps to establish a continuity with the old designs. Moreover, they also include the nominal value expressed in numbers in the four corners of the banknote. Thirdly, the official seals we identified in Section 4.2 not only are maintained, but they are situated in the exact same positions they were previously. Finally, also in the new series a central position is given to the portrait of the historical character that identifies each note. Hence, we can see how a *visual* type of continuity is maintained from one series to the other, probably as a means of expressing another type of continuity (we will see an example of the contrary in Chapter 10 when studying the Argentine peso).

Continuity is also maintained in the correspondence between historical characters and nominal values. The portraits included in the five new banknotes of the US dollar are those of the same individuals that were depicted in the same notes of the old system. The decision to maintain such a degree of iconographic continuity is not a given of the discursive genre, as we will see in Chapter 5. The designs of the US dollar are particularly conservative in this sense: as already mentioned, the current iconographic elements, including the main characters, were introduced as early as 1929, and some even before.[8]

Figure 9 The five banknotes issued between the old and new series, including ovals around the portraits of the characters.
Source: numista.com.

The most visible changes from the design of the front sides of one series to the other are three. First, the removal of the oval embracing the main character. Second, the more realistic type of portrait used. Finally, the inclusion of new iconographic elements in the designs.

The disappearance of the oval occurred gradually in time, and not radically from one series to the other. Figure 9 presents the front designs of the $5, $10, $20, $50 and $100 banknotes that circulated between the old and the new systems. These banknotes, introduced between 1996 and 2000, were the first ones since 1929 where a change in design was implemented.

In that intermediary series, the oval frame surrounding the portrait was maintained. This is a graphic decision that produces two sense effects, both linked to continuity. On the one hand, the oval can function as a marker of continuity with the previous series, which was used for decades. Since that series was historical and well known, the oval can function as a sign of continuity with the past, tradition and custom. But since in the second half of the decade of 1990s only a few banknotes were redesigned, a continuity had to be maintained

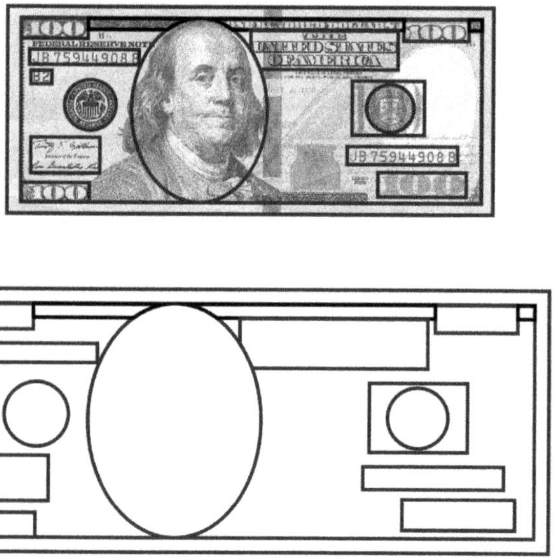

Figure 10 Topological grid of the US dollar from the new series.
Source: Author's own elaboration.

with other banknotes of the system that would not be redesigned, notably the $1 and $2 notes.

Another main visual change from the old series to the new one, passing through the intermediary series that kept the central ovals and replaced the old portraits with the current ones, is the size of the portrait of the historical character, which in the intermediary series is bigger than before. While this might be an arbitrary decision motivated by trends in the field of graphic design, it can also be interpreted as establishing a coded relationship between the size of the figure and the importance given to it. Following this logic, there would be a relationship between the opposition /big/–/small/ and that of /more important/–/less important/.

Figure 10 presents the topological grid used as the basis for the new series. The most evident change regarding the grid sustaining the classic notes is that the location of the country's name has now a clearly determined place in the visual composition. However, differences in the stylization of the name still exist.

The US dollar is hence a good example of how a currency system can construct its unicity and systematicity thanks to a visual type of semiosis, using specific

Figure 11 Painting of Alexander Hamilton by John Trumbull, and the portrait used in the $10 note.
Source: US Currency Education Program.

design elements that belong to the visual domain to mark continuities between different series. As we will see in the upcoming chapters, this is not always the case in the genre of currency design.

After having dealt with the US dollar as a visual system (that is, with a focus on format and layout), let us know study the specific content elements that are used in the seven banknotes that compose the system. In the front side of each banknote, we encounter a portrait of a single individual. Each of these portraits depicts a man, leaving aside women. These men are depicted frontally, in a decision that differs from the one used in the coins of the system, where profile portraits are the standard.

Some of the characters portraited 'look at us in the eye', whereas others not. While we could try to attribute some sense to this opposition (/eye contact/–/no eye contact/), we can reasonably assume that this feature depends on the image that was used as the source for the portrait we find in the banknotes. For example, we know that the portrait of Hamilton we encounter in the $10 note is based on an 1806 painting by John Trumbull (Figure 11).

The seven men depicted in the banknotes wear suits that we can relate to a past era, like those we see in epoch movies and series. Moreover, thanks to our cultural competence, we can read these suits as expressing power positions, usually in economic and political terms. These attires also connote a degree of formality.

Each portrait is accompanied by a tag, stylized in an antique fashion, including a name. Thanks to the topological choice of positioning the tag *near* the portrait, we can recognize it as a verbal text that functions as the anchorage of the figure we see. This is the same logic that applies to the descriptions used as footers of images such as the ones used in this book: thanks to proximity, we can associate verbal text and image as being related. Moreover, thanks to cultural habits, we can expect the text to refer to the image. Curiously, tags used on the US dollar banknotes only include the surnames of the individuals depicted in the portraits: 'Washington', 'Jefferson', 'Lincoln', 'Hamilton', 'Jackson', 'Grant' and 'Franklin'.

Design decisions like these are meaningful and produce specific sense effects because other decisions could have been taken instead. Instead of using only the surnames of these seven men, the inscription could have used a combination of first and surname or only their first names. In terms of personal identification, what gives an individual a nominal identity is the combination of name and surname. There are many Jacksons that are not the Jackson we see in the portrait. While using only the first name could convey a sense of extreme familiarity and even informality, the option for using surnames only can be regarded as a strategy sustained by a process of *mythification*: the choice to use only the surname of these seven men seems to be based on an assumed understanding by the enunciator that the addressee *should know* which Jackson, among the many existing Jacksons, he or she is looking at, because this one is *the most relevant* of all existing Jacksons, the one we all should know as members of the US-American semiosphere and the first one we should think of when thinking of a Jackson.

Evidently, this assumption is also mediated by the type of discourse the design of banknotes expresses. Most probably, if any US-American – or, more broadly, anyone familiar with the US-American semiosphere – were asked to mention the most famous Jackson in the country, many would think of singer Michael Jackson. However, since banknotes and coins express an official type of discourse, that interpretative hypothesis can be discarded, because in official terms 'Jackson' stands for *Andrew* Jackson.

When considering the seven men we encounter on the US dollar banknotes, we can quickly identify a common productive matrix that is anchored on a specific local encyclopaedia. These men were key figures in the process of constructing the United States both as a nation and as a political entity in the form it currently has – sovereign and independent. An observer not necessarily familiar with US history might assume they were all presidents of the country, which is the highest role within that political system. This interpretation could be reinforced by the formal and classical attire these men use in the portraits. In such a case, the selection of historical characters to be portraited in the banknotes would have been justified by their belonging to a reduced portion of the local encyclopaedia, defined intensively using the criterion 'politicians that were presidents'.

Although this is not the case – Hamilton and Franklin were not presidents of the United States – this hypothesis regarding the generative mechanism used to select characters to be included in the banknotes is backed by the inclusion of former presidents William McKinley, Grover Cleveland and James Madison in designs that were withdrawn. However, Salmon P. Chase, who was not a US president, was also part of those banknotes.

The repertoire of US presidents could also include more recent ones. However, the seven men depicted in the current banknotes (and those included in the withdrawn ones) could be clearly located in a distant past, that is, as part of US history, and specifically between a period that spans between 1706 (birth of Benjamin Franklin) and 1885 (death of Ulysses Grant). Therefore, we can identify two of the traits that characterize the encyclopaedic repertoire chosen for the selection of characters to be depicted in banknotes: politics and history. The men included in the banknotes are all statesmen from a past era, a foundational era of the US-American nation. Independently of whatever might happen in the present or in the future, it is in this 'glorious past' that the grounds of the nation are to be found.

Hence, a possible reading of this selection of historical characters can be done through the lens of the mythology around the US Founding Fathers, as identified by historian Richard B. Morris (1973). For Morris (1973: 1),

> These men, extraordinary by the standards of their day as well as by our own, faced the sternest tests confronting our national history, the tests of achieving independence and building a durable nation. Incapable of self-delusion, they were prepared to assume the risks of revolution, confident that America would achieve its freedom from colonial rule and that a republic of free peoples would prosper and serve as an example to a world aching for liberty.

According to Morris, the Founding Fathers are John Adams, Benjamin Franklin, Alexander Hamilton, John Jay, Thomas Jefferson, James Madison and George Washington.[9] As we can see, Abraham Lincoln, Andrew Jackson and Ulysses Grant, whose portraits are featured in the US dollar banknotes, are not part of the list.

Despite the reason why they were chosen to be featured as the banknotes' main figures, all these individuals serve as what semioticians would call *tokens* of the same *type*, that is, units belonging to the same group. That group is the one composed by those men whose actions led to the architecture and construction of the United States as an independent and sovereign nation. Due to the colonial nature of its origins, that national construction was not a given, but had to be actively constructed – both politically and discursively. In this sense, if a banknote of $200 were to be created based on the encyclopaedic repertoire that we can identify as the one used to sustain the choice of characters to be depicted in the banknotes that compose the system, we could expect to find another individual (token) – and probably a man from the past – belonging to this group (type) depicted in its main portrait.

The hypothesis that the US dollar banknotes were designed through the mediation of discourses of the historical construction of the nation becomes stronger when looking at the reverse of the banknotes, at the new design elements included in the contemporary series and at the design of the US dollar coins.

If we look at the reverse of the seven banknotes from Figure 4, we find differences between the classic and the contemporary series. In the new designs – $5, $10, $20, $50 and $100 – we find buildings: the Lincoln Memorial ($5), the building of the US Treasury ($10), the White House ($20), the US Capitol ($50) and the Independence Hall ($100). These depictions are not original but were inherited from previous series. Moreover, except for the Independence Hall, which is in Philadelphia, all the other buildings are in Washington, DC, the capital of the United States.

Although these buildings might be valuable in themselves as expressions of architectural heritage, here they stand for something else: they are symbols of the state and, with it, of the institutions that sustain the United States. In this sense, as Steven Levitsky and Daniel Ziblatt (2018: 213) argue, 'the genius of the first generation of America's political leaders was […] that, in addition to designing very good institutions, they […] established a set of shared beliefs and practices that helped make those institutions work'. In this sense, the buildings we encounter in the reverse of the US dollar banknotes also could be read as expressing those beliefs and practices. Here texts (buildings) stand for something else (shared beliefs and practices, institutions).

The $1 and $2 notes are exceptions to the use of this encyclopaedic repertoire. The previous design of the $2 note included a depiction of Monticello, a plantation owned by Thomas Jefferson located in Charlottesville, Virginia. When the banknote was reintroduced in 1976, it underwent a redesign. The building, which would have been a systemic choice if considering the other buildings used in the reverse of the banknotes of the series, was abandoned. Instead, an image was chosen that introduces some novelty into the semiotic system: the depiction of a historical event.

This event is the Declaration of Independence from 1776, as painted by artist John Trumbull. This is a meaningful design choice for various reasons. On the one hand, it introduces an evident *narrative* component into currency design, focused on a specific event that is regarded as crucial in the history of the nation and the state. Before this design choice was introduced, US dollar banknotes depicted only the *characters* of that history and some of its *places*, but not the *events*. From a semiotic perspective, although narrativity was already present in the system, the inclusion of a historical event adds a different type of discursive and figurative strategy, linked to narratives and storytelling.

On the other hand, the selection of this specific event leaves aside other events that could have been used. Many episodes of the long and rich history of the United States could have been chosen to introduce historical events in currency design. However, the one that was chosen is among those considered more relevant, if not the most: the moment of the birth of the nation, both in political and symbolic terms.

The banknotes from the new series also include some extra design elements. These are all symbols related to the identity of the nation, such as the Great Seal of the United States, the flag, an eagle and the torch of the Statue of Liberty, to mention only a few. The $100 note, besides the golden feather and inkwell that we find next to Franklin's portrait, includes a written text. This text is a fragment of the Declaration of Independence. Above it, the date '4 July 1776' is featured. Reproducing the text of the declaration and including a depiction of the moment of its signature are two different modes of bringing this event to life in figurative terms, that is, of rendering it recognizable in visual articulations that we can read as expressing it.

The $1 banknote deserves a special discussion, since the design used in its reverse is evidently discontinuous – and disruptive – with regard to the rest of the units of the system. According to Heinz Tschachler (2010: 16), this note is 'truly unique in that no other piece of paper money, American or non-American, communicates such abundant information about the nation's history, the structure of the nation, and its highest goals and aspirations'. This is the case thanks to the design of its reverse.

In the centre of the design, we encounter the word 'ONE' written in all-caps and stylized in a big size. On its sides, we see two circles presented in a symmetrical disposition regarding the vertical axis of the image, each of them containing an image within. Below these circles, we read 'The Great Seal' and 'of the United States', also spelled in all-caps. Nothing in the design clarifies that what we see in those circles are the *two sides*, front and reverse, of the Great Seal of the United States, described in the written text under them.

In the reverse of the $1 banknote, we do not encounter any buildings or historical events, as is the case with the other banknotes currently circulating. What we find is a different type of discursive construction of the idea of the nation – one based on using the Seal, one of the official symbols that were created by the political power to stand for it, and specifically to be used by state authorities to certify authenticity. Created in 1782, the Great Seal is a two-sided visual text used to represent the power and agency of the national state in administrative terms.

On its front side, it depicts the national coat of arms. This symbol consists of a shield with thirteen vertical stripes – standing for the thirteen original colonies – depicted over an eagle with the wings and legs spread, which is holding an olive branch in one talon and thirteen arrows in the other, and a ribbon with the inscription 'E PLURIBUS UNUM' in its beak. This inscription is also present in the reverse of the six coins of the system. As the US Mint website indicates, while the olive branch expresses /peace/, the arrows express /war/, and the inscription is the national motto, standing for 'Out of many, one'.[10] This paratext also clarifies that many of the symbols used in coins have ancient Greek and Roman origins and were also widely used in the eighteenth and nineteenth centuries.

In the reverse of the Great Seal, we encounter the image of an unfinished pyramid with a triangle containing an Eye of Providence on top, surrounded by a halo. The pyramid has the inscription 'MDCCLXXVI', a denomination in Roman numbers which stands for 1776, the year of the Declaration of Independence. Moreover, it is surrounded by two inscriptions, in Latin: 'ANNUIT COEPTIS' and 'NOVUS ORDUM SECLORUM'. The choice of Latin, an ancient and dead language that has no relation whatsoever with the territory of the United States, also produces sense effects, because it connotes a distant and classical past, which can be considered as one of the main pillars of contemporary Western civilization.

As is the case with other banknotes, the $1 taps in a more evident manner into what we could identify as a quite specific discursive strategy: using isotopies conflating the meaning and significance of the US nation with those of the state linked to it. Since the US dollar is a *national* currency created and regulated by the United States to be used – originally – within its territory and by its citizens, we can expect to encounter in its design semiotic resources that express that differential national identity. As Tschachler (2010: 4) argues, 'Americans united politically before they created a monetary union and integrated economically'.

Tschachler (2010: 17) argues that in the US dollar designs, 'the presence of the United States as a fiscal and/or monetary community is established in words and in image'. We encounter this presence as a sense effect achieved using various semiotic resources, such as handwritten signatures and, especially, symbols such as the seal of the Federal Reserve and the seal of the US Treasury (Figure 6). Signatures and the two seals are accompanied by the full name of the political entity sustaining the currency, 'The United States of America', located in a prominent position within the design. This would be enough to recognize these banknotes as Federal Reserve Notes dependent on and backed by the United States.

However, other design elements expressing other types of discursive contents are used as well. The repertoire of characters, buildings, symbols and a single event (the Declaration of Independence) construct sense on a different level, one that is not related to the United States as a fiscal or monetary community, but as a nation. This is a nation that was created by the men celebrated in banknotes because they, as a collective identity (a group), signed its birth certificate. Moreover, the national state is recognizable through a series of impressive buildings that, in the US social imaginary, function as symbols of the nation because they are linked to the state and its institutions.

Nevertheless, a third discursive force is present in the designs and complements those of the nation and the state: religion. If we look at the reverse of the seven banknotes, in each of them we find the inscription 'In God We Trust'. This inscription, introduced by law in 1955, brings into play religious discourse, and by combining it with the discourse revolving around the nation and the state, it conflates them and gives the nation a 'divine imprimatur', as Tschachler (2010: 17) argues. This is the case because this inscription

> encodes the conviction that the contract governing the relations between the state and the citizens derives its legitimacy from God. In plain English, it means that the people of the United States should trust that God has empowered the state to fulfil the promises and obligations articulated on the note, in particular the paying back of debts.

The 'divine imprimatur' is also present in the coin system, since every coin includes the inscription 'In God We Trust'. As Gabriel (2016: 27, my translation) argues, this inclusion can be read as a strategy to express that 'trust in the currency is to be stabilised transitively via the trust in God'. Besides, all the coins include the word 'Liberty', and we can see how the iconographic elements used to adorn them respond to the same productive matrix we identified in this chapter. Moreover, the inclusion of the world 'Liberty' also can be related to the elements of the Statue of Liberty included in the banknotes.

The only difference that seems relevant to comment upon is that the repertoire of statesmen used in coins is not any longer limited to a distant and foundational past, but include also more contemporary characters that were active in the twentieth century, such as Franklin D. Roosevelt and John F. Kennedy. This is an interesting choice that broadens the repertoire of statesmen celebrated in currency design. In their reverses, the coins with a standard circulation include either symbols related to the state (Lincoln's Union shield, the Presidential Seal, the eagle) or buildings (Monticello).

All these choices, which are discursive ones that tap onto preexisting cultural repertoires and use them strategically to produce visual texts, can be read as expressions of what Tschachler (2010: 4) sees as the essence of the design of the dollar, a currency that functions as 'a symbol of and proxy for the power of the American nation'.

Drawing on Greimas's narrative scheme, we could make sense of this discourse in terms of a Subject – collective in nature and composed of the statesmen depicted in the banknotes and some of the coins – that envisioned, fought and worked to achieve a state of conjunction with a specific Object of Value: the creation of the American nation as independent and sovereign, and a corresponding state whose boundaries coincide with those of the nation. Various Anti-Subjects opposed this specific Narrative Programme, but in the end, the historical characters celebrated in banknotes and coins were successful, as evidenced by the Declaration of Independence, the only historical event immortalized in the design of the US dollar. Therefore, as an exemplary national type of currency, the US dollar presents us with a glorification and celebration of the process of foundation of the US-American nation, led by some men who should be clearly identified and celebrated, but also by the US-American people, as evidenced in design elements such as 'We The People', or the plural 'We' in 'In God We Trust'.

* * *

The purpose of this chapter was to study the banknotes and coins of the US dollar through the semiotic perspective we embrace in the book. Working with the visual dimension of the banknotes and coins of the US dollar, we saw how the enunciation of the visual texts belonging to this currency system is strongly shaped by discourses revolving around nationhood and statehood, through the mediation of references to religion.

Moreover, we saw how these discourses come to life figuratively in this currency system through the highlighting of a group of men, and concretely statesmen, whose action was fundamental to bringing the national state to life as an independent and sovereign one, together with a selection of buildings and some specific symbols – many of them official – that express that political identity. The design of coins adds two more contemporary characters, namely from the twentieth century.

In the glorious national story told in the US dollar, two major absences are evident: women and minorities. The only exception is the inclusion in the $1 coin of a portrait of Sacagawea, an indigenous woman whose identity combines these two distinctive traits that are absent from the rest of the pieces of the system. Nevertheless, when approached using Greimas's actantial roles, her role in US history is not that of a member of the collective Subject that constructed the nation, but rather that of a Helper, who supported the Subject in implementing its Narrative Programme.

The issue of feminine presence in the US currency iconography has been an object of discussion and action in recent years. In 2016, after an advocacy campaign,[11] an agreement was reached to redesign the $20 banknote replacing with the portrait of a woman Andrew Jackson, accused of being a slave trader. This is an example of how ongoing discursive disputes can impact currency design, as it occurs with other discursive practices. The selected woman was Harriet Tubman, who was also a Black (Lusane, 2022). Tubman was selected from a shortlist that also included Eleanor Roosevelt, Rosa Parks and Wilma Mankiller. Tubman's inclusion in the $20 note was never implemented.

More recently, a special series of the 25 cents coins was released. With the name 'American Women Quarter Program', the plan was to mint five new designs of this coin per year, between 2022 and 2025, honouring a total of twenty notable women. These designs are to be found in the reverse of the 25 cents coin, whereas the front is still reserved solely for the portrait of George Washington.

Despite being a national currency linked to the United States as a state, the US dollar circulates in several other countries, and some even use it as an official currency. This is an interesting situation because the discourses we just analysed are expected to be meaningful for individuals who identify with the US-American nation and state – namely, its citizens and those residing in the country. In cases of external circulation, meaning and sense also are involved, although for outgroups. As Tschachler (2010: 7) argues, 'the lowly paper dollar is one of those everyday, self-evident things that are most taken for granted but that for that very reason may well be the most important ones for revealing and understanding of American culture'.

5

Canadian Dollar

In Chapter 4, we began the analytical work studying the US dollar. As we argued, that currency system will serve as a benchmark of the genre of currency design. This is the case because some of the traits of that currency are dominant in the discursive genre that interests us in this book. In this chapter, we move further north in the American continent and study the Canadian dollar, which is also a currency linked to a national state. In the analysis, we shall see how a different discursive universe is presented in the design of this national currency.

5.1 Context

The Canadian dollar is the official currency in Canada. It is regulated by the Central Bank of Canada, founded in 1934. The first series of the Canadian dollar was produced in 1935. It was only relatively late, in 1949, that the country had a single and homogeneous paper currency, which aggregated the variety of coins and banknotes in circulation and whose responsibility was in the hands of the state, precisely through the supervision of the central bank (Gilbert, 1999: 25).

This change involved a need of making banknotes look not only more modern but also distinctively Canadian, in the sense of a conflation of visual elements that express both Canadian nationhood and statehood. This was done replacing the allegorical and mythological figures used in previous currencies and series – such as Britannia, Justice and Neptune – notably in the nineteenth century, with Canadian landscapes (Gilbert, 1998, 1999), as we will see below.

The latest series of the Canadian dollar was introduced between 2011 and 2013 and is called 'Frontiers'. The banknotes that compose it are made 100 per cent in polymer. Since this is the last complete series, this is the one we will analyse. However, a new series is currently being designed and gradually introduced: it already counts with a new C$10 note. For the first time in the country's history, this new design shifted the paper orientation from horizontal to vertical, and it has been announced that the designs of the upcoming series will all be vertical.[1] The first banknote of that new series features Viola Desmond, a historical character that combines two of the main traits that were absent in the US dollar: she is a woman and stands for a minority.

The currency used in Canada was one of the first currencies to be approached by scholars interested in the relationship between currency and discourses of the nation. In her research, Emily Gilbert (1998: 65) argues that, throughout history,

> a range of images have been used on Canadian paper money: from urban vistas to icons of empire; from portraits of the monarchy to those of bank officials; from bucolic natural landscapes to images of mining and industry; from local trains to a plethora of anonymous trains and steamships; from innocent children to barely clothed buxom women.

As we will see, the latest series of the Canadian dollar evidences this multiplicity of discursive universes used for currency design, as do some of the previous series, to which we will refer as well.

5.2 Banknotes and coins of the Canadian dollar

The corpus is composed of five banknotes and seven coins, as presented in Figures 12 and 13. The current banknotes belong to the seventh series of the Canadian dollar and were introduced between 2011 and 2013. Besides these five banknotes, the newly designed C$10 banknote (Figure 14), introduced in 2018 and with a vertical design, already circulates in the country. Hence, we should consider it as part of our analytical corpus. As is argued below, the new banknote has some discontinuities regarding the series it will replace.

In terms of the units that compose the system, we can already identify some commonalities and differences with regard to the units that were part of the US dollar system. To begin with, the Canadian dollar system has less banknotes and does not have banknotes for low denominations, namely 1 and 2. The higher nominal value in both systems is 100, and the nominal units coincide: 5, 10, 20, 50 and 100. Regarding the coins, the Canadian dollar includes also a coin of C$2, introduced in 1996 and that has kept the same design since then (with the

Figure 12 The five banknotes of the Canadian dollar 'Frontiers' series currently in circulation.
Source: Bank of Canada.

exception that the portrait of Queen Elizabeth II has been replaced with that of King Charles III). Apart from that, the segmentation in decimal nominal units is the same between the two currency systems: the decimal units to be found in coins of the Canadian dollar are 1, 5, 10, 25 and 50, just as is the case in the US dollar.

Tables 3 and 4 list the differential design elements identified in banknotes and coins of the Canadian dollar's current series. Upon a quick look at these two tables, we can already realize how the iconographic universes chosen to decorate the banknotes and coins of the Canadian dollar partially differ from those used in the US dollar. However, others are common.

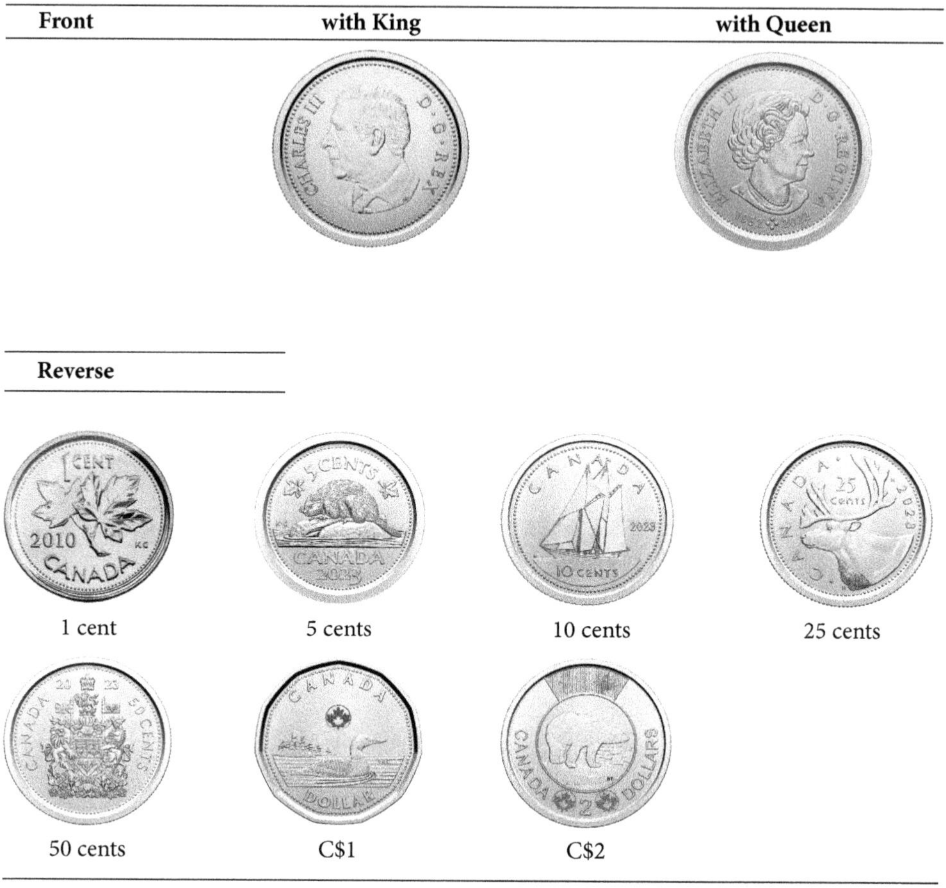

Figure 13 The seven coins of the Canadian dollar with current standard circulation.
Source: The Royal Canadian Mint.

Figure 14 The new C$10 banknote.
Source: Bank of Canada.

5.3 Analysis

The 'Frontiers' series consist of five banknotes. At first sight, we realize how they differ in several aspects from those of the US dollar. To begin with, the currency system of our interest in this chapter is 100 per cent designed using polymer, which allows for an inclusion of security features that are not possible to be included in a banknote made of a fabric based on a combination of cotton and linen. These security features – the most visible of them being the transparent mark located on the right side of the Canadian dollar notes – is strongly integrated in the overall design of each banknote.

Besides, the Canadian dollar is clearly identifiable as a visual system thanks to its salient colourfulness. In this system, five very different colours have been chosen to give each banknote a distinctive identity. Throughout history, green dominated the chromatic dimension of the US dollar, and some subtle colour details were included in the current designs of the $5, $10, $20, $50 and $100 notes. According to Laura Millard (1993: 31), 'unlike the tradition of American paper currency which has not deviated from its "green-back", Canadian bank notes have undergone numerous design and imagery changes', as we shall see in this chapter.

Table 3 List of Distinctive Design Elements Identified in the Five Banknotes of the Canadian Dollar 'Frontiers' Series.

Value	Front	Reverse
C$5	A portrait of Sir Wilfrid Laurier, with a text indicating his name and that he was prime minister of Canada from 1896 to 1911 In the translucid strip, a depiction of the Mackenzie Tower of the West Block of the parliament in Ottawa	Depictions of Canadarm2 and Dextre, part of the mobile servicing system on board the International Space Station (ISS), an astronaut and the Earth seen from space, showing the territory of Canada[a]
C$10	A portrait of Sir John A. Macdonald, with a text indicating his name and that he was prime minister of Canada from 1867 to 1873, and from 1878 to 1891 In the translucid strip, a depiction of the Library of Parliament in Ottawa	Depiction of The Canadian, the transcontinental train, and mountains that are part of the Canadian Rockies in Jasper National Park[b]
C$20	A portrait of Queen Elizabeth II without any explanatory text In the translucid strip, a depiction of the Peace Tower from the national parliament in Ottawa	Depiction of the Canadian National Memorial in Vimy, France, including the Canadian flag on top, and poppies[c]
C$50	A portrait of William Lyon Mackenzie King, with a text explaining that he was prime minister from 1921 to 1930 and from 1935 to 1948 In the translucid strip, a depiction of one of the four towers that stand along the northern perimeter of Centre Block of the parliament	Depiction of the CGCS *Amundsen*, a research icebreaker ship, an inscription in the Inuktitut language, a map showing Canada's northern regions and a compass in the background[d]
C$100	A portrait of Sir Robert Laird Borden, with a text indicating that he was prime minister of Canada from 1911 to 1920 In the translucid strip, a depiction of the East Block tower of parliament in Ottawa	Depiction of a researcher using an electronic microscope, an electrocardiogram track, a bottle of insulin and a depiction of DNA strand[e]

Source: Author's own elaboration.

[a] Cf. www.bankofcanada.ca/banknotes/bank-note-series/frontiers/5-polymer-note.

[b] Cf. www.bankofcanada.ca/banknotes/bank-note-series/frontiers/10-polymer-note.

[c] Cf. www.bankofcanada.ca/banknotes/bank-note-series/frontiers/20-polymer-note.

[d] Cf. www.bankofcanada.ca/banknotes/bank-note-series/frontiers/50-polymer-note.

[e] Cf. www.bankofcanada.ca/banknotes/bank-note-series/frontiers/100-polymer-note.

Table 4 List of Distinctive Design Elements Identified in the Seven Coins of the Canadian Dollar.

Coin	Front	Reverse
1 cent	A profile portrait of King Charles III, looking to the left, his name and the inscription 'D.G. REX'	A maple twig with two leaves
5 cents		A beaver standing on a log in the water
10 cents		A depiction of the Bluenose, a Canadian schooner, sailing
25 cents		A caribou
50 cents		Canada's coat of arms
C$1		A loon swimming on a water surface
C$2		A polar bear standing on an ice flow

Source: Author's own elaboration.

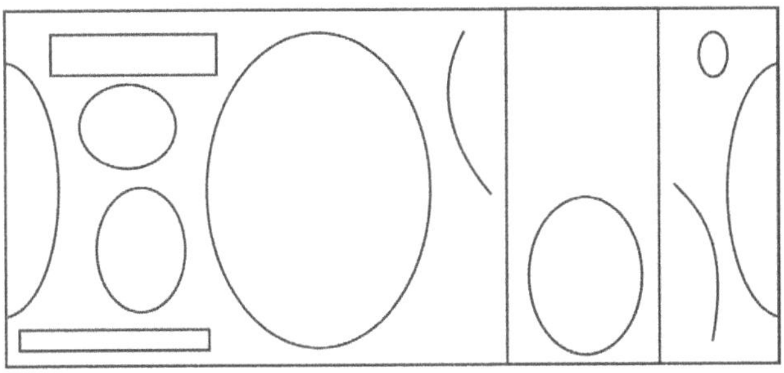

Figure 15 Topological grid of the 'Frontiers' series of the Canadian dollar.
Source: Author's own elaboration.

As was the case in the US dollar, also in the banknotes of the Canadian dollar we can identify a clear topological grid underpinning the design. Together with colour, this is one of the semiotic resources used to contribute to the sense effect of a system (Figure 15). Several design elements are used for this purpose, such as the positioning in that grid of the main character, the translucid security strip, the indications of the nominal value and the reference to the Bank of Canada, among others.

Of particular interest for our analysis is the maple leaf, which is also positioned in a clear place in the five banknotes of the series. The maple leaf functions as a symbol of Canadian national identity thanks to cultural codification. According to Emily Gilbert (1999: 32), this sign has been associated with Canada since the seventeenth century. The salience of this symbol is evident when looking at Canada's national flag, where it is positioned in the centre. As Gilbert (1999: 32) shows, the first Canadian decimal coins, issued in the Province of Canada in 1857, already featured maple leaves as part of their iconography. Currently, maple leaves can be found in the reverse of five of the seven Canadian dollar coins.

When studying the US dollar, we saw how looking at past designs can help us understand the genesis and sense of the current ones. In that case, we saw how the current designs can be traced back to 1929 (some even to 1914), that is, around one century ago. Although our focus of interest is set in the series that currently circulate, looking at past designs can serve us to properly grasp the sense of the current designs thanks to the intervention of a relational premise, that is, of the relationships of continuity and discontinuity we can identify between series.

Therefore, in our analysis of the seventh series of the Canadian dollar, we will consider previous series as well. When studying them, we will identify some continuities and discontinuities that will allow us to propose hypotheses about the generative matrix used to create the designs. Figure 16 presents the banknotes of the sixth series of the Canadian dollar, 'The Canadian Journey' – 'L'épopée Canadienne' in French,[2] and Figure 17, those belonging to the fifth series, 'The Birds of Canada'.[3] Already in the names we can see different semiotic strategies in play: while the former is conceived of as a journey (or an 'epic', in the French version), the latter focuses on identifying individual bird types imagined as typically Canadian.

By looking at them, we see how the three series of the Canadian dollar introduced so far have various elements in common. To begin with, the segmentation of nominal values is the same, except for the C$2 and the C$1,000 banknotes of the 'Birds of Canada' series, which were removed from the following series. Moreover, the colours used in each banknote are maintained between the three series, although their intensity changes, probably due to the physical characteristics of the material used to create the banknotes. The historical characters used in the front side of each banknote are also maintained from one series to the next, even if the portraits used are different (the three series include different portraits of each depicted character). Finally, the banknotes of the three series include depictions of portions of the national parliament, a building located in Ottawa, although they do this differently. Thanks to their continuous presence, all the listed elements serve to construct a sense effect of continuity between the current series and the two previous ones.

Figure 16 The five banknotes of the 'Canadian Journey' series (sixth series) of the Canadian dollar.
Source: Bank of Canada.

In topological terms, each of these three visual systems seems perfectly planned, with every design element located in a clearly delimited and fixed place. Thanks to the use of design elements, we can recognize the internal systemic relationships existing not only between the banknotes that compose each system but also between the three systems as variations of the same national currency. Hence, we can claim that there is a historical but also a thematic and a visual continuity between the last three series.

Figure 17 The seven banknotes of the 'Birds of Canada' series (fifth series) of the Canadian dollar.
Source: Bank of Canada.

Moving into the analysis of the content we find on the banknotes of the Canadian dollar, we realize that contrary to the case of the US dollar, whose banknotes include seals that express the state's identity, those of the Canadian dollar are less loaded with this type of signs. In fact, besides the name 'Canada' located on the top left of the front side of the banknotes and the reference to the 'Bank of Canada' – both in English and French – there are no other references to the state responsible for these banknotes. Particularly, there are no coded signs such as state symbols – flags, coat of arms and so on – expressing it.

This is why we could argue that the inclusion of the maple leaf as a distinctive design element serves as a semiotic resource to reinforce the isotopy of the Canadian identity, albeit it does not do it in statal terms, but in national ones. That national presence is done through the mediation of a leaf, which is an element belonging to the natural realm. Below we shall discuss the role of nature, landscape and territory in discourses of Canadian identity, but we can already advance that nature can also be used as a means to convey an idea of the nation.

It is interesting to note how Canada's coat of arms, an official symbol of the state used in previous series of banknotes, was replaced in the current series by the maple leaf. This design element also functions as a sign of Canada, albeit not of the institutional order of the state. In terms of the nature of the sign, while the coat of arms is clearly an arbitrary symbol created for specific purposes, the use of a natural element is less arbitrary and partially grounded on the flora found on the territory associated with the nation. While both signs are arbitrarily selected to signify, their arbitrariness differs.

We can identify two encyclopaedic repertoires used for the design of the front sides of the banknotes. These consist of individuals and buildings. Hence, we encounter the same repertoire we identified on the iconography of the US dollar. Moreover, all the individuals included in the two currency systems held state positions, and the buildings depicted are linked to the state's architectural materialization.

However, there are differences between the two currency systems regarding how these two thematic repertoires are used. Perhaps the most salient one is temporality. In the Canadian dollar banknotes, the temporal selection is closer to our time: the four prime ministers depicted in the banknotes held office between the second half of the nineteenth and the first half of the twentieth centuries: Laurier was prime minister from 1896 to 1911; Macdonald, from 1867 to 1875 and from 1878 and 1891; King, from 1921 to 1930 and from 1935 to 1940; and Borden, from 1911 to 1920. This selection allows us to see a different temporal focus than the one we encountered in the US dollar, much more focused in a distant and foundational past.

The oldest date, 1867, is that of the birth of Canada as a confederation. Hence, it functions in a similar manner than 1776 in US history. Two different dates fulfil a similar function: that of providing national history with a date of origin, which is used in discourse as a cut to distinguish a present from a past, and hence a discontinuity. In the Canadian case, that discontinuity means having gained sovereignty with regard to the UK.

As we can see, the temporal selection of the repertoire of historical characters we encounter in Canada's banknotes as one closer to our time is not fully arbitrary but partially motivated by historical facts. In this sense, the four statesmen we encounter in four of the five current banknotes are equivalent to those included in the US dollar ones: these are the politicians that shaped the nation as we know it. Since in Canada that process occurred almost one century later than in the United States, the historical characters depicted belong to a more recent time.

Regarding the use of buildings, the towers used in the translucid security strip of the current series all belong to the same building. This differs from the strategy used in the US dollar: whereas in that currency system the national state was brought to life figuratively thanks to a group of buildings that together express the state's institutions, in the Canadian dollar the focus is set on the national parliament, a building located in Ottawa, which is the country's capital and hence equivalent to Washington, DC, in the United States. The towers and spaces depicted in the banknotes of the Canadian dollar function metonymically, that is, as part of a figurative strategy where the part stands for the whole, and the whole stands for something else thanks to how the meaning of that something else can be condensed in a single official building. While the discursive strategy of using architectural heritage to express the state is the same in the Canadian and US dollars, the figurative strategy differs.

Similar to what occurs in the US dollar, four of the five portraits included in the banknotes depict men. Thanks to the text located below each portrait as anchorage, we learn that all of them were prime ministers. It is this political role as state officials that justifies their inclusion in the banknotes. While the US dollar banknotes included only the surname of the character depicted, more information is included in the Canadian dollar, which helps the non-native reader to understand who these men were, why they are celebrated in banknotes and when they held office.

For our purposes, the most interesting banknote of the series is the C$20 one because it evidences a clear discontinuity. Not only does this banknote include the sole woman of the system, but it also evidences a different reason sustaining the iconographic choice. That note currently includes a portrait of Queen Elizabeth II, former queen of Britain and, as such, ruler of the British Commonwealth, the political structure to which Canada belongs as an independent country. Until recently (2023), the queen's portrait was included as well in the front sides of the seven coins, albeit as a profile portrait. After her passing, it was replaced by a profile portrait of King Charles III, as will her portrait in the C$20 note soon.

Different from the rest of the banknotes of the series, the C$20 one does not include any anchorage text. This design choice can be interpreted as an assumption, occurring in the pole of enunciation, of a stronger mythification of the reigning monarch, who is supposed to be known by anyone holding the note. The interpretative hypothesis here is that anyone encountering that image should know who he or she is looking at, different from what occurs with the four prime ministers depicted in the remaining banknotes.

We will come back to the role of the reigning monarch in Chapter 6 when studying the pound sterling. For now, it is interesting to consider two issues. A first issue regards how the depiction of the monarch is dependent on an extra-discursive fact, which impacts the continuity of the design: the portrait included in currency design will be that of the individual holding that role *in the present*. This is different from what occurs with the four prime ministers included in the other banknotes, who no longer occupy that institutional role in the government. In fact, except for totalitarian states, it does not seem common to encounter portraits of current elected officials in currency design. When Queen Elizabeth II passed away in 2022 and the throne was taken over by the heir, King Charles III, arrangements began being made to replace her portrait with his, both in the pound sterling and in the C$20 banknote.

The Bank of Canada announced that the new banknote featuring King Charles III shall begin circulating in 2027.[4] Also the portrait featured on the front of the Canadian coins depends on who actually holds the throne. The first series of Canadian coins included a portrait of Queen Victoria, and these were followed by portraits of Kings Edward VII, George V and George VI, Queen Elizabeth II and, as of 2023, King Charles III. In these changes, while the actual individual was replaced, the productive matrix was maintained.

A second issue of interest to us, also related to the figure of the reigning monarch, is that the current design of the Canadian dollar seems to be grounded on a dichotomy between two discursive poles linked to the country's particular political status. One pole is that of the Canadian/national/local, and the other is that of the Commonwealth/imperial/overseas. Following Gilbert (1999), we could argue that what is activated in the design choice for this banknote is Canada's identity of belonging to the British Commonwealth, despite being an independent country with enough semiotic resources at disposal to construct that identity. In fact, as Gilbert (1999: 33) claims, Canadian currency historically 'reflected this anglophilia in that local images were juxtaposed with portraits of the monarchy, symbols of Britannia, etc.'.

In this sense, while the four banknotes featuring prime ministers are clearly and distinctively Canadian thanks to the chosen encyclopaedia being clearly bound to that specific semiosphere, the C$20 banknote combines elements belonging to these two discursive poles: one local and the other imperial. This raises the question of how these two encyclopaedias come into being through signs in the generative moment, plus a need to map these cultural repertoires and choose signs among them to figurativize these identities in the specific designs used in currency. Moreover, the choice for these poles could also be interpreted as expressions of conservatism or progressivism, a debate that characterizes Canada's politics even today.

The inclusion of the UK reigning monarch in Canadian currency is not novel but inherited from the past. Following Queen Elizabeth II's taking over the throne in 1952, she became the central character used for Canadian currency in the series issued in 1954 – the Canadian dollar's third series. Let us now explore this historical path because it will be useful for us to study the reverse of the banknotes of the current series.

The first series of the Canadian dollar dates from 1935, the year after the Central Bank of Canada was created. Each of the banknotes of that series includes a portrait of a member of the royal family, except for two, which depicted Macdonald and Laurier. In that series, the C$20 note included a portrait of Princess Elizabeth as a child.[5] In the new series (second series, from 1937), her portrait was removed because all the designs had the same portrait: that of the king (and two had Macdonald and Laurier). However, the portraits of Macdonald and Laurier were maintained in this series, constituting two exceptions to the centrality given to the monarch in banknotes.

In 1954, the Bank of Canada introduced the third series.[6] Following the productive matrix of the second series, which included the portrait of King George VI in every front side (except the two banknotes depicting Macdonald and Laurier), and as is the case with the pound sterling, the queen's portrait was the main iconographic figure, and it was included in the front designs of every banknote. As a result, since the eight banknotes looked alike, colour was used to differentiate them (Figure 18).

CANADA
ONE DOLLAR 1 UN DOLLAR
BANK OF CANADA - BANQUE DU CANADA
ONE UN
ONE DOLLAR UN DOLLAR
BANK OF CANADA — BANQUE DU CANADA
CANADA
TWO DOLLARS 2 DEUX DOLLARS
BANK OF CANADA - BANQUE DU CANADA
TWO DEUX
TWO DOLLARS 2 DEUX DOLLARS
BANK OF CANADA — BANQUE DU CANADA
CANADA
FIVE DOLLARS 5 CINQ DOLLARS
BANK OF CANADA - BANQUE DU CANADA
FIVE CINQ
FIVE DOLLARS 5 CINQ DOLLARS
BANK OF CANADA — BANQUE DU CANADA
CANADA
TEN DOLLARS 10 DIX DOLLARS
BANK OF CANADA - BANQUE DU CANADA
TEN DIX
TEN DOLLARS 10 DIX DOLLARS
BANK OF CANADA — BANQUE DU CANADA
CANADA
TWENTY DOLLARS 20 VINGT DOLLARS
BANK OF CANADA - BANQUE DU CANADA
TWENTY VINGT
TWENTY DOLLARS 20 VINGT DOLLARS
BANK OF CANADA — BANQUE DU CANADA
CANADA
FIFTY DOLLARS 50 CINQUANTE DOLLARS
BANK OF CANADA - BANQUE DU CANADA
FIFTY CINQUANTE
FIFTY DOLLARS 50 CINQUANTE DOLLARS
BANK OF CANADA — BANQUE DU CANADA
CANADA
ONE HUNDRED DOLLARS 100 CENT DOLLARS
BANK OF CANADA - BANQUE DU CANADA
ONE HUNDRED CENT
ONE HUNDRED DOLLARS CENT DOLLARS
BANK OF CANADA — BANQUE DU CANADA

Figure 18 The eight banknotes of the third series of the Canadian dollar.
Source: Bank of Canada.

About this series, Gilbert (1999: 39) writes that 'the consolidation of a single, national currency in the 1950s was an expression of internal and external territorial coherence, reinforcing national borders both domestically and with respect to foreign powers'. The banknotes of the 1954 series include some design elements that remind us of those used in the US dollar, such as the inclusion of economic value in the four corners of the note, or the internal coloured frame used, combined with a light-coloured background. These similarities can help us visualize the conditions of production of these texts, which reflect styles and dominant visual strategies at a specific time of history – all of them quite distant from our day and age and bearing marks of the styles of the first half of the twentieth century.

The design of the 1954 banknotes is a good example of the coexistence of imperial with local discourses. The front designs are clearly dominated by the portrait of the reigning monarch, which catches the eyes immediately. However, these designs also include the Canadian coat of arms in their background. The reverse of these banknotes, however, presents contents that are clearly linked to the discursive pole of the local, distancing currency design from the imperial discourse linked to the monarch and the Commonwealth. In this case, this occurs not thanks to design elements relating to the state, such as buildings, state symbols or foundational events, but in terms of *territory*. What we find in these banknotes are *landscapes*, something we did not encounter in the designs of the US dollar.

Laura Millard (1993: 33) identifies the following landscapes as part of that series: Prairie View Saskatchewan (C$1); View of Upper Melbourn, Richmond, Quebec (C$2); Otter Falls at Mile 996 of the Alaska Highway (C$5); Mount Burgess, Alberta (C$10); Laurentian Winter (C$20); Atlantic Seashore (C$50); Okanagan Lake, British Columbia (C$100); and Anse St. Jean, Saguenay River, Quebec (C$1,000). According to Gilbert (1999: 37), these landscapes 'not only reinforce the connections between the official forms of the state and the historical role of landscape and nature in the Canadian imagination, but they also – especially in their comprehensive inclusion of distinct Canadian regions – reflect the territorial cohesion brought about by the Bank of Canada notes'.

We will take the designs of the 1954 series as the point of departure for our analysis of the current series. As we have just seen, on the reverse, these banknotes depict landscapes, untouched by humans and without human presence, and, therefore, somehow depicted in a bucolic and idyllic manner. In fact, officials from the Bank wanted these landscapes to show 'little or no evidence of human activity' as a means to function as 'the natural starting point for an evolving manifestation of official identity'.[7]

If we now turn to the designs of the fifth series (see Figure 17), we see that a selection of birds is used as the main encyclopaedic repertoire. In fact, the purpose of that series, called 'The Birds of Canada', was to depict birds considered indigenous of the Canadian territory, together with a background that stands for the landscape each of those birds typically inhabits. The choice was partially grounded on 'their political neutrality' and considering 'their visual simplicity'.[8]

Although in this series the focus was set on elements belonging to the specific domain of fauna, the underlying discourse is still anchored in the domain of nature. This is the case because nature is a useful resource to construct an idea of Canadian identity, specifically through the mediation of territory and the lifeforms one encounters there. This discourse anchored in nature is the same one sustaining the inclusion of the four animals that we encounter in the reverse of the current coins of the Canadian dollar.[9] We did not find anything similar in the designs of the US dollars: the territory of the United States and its geographical, natural and faunal diversity are absent from currency design.

As we will see in upcoming chapters, using the domain of nature in currency design is a common discursive strategy as a distinctive repertoire to figurativize a distinctive collective identity segmented in national terms. However, in semiotic terms, this option places the state, the nation and the inhabitants of the territory on a second plane as cultural repertoires that can be used in currency design. These are much more visible when currency design draws on discourses of human action and, in gross terms, what we could refer to using the – not unproblematic – nouns 'culture' and 'civilization', as opposed to that of nature.

If a state is an entity composed of three major elements – a territory, a government and a people – then territorial features and facts are a constitutive element of the state. However, they are probably less salient and evident to express statehood as people and government are. These two are the ones generally chosen throughout history as the standard for currency design, as we saw in the US dollar.

Something similar occurs with the construction of national identity in discourse: discourses revolving around nature, notably through landscape, territory, flora and fauna, are certainly intertwined and entangled with discourses and social imaginaries of the nation, even if they are probably more peripheral than other contents such as those linked to human action and agency. Once a national identity has been segmented from the continuum of all national identities thanks to establishing oppositions with other national identities, that segmented unit must be filled with specific content. Nature is one of the discursive repertoires that can be used for this purpose. This explains why some national identities can be characterized – even if partially – by the presence of geographical elements such as a seashore or mountain ranges in the territory linked to the nation.[10]

The option for the domain of nature is common to the third and fifth series of the Canadian dollar and to the fourth series as well, called 'The Scenes of Canada' (Figure 19) and introduced in 1969.[11] However, there are differences that already relate to the designs we find in the current series. The images we find in the reverse of the banknotes of the fourth series include, besides landscapes – notably, mountains and a lake in the C$20 note – *humans and human action*.

In this series, Canada is not anymore depicted through territory in the sense of a pristine, bucolic and idyllic landscape, but something that humans use for their purposes, and above all as a space where they achieve things relevant to them. That is why in the reverse of the banknotes of this series, we find boats, harbours, buildings (including the parliament building in Ottawa, still used in the current banknotes), humans using different techniques to fish, a refinery and social institutions such as the Royal Canadian Mounted Police. As written in one paratext by the Bank of Canada, 'on the reverse, this series did not feature "the great lone land" but a landscape that is transformed by humans, both by traditional activities and with industry'. Although nature is still present in the banknotes of this series, it is not anymore untouched and pristine as in the previous and posterior ones – it is a nature seen through the eyes of humans and made sense of, both in functional and symbolic terms, by the people inhabiting it: the Canadians.

Why such a recurrence of territory and landscape? For some commentators, it is related to the lack of the standard elements that serve to construct the idea of a nation such as language, religion or ethnicity. This has given place to what Daniel Francis (1997: 8) calls 'a civil ideology', that is, 'a framework of ideas and aspirations which expresses itself in allegiance to certain public policies and institutions'. Gilbert (1999: 37) argues that 'landscape images strengthen the

BANK OF CANADA – BANQUE DU CANADA
ECK6000307
ECK6000307
UN 1 ONE
DOLLAR
CANADA

ONE
1
UN
BANQUE DU CANADA - BANK OF CANADA

BANQUE DU CANADA - BANK OF CANADA
RV8732294
RV8732294
TWO 2 DEUX
DOLLARS
CANADA

DEUX
2
TWO
BANK OF CANADA-BANQUE DU CANADA

BANK OF CANADA - BANQUE DU CANADA
CP0783904
CP0783904
CINQ 5 FIVE
DOLLARS
CANADA

FIVE
5
CINQ
BANQUE DU CANADA - BANK OF CANADA

BANQUE DU CANADA - BANK OF CANADA
ETG2210479
ETG2210479
TEN 10 DIX
DOLLARS
CANADA

DIX
10
TEN

WX1788678
WX1788678
VINGT 20 TWENTY
DOLLARS
CANADA

TWENTY
20
VINGT
BANK OF CANADA - BANQUE DU CANADA

BANQUE DU CANADA - BANK OF CANADA
EHN8026331
EHN8026331
FIFTY 50 CINQUANTE
DOLLARS
CANADA

CINQUANTE
50
FIFTY
BANK OF CANADA-BANQUE DU CANADA

Figure 19 The seven banknotes of the 'Scenes of Canada' series (fourth series) of the Canadian dollar.
Source: Bank of Canada.

terms under which national currencies have been characterized in the Canadian context'. According to Benoit Raoulx (2022), the immensity of the Canadian territory has been a challenge to nation-building, because there is an 'excess of geography'. As the author claims, when studying the Canadian case, it is necessary to 'emphasise the plurality of space in order to highlight not only the diversity of Canada, but also the complexity associated with the political and cultural construction of this country, where identities and scales of reference are multiple, sometimes in tension and in renegotiation' (Raoulx, 2022: 9, my translation).

The 1969 series marks a transition towards the current one. To begin with, it modifies the colour scheme of the previous series – blue for C$5, purple for C$10, green for C$20, red for C$50 and yellow/brown for C$100. These are the colours that Canadian banknotes had since then and still maintain. Moreover, this series introduced the portraits of the four prime ministers that are still featured currently. This means a continuity of over half a century.[12]

The reverse designs of the banknotes of the series 'The Canadian Journey' (Figure 16) expand this strategy, leaving aside the focus in nature and giving more relevance to human action. In their reverse, these banknotes depict children enjoying the snow, peacekeeping forces, a war memorial, artworks, activism and works of technological innovation. This series also introduces another design element: written quotes. Table 5 presents the quotes and their sources.

The quotes add extra meaning related to Canadian identity, either because they were written by Canadian authors or because they are meaningful within the Canadian semiosphere. Moreover, some of the specific contents they express also contribute to such a sense effect. When reading them, we encounter references not to landscape, territory and nature, but to situations and contents that relate to humans, such as ice skating, war, art, human rights activism and exploration.

Table 5 Quotes Included in the Reverse of the Five Banknotes of the Canadian Dollar's 'The Canadian Journey' Series.

Value	Quote	Source
C$5	'The winters of my childhood were long, long seasons. We lived in three places – the school, the church and the skating-ring – but our real life was on the skating-ring.'	'The Hockey Sweater', a short story by Roch Carrier, published in 1979
C$10	'In Flanders fields the poppies blow Between the crosses row on row, That mark our place, and in the sky The larks, still bravely singing, fly Scarce heard amid the guns below.'	'In Flanders Fields', a 1915 poem by John McCrae (1872–1918)
C$20	'Could we ever know each other in the slightest without the arts?'	*The Hidden Mountain*, a 1961 novel by Gabrielle Roy (1909–1983)
C$50	'All human beings are born free and equal in dignity and rights.'	Universal Declaration of Human Rights (1948)
C$100	'Do we ever remember that somewhere above the sky in some child's dream perhaps Jacques Cartier is still sailing, always, on his way always about to discover a new Canada?'	'Jacques Cartier in Toronto', a poem by Miriam Waddington

Source: Author's own elaboration.

Except for the Universal Declaration of Human Rights, all the source texts were written by Canadian authors. In semiotic terms, these quotes can function as *interpretants*, that is, as texts that mediate how we make sense of the images we see. Although these texts do not fulfil a function of anchorage (as the name located below a portrait does), they are meaningful, and we might use them in our efforts to make sense of the images we find in the banknotes.

In their reverse, each of the five banknotes of the 'Frontiers' series includes various design elements used to convey specific themes. In the back of the C$5 note, we encounter astronauts and machines that we can recognize as spaceships and tools related to them. Thanks to the anchorage text used, we know these mechanical innovations have proper names: 'Canadarm2' and 'Dextre'. Moreover, in that banknote we can see the Earth, in another reference to (Canadian) territory. These contents, already present in the previous series' C$100 banknote in the form of a satellite and a parabolic antenna, propose a discursive selection that is radically different to the one used in the 1954 series.

We can map this difference using sets of oppositions such as natural/artificial, premodern/hypermodern, given/made, in-Canada/outside-Canda or others.

Despite the temporal and discursive distance that separates the idyllic landscapes used in the banknotes of the 1954 series and the theme of space innovation and exploration, both are used because they can be read as *distinctively Canadian*. Similarly, the C$10 banknote presents The Canadian, a transcontinental train that functions as an expression of innovation and technical competence and that is usually regarded as one of Canada's foundational myths (Francis, 1997). The C$50 note includes an image of the CCGS *Amundsen*, a research icebreaker ship, and the C$100 one, a bottle of insulin, the graphic representation of DNA and a (female) researcher using an electronic microscope.

The C$20 note is exceptional as well in terms of the design of its reverse. In it, we encounter a memorial, that is, a material construction meant to remember and commemorate past events, usually somehow traumatic.[13] However, despite the number of memory sites one imagines could be found in the Canadian territory, the memorial depicted on the banknote is in France. This choice seems meaningful due to the strong bonds of France and French communities with Canada's national identity, characterized by bilingualism and the existence of French-speaking communities in the Canadian territory.

As such, also on its reverse, this banknote presents a discontinuity regarding the visual system it belongs to. In the current series, the dominant topic is that of innovation (hence the name 'Frontiers'). This is a discourse that links the past and the present with the future and with the realm of what is possible thanks to the possession of competences and resources, which materialize in specific technological devices. The use of the war memorial included in the C$20 note draws on discourses of the past, a past that is remembered and celebrated from the present. In either case, albeit with differences, it is thanks to Canadians that the elements depicted in the banknotes occurred.

As we could see in this chapter, the discourses we encounter on Canadian banknotes have oscillated throughout history between different poles. Beginning with the natural, untouched and bucolic landscape as a national asset in terms of territory, the Canadian dollar now carries a different type of social discursivity, one giving almost total centrality to human action and power. On the front side, we see individuals that are relevant to the Canadian state in terms of its construction and of institutional national memory. On the reverse, we encounter elements that thematize the potential of human competence – and, specifically, Canadian competence – and what humans can do with the limits nature imposes on us.

The design of the 'Frontiers' series is strongly based on the ideas of progress and innovation, which are thematized in the reverse of the banknotes through four major themes: space and robotics innovation (C$5), engineering and transport innovation (C$10), geographical research (C$50) and medical innovation (C$100). These innovations are not located in a distant past but are recent. Therefore, if the design of the US dollar is focused on a distant and foundational past, something different occurs with the Canadian dollar, which draws on discourses that are contemporary.

How could we explain this difference in the focus for visual creation? What motivates an enunciator to opt for one or the other discursive strategy when designing banknotes and coins? Some reasons can be found in the historical processes leading to the creation of each national state. According to Daniel Francis (1997: 15–16),

> Canada accepted its autonomy as a country gradually, almost tentatively, as opposed to many other countries which seized it enthusiastically and proclaimed it defiantly. As a result, we have no myth of creation, no narrative which celebrates the birth of the nation, not even a central image like Uncle Sam or John Bull to personify the community and sum up what it stands for. We have no Founders, at least none whom we celebrate.

If we accept this interpretative hypothesis, we can see how different historical processes can lead to a preference for different discourses to be used to express and convey the idea of the nation. Comparatively, the cases of the US and the Canadian dollars are useful to see this difference.

As mentioned at the beginning of this chapter, a new C$10 banknote was introduced in 2018, and it was announced that new designs – belonging to a new series – will be gradually introduced in the upcoming years. The design of this new banknote presents continuities and discontinuities with the current and the previous series. In terms of continuity, the new C$10 note maintains the purple colour that gives it a differential chromatic identity within the system. Moreover, it also includes only one historical character in the front, accompanied by an image of a portion of the national parliament.

However, everything else seems to be different, beginning with the orientation of the paper, which changed from horizontal to vertical. This means a major change in the history of the Canadian dollar's design. Another major discontinuity is the inclusion of a portrait of Viola Desmond as the main character, a Black businesswoman who was an advocate of social justice. This choice left aside the portrait of John A. Macdonald, used as the main figure of the C$10 note since 1969.

This substitution means a rupture not only with *historical* continuity (that is, tradition) but also with *thematic* continuity, since Viola Desmond never held a government position. This is a major change in the generative matrix used to design the banknotes of the Canadian dollar. This matrix was based in having been a statesman or -woman. This is the condition that, up to now, seemed necessary for someone to fulfil to be included in a banknote. With the inclusion of Desmond, this is not the case anymore. Now anyone active in the political domain of social life, such as an activist for social justice like her, can be expected to be encountered as the main figure of a banknote. Finally, another relevant element of discontinuity with the past is that, now, a second woman is featured in the banknotes besides Queen Elizabeth II. As we know, the queen's portrait will be replaced soon.

A further relevant element of the new C$10 note is the stronger presence of symbols of Canada in terms of the nation and the state. Now, the maple leaf is used a couple of times. Moreover, the coat of arms has been reintroduced, together with a Canadian flag. In the reverse, we encounter a different type of building than the one we were used to seeing in the Canadian dollar banknotes: the Canadian Museum for Human Rights, located in Winnipeg, Manitoba. The back design also includes a feather, a sign that can be interpreted as standing for aboriginal First Nations, and an excerpt from the Canadian Charter of Rights and Freedoms (section 15), which reads: 'Every individual is equal before and under the law and has the right to the equal protection and equal benefit of the law without discrimination.'

To understand these changes, it is necessary to analyse the conditions of production of this new design, that is, the social, political and cultural constraints that, in a given time and space, shape textual production thanks to the salience and relevance of specific discourses, topics and struggles. In examining the conditions of production, we can think how political issues relevant to the context in which a series is produced leave traces in the designs. In the case of Canada, the ongoing discussions about multiculturalism (Le Jeune, 2023) and the different communities that inhabit the country (Bernd, 2018) seem to be relevant here.

Hence, currency design can function as an entry point not only to the national semiosphere but also to the topics, themes and issues that are and were relevant for a given community in a specific time of their history, such as social equality. The rupture that the new design of the C$10 note brings certainly evidences a discursive change of this type. Namely, in recent years, the Bank of Canada appointed an Indigenous Advisory Circle, whose task is, as expressed in its website, to 'provide advice and recommendations on how Indigenous Peoples in Canada might be represented on future bank notes through the use of symbols, images, patterns and other forms of visual iconography'.[14] Moreover, the Bank has actively engaged with citizens in the selection of new historical characters, as well as in supporting the overarching principles sustaining national currency design. As times change, so do the design elements we encounter featured in currency.

* * *

As we have seen, the Canadian dollar challenges our synchronic approach (that is, the decision of working with the banknotes and coins currently circulating). This challenge shows us how currency design is an evolving and changing discursive genre and how working with a specific series is a decision that might be comfortable from a methodological point of view, but not accurate in terms of what a community might be encountering in currency in the daily lives of its members. Moreover, in the chapter we saw how working with material culture is not something done once and for ever but needs regular revisits and updates: in some years from now, the current series will be past, and the analysis should be partially redone in light of the new vertical banknotes.

In terms of content, and to sum up, when studying the banknotes of the Canadian dollar, we encounter a gradual transition over history of the contents that are used to convey the idea of a Canadian identity. These began with a strong anchorage in territory and landscape as expressions of discourses of the natural and the prehuman. As times passed and new series were created, the design of the Canadian dollar began shifting to the realm of culture, humans and their action in the national territory. In this sense, the purple-coloured, empty and quasi-idyllic landscape included in the C$10 banknote from 1954 is substantially distant – not only temporally but also discursively – from the hypermodern and contemporary building included in the newest C$10 note. The museum depicted, as well as the innovations included in the current 'Frontiers' series, is strongly dependent on human action and achievements, that is, on what Canadians, as a collective actor with agency, notably do – and can do – in the national territory and with the natural resources their nation provides them with. But they also go beyond: they break the barriers of space and innovate, pushing the frontiers further.

6

British Pound Sterling

After studying the US and the Canadian dollars, in this chapter we cross the Atlantic Ocean and begin the journey of examining the design of banknotes and coins currently used in European countries. This chapter studies the pound sterling, the official currency of the United Kingdom of Great Britain and Northern Ireland, as well as of other territories that are connected to the UK. This is a currency that has attracted scholarly attention (Blaazer, 1999, 2002, 2016; Dittmar, 2009; Hewitt and Keyworth, 1987; Hewitt, 1999), although researchers who studied it did not use a semiotic perspective.

Our study of the British pound sterling shall bring to the fore the differences that exist between this currency and the US and Canadian dollars. As we saw in Chapter 4, in the US dollar we encounter design elements that express a narrative of notable statesmen that created the United States as an independent and sovereign nation. In the banknotes, besides the prominence given to these statesmen, we encounter buildings and a concrete historical event (the act of the birth of the nation), all linked to the creation of the nation and hence contributing to a foundational myth expressed in currency design.

As we shall see in this chapter, in the pound sterling we find a different type of narrative, evidencing a different discursive strategy. A strategy such as the one we find in US dollar banknotes is not easy to implement in the British case due to how history developed. A quick look at the banknotes of the pound sterling can help us recognize some of the main differences, the most salient of them being the absolute centrality that is given in this currency system to the reigning monarch (as opposed, for example, to past monarchs, which also could be celebrated in currency). Hence, to highlight only one difference, from a collective type of actor in the US banknotes, we now encounter a focus on an individual actor or, more precisely, a political role that involves only one individual.

Therefore, when comparing the design of banknotes and coins of the pound sterling with those studied in the previous chapters, we should be able to identify different semiotic strategies to express nationhood and statehood in currency design, with the focus set on different cultural repertoires.

6.1 Context

The pound sterling is the official currency of the UK. Since 1971, it has been a decimalized currency system: one pound is composed of 100 units called 'pence', in plural, and 'penny', in singular. The banknotes we will study in this chapter are issued by the Bank of England, whereas the coins are designed, minted and supervised by the Royal Mint. In 1983, the £1 note was replaced by a coin.

The pound sterling is also used in other countries and territories, some of which are allowed to print their own banknotes using their own designs. The entity that issues and regulates the pound sterling we all know is the Bank of England, which was created in 1694 as a private institution, and nationalized in 1946. Since then, it became in practice the UK's central bank, even if it maintained its original name (and some visual elements, as we shall see) referring to England, one of the four political entities that compose the UK.

As a political entity, the UK comprises four countries: England, Scotland, Northern Ireland and Wales. Therefore, as David Blaazer (2002: 12) argues, the history of the pound sterling is not only complex but also multinational. In his view, 'Images from English, Scottish and Irish paper money show not only how their national rhetoric has reflected competing ideas about the relationships between the components of the UK, but also how paper money has both reflected and shaped the divergent roles money has played in the nations' respective histories' (Blaazer, 2002: 12).

Even if the pound sterling is the only valid currency in the country, the Bank of England is not the only institution allowed to issue banknotes in the UK's territory, as is generally the case in countries around the world. Since 1921, the Bank of England has the monopoly of issuing banknotes in England and Wales, two of the UK political entities. However, three private banks in Scotland (Bank of Scotland, The Royal Bank of Scotland and Clydesdale Bank) and three in Northern Ireland (Bank of Ireland, Danske Bank and Ulster Bank) are allowed to print pound sterling banknotes as well. These banknotes have different designs than the ones we will study in this chapter, which are those that come to mind when thinking of the pound sterling.

When the euro was introduced as the EU's common currency, the pound sterling was one of the national currencies that were not abandoned in favour of the new common currency. As scholars argue (Blaazer, 1999, 2002, 2016; Hewitt, 1999), there was a strong opposition in the UK to joining the monetary union because the British pound was, following David Blaazer (2016: 53), 'deeply entwined with British national identity and prestige'. Therefore, the idea of giving up the national currency triggered 'a visceral fear that to surrender the pound was to commit a devastating act of national self-effacement' (Blaazer, 2016: 53).

6.2 Banknotes and coins of the pound sterling

Currently, two designs of the pound sterling circulate in the UK, both created by the Bank of England and pertaining to the G series. The one we will use as our corpus here is the latest of them, which began circulating in June 2024. The previous designs were set in circulation between 2016 and 2021. As we shall see, the changes from the previous designs to the new ones are minimal – actually, they consist of one substantial substitution.

As a currency system, the pound sterling is composed of four banknotes (Figure 20) and eight coins (Figure 21). As such, this is the currency system with fewer banknotes and more coins of the currencies we study in the book.

As is clearly visible in Figure 20, in the pound sterling we encounter a different design strategy than those we dealt with in the currencies studied in the previous chapters. Here, on the front side, the four pound sterling banknotes include the same major design elements. The most salient difference between them is the use of colour, although some minor security elements also differ and help give each banknote its identity. In this sense, if in the two currencies studied so far we could postulate the idea of an intended 'banknote identity' as a sense effect to be constructed through some distinctive visual elements used in each banknote, in the case of the pound sterling's banknotes, the visual differentiation between them is minimal and, above all, based on the chromatic dimension.

Value	Front	Reverse
£5		
£10		
£20		
£50		

Figure 20 The four banknotes of the pound sterling (G series) circulating since 2024.
Source: Bank of England.

Moreover, the banknotes of the pound sterling introduce a feature – relating to format – that we did not encounter when studying the US and Canadian dollars: the variation of size of the banknotes. In these notes, as nominal value augments, so does the size of the banknote: whereas the £5 banknote has a size of 12.5×6.5 cm, the £10 note measures 13.2×6.9 cm, the £20 note measures 13.9×7.3 cm, and the £50 note measures 14.6×7.7 cm. As we saw in Chapter 3, size can be used to signify. While in the case of US and Canadian dollars this was not a pertinent trait to approach sense-making, in the case of the pound sterling it does signify. This occurs thanks to a codification that relates size with economic value, in a relationship that pairs /low/ with /small/ and /high/ with /big/. Once again, we can see how signification depends on the relationships that are established between the units of a given system.

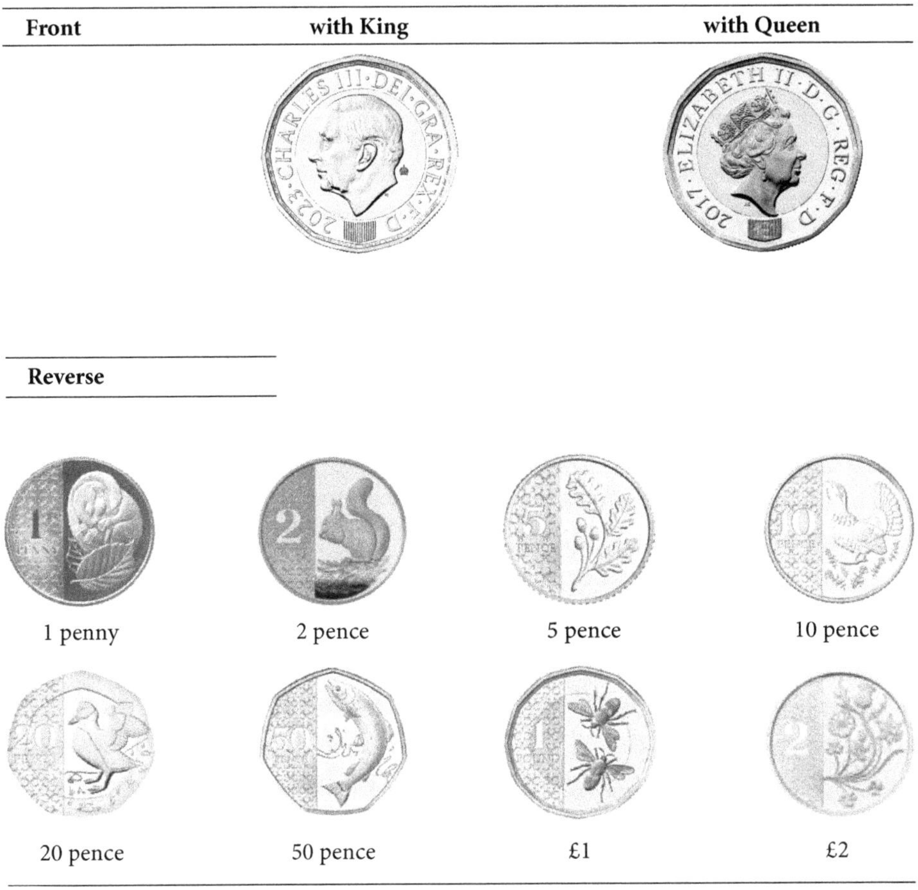

Figure 21 The eight coins of the pound sterling.
Source: The Royal Mint.

In the case of the pound sterling, size can be regarded as another trait to achieve banknote identity, in a system where the designs of the front side of each banknote do not contribute to this. In this sense, a description (intended to be definite) such as 'the banknote depicting King Charles III' does not refer to a specific banknote, whereas 'the bigger banknote of the pound sterling' or 'the red note' do.

The idea of banknote identity gains relevance when looking at the designs used in the reverse of the four banknotes of the pound sterling. Table 6 lists the design elements included in the front and reverse of each banknote.

Table 6 List of Distinctive Design Elements Identified in the Four Banknotes of the Pound Sterling.

Value	Front		Reverse
£5	A portrait of King Charles III A depiction of the building of the Bank of England	An image of Elizabeth Tower of Westminster Palace on the translucid security window	A portrait of Sir Winston Churchill A depiction of Westminster Palace Nobel Prize in literature medal
£10		An image of Winchester Cathedral on the translucid security window	A portrait of Jane Austen An illustration of Elizabeth Bennet (fictional character from the novel *Pride and Prejudice*) A depiction of Godmersham Park House
£20		An image of Margate Lighthouse and Turner Contemporary (gallery) on the translucid security window	A portrait of J. M. W. Turner A depiction of Turner's painting 'The Fighting Temeraire'
£50		An image composed of lines on the translucid security window	A portrait of Alan Turing Images of a matrix table and mathematical formula, ACE Pilot Machine, binary code, Bombe technical drawings and technical drawings from the ACE Progress Report

Source: Author's own elaboration.

If we look at the coin system, just as it was the case with those of the Canadian dollars, we see that the designs include a profile portrait of the reigning monarch. The new designs used on the reverse of the coins are part of the 'Flora and Fauna' series and include animals – hazel dormouse, red squirrel, capercaillie, puffin, Atlantic salmon and bees – except for the 5 penny and £2 coin, which include plants – an oak tree leaf and the four 'national' flowers. Hence, these new designs tap on an encyclopaedic repertoire that we already encountered when studying the Canadian dollar, but that is new to the design of the pound sterling: nature and, specifically, flora and fauna.

When discussing the Canadian dollar, we saw how landscape and fauna were relevant themes to construct Canadian identity through the mediation of these types of discursive contents. This was not the case in the US dollar, and neither has it been historically in the British pound sterling.

These new coin designs substitute the previous ones, which consisted of different portions of the UK's coat of arms, an image of the four national flowers in the £1 coin[1] and one of Britannia in the £2 coin.[2] In the remainder of the chapter, we will leave aside the coin system from our analysis, since it will not add much novelty regarding the semiotic strategies studied so far. However, we will consider the designs of Britannia and of the national flowers.

6.3 Analysis

When looking at the design elements that allow us to recognize the relationship between the four current banknotes of the pound sterling as part of the same visual system, we have the advantage of encountering the same design in their front sides, apart from those elements that grant each banknote its economic value. This means a continuity that helps to visualize the systemic nature of the currency system as a visual system. The same occurs with the coins, whose front sides are also designed using almost the same image, while differences are to be found in colour and shape.

If we draw on the three main categories of plastic semiotics introduced before, we can argue that differences between the front sides of the units of the pound sterling, including both banknotes and coins, are primarily chromatic and eidetic, but not topological. That is, they differ in colour and the forms used, but not in how they articulate the space within the frame that delimits each visual unit.

The new designs of the pound sterling including the portrait of King Charles III were formally unveiled in 2023, and they started being issued in 2024. The new design was motivated by two related events, none of them involving issues of banknote security or preventing counterfeiting, which are what usually motivates change in currency design. Those events were the passing of Queen Elizabeth II, in September 2022, and the taking over of the throne by her son, Charles III, shortly after. An historical event – the death of the reigning monarch – was the source of the decision to redesign the circulating currency.

This redesign was necessary in light of the discursive strategy sustaining the design of the pound sterling. As is evidenced in the front designs of banknotes and coins, this strategy consists in giving an absolute centrality to the figure of the reigning monarch. This choice expresses what semioticians call a euphoric – positive – axiologization. Discourse can depict things and events in different manners, depending on how the enunciator evaluates them. This depiction can be done using an axiological continuum that ranges between a negative and a positive pole. As a default, and thanks to the nature of the discursive genre we are dealing with, we could argue that we can expect whatever we find on the design of a given currency to be positively axiologized (if not by the community, by the institutional enunciator responsible for the designs).

In the case of the pound sterling, what seems to be axiologized is *the political role*, and not necessarily the individual holding it. Whereas in the back of the pound sterling banknotes we encounter individuals that are positively axiologized thanks to their specific action and specific contributions to British culture and society, the front designs of banknotes and coins evidence an axiologization of a state role that can be occupied by different people. Although the individuals occupying the role can be – and probably will still be – positively axiologized after their passing, the trait that matters for someone to be featured on the banknotes and coins is the role being held, and not the person. Or, to be fair, it is the person, but as long as he or she occupies that role.

In the pound sterling, the positive axiologization of this role is expressed thanks to a textual strategy of repetition. This strategy consists of repeating the portrait of the monarch not only in the four banknotes that compose the system but also within each banknote: in the main portrait and in the translucid security window.

In this currency, we can identify a direct link between the designs of banknotes and coins and facts of the natural world, such as the passing away of a human being. These two poles coexist in a relationship where the former is dependent on the latter. Hence, when the reigning monarch changes, currency design should change as well, as does the design of the UK's coat of arms.[3] Nothing like this can occur in the designs of US and Canadian dollars, where all the currency pieces include historical characters that are already deceased. Except, of course, on Canada's C$20 note, which includes the portrait of the UK's reigning monarch and head of the Commonwealth.

The strategy we encounter when studying the British pound sterling is different to that we usually encounter when studying currency design as a genre. Usually, characters included in banknotes and coins are historical, not actual. Moreover, they are usually long deceased. In these cases, textual creation is grounded in a collective memory that draws on the past. As such, discursive constructions of this type are composed of facts and events that are finished and closed, and not of current events, which are still open and can change.

When studying the US and Canadian dollars, we saw that the selection of characters depicted in banknotes and coins was mediated by two main traits: they were individuals that held government positions, and they are long deceased. Combining these two traits, the people depicted there belong to the nation's collective memory. Even the most contemporary characters featured in US coins, such as F. D. Roosevelt and J. F. Kennedy, are not alive anymore, although their temporality is much closer to our time than that of other characters used in the design of US dollar banknotes.

How could the Bank of England lose this dependence on facts that precipitate change in the design? Although the death of a reigning monarch is an event that occurs relatively seldom, the relationship between who occupies the role and what portrait and secondary elements to include in currency design could be easily left aside, for example, creating a new denomination with a new design whenever a monarch passes away. This means that, for example, a note of £200 could be created featuring a portrait of Queen Elizabeth II.

As mentioned above, the discursive strategy of giving absolute centrality to the reigning monarch in currency is interesting because it depends on the political role of the monarch, and not on the specific things he or she has done. There is only one monarch in the UK, and what grants the person occupying that role a presence on the front side of the banknotes is the fact of being the monarch, independently of what the specific person occupying the role might do. This differs from the selection of historical characters to be included in currency, which is usually grounded on what they have done and how they have contributed to the nation, as is the case with the four individuals depicted in the reverse of the notes of the pound sterling.

If we compare the front designs of the banknotes of the pound sterling introduced in 2024 with those it replaced (Figure 22), we can see that the only difference lies in the figure of the monarch. Nothing else was changed, neither in the front nor in the reverse. Therefore, the historical fact of the queen's passing is articulated in the visual texts of the pound sterling only in the front side of the banknotes.

Besides the centrality given to the figure of the monarch, banknotes of the pound sterling are loaded with signs and symbols that express nationhood. The dominant ones are of an institutional nature and express the identity of the Bank of England. The most salient of these signs is the image depicting the bank's main building, which is visible in the front side of the four banknotes, next to the portrait of the monarch. Whereas other currency systems choose different buildings (or portions of them) to express institutionality through architectural heritage, the pound sterling uses only the building of the bank issuing the notes, perhaps as a mode of affirming its positioning as the maximum authority

Figure 22 Comparison of the two designs of the £5 banknote of the G series, one depicting King Charles III; the other, Queen Elizabeth II.
Source: Bank of England.

governing them, together with an intention to connote solidity and wealth as the basis for trusting it.

Other signs included in the front of the current banknotes function as isotopies to express the identity of the Bank of England. Isotopies are relationships between design elements that contribute to expressing the same content. In the genre of currency design, we can speak of isotopies when different design elements (located in the plane of expression) are related to the same unit in the plane of content.

The first isotopic resource used to express the identity of the Bank of England is its written name. The name 'Bank of England' is repeated in each banknote, the three most visible appearances being the one located above in the centre, as a sort of header for the banknote, both in the front and the reverse (although with different typefaces) and the one included in the translucid security oval window.

A third visual element used to express nationhood through the institutional role of the Bank of England is the seal located in the bottom left corner of each banknote. Whereas in the US dollar banknotes we found the Great Seal of the United States as a design element, here we encounter the seal of the bank, which also stands for the state due to its institutional nature.

Although the design of the seal included in each banknote differs (Figure 23), the four designs reproduce the Bank of England's seal. Since its foundation in 1694, the Bank has used the image of Britannia as part of its seal and logotype.

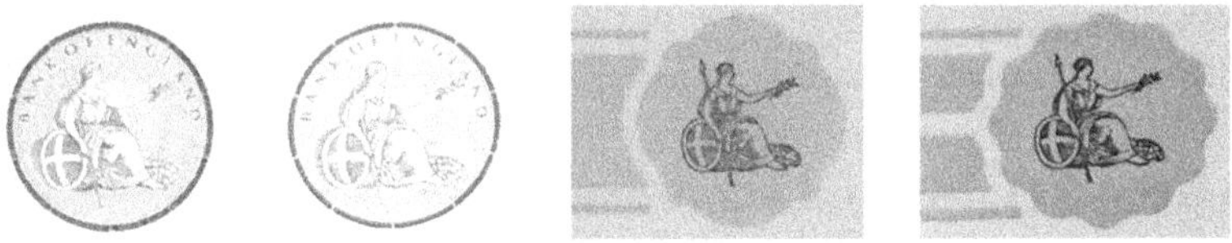

Figure 23 The four seals of the Bank of England depicting Britannia on the four banknotes of the pound sterling.
Source: Author's own elaboration.

The image we encounter on the banknotes of the pound sterling is based on an older version of the Bank of England's logotype. Since the Bank updated its logotype recently, we could expect that the design based on it will also be updated in the future. This would be another example of an external fact (an organization updating its visual identity) impacting currency design.

The image of Britannia included in the banknotes of the pound sterling is of interest for our purposes because it introduces a discursive strategy that we have not encountered so far in our analyses. This strategy consists in using allegories or personifications of the nation (de Heij, 2012: 95–7). In figurative terms, the strategy consists of using a specific anthropomorphic character to conventionally express an abstract idea linked to a collective identity segmented and defined in national terms.

In this sense, allegories belong to a discursive domain where specific contents linked to national identity are related to specific human-like figures. However, this is not the only type of codification between national identities and other discursive universes we can encounter. As a means of example, nations and national identities can also be expressed using animals, such as the bald eagle standing for the United States, the dragon standing for China and the bear standing for Russia.

Although at some point of their history the US and Canadian dollars had allegories in currency, there are two major differences with those historical uses of allegories and the one we encounter in the pound sterling. On the one hand, our analyses (focused on the present age through circulating currency) did not bring us to them because they did not seem relevant to understanding the meanings and sense conveyed by the designs of banknotes and coins currently used. On the other hand, these allegories were either mythical or referred to abstract concepts such as commerce, agriculture and justice, and were not strictly personifications *of the nation*.

Contrary to the characters we have encountered so far in our analyses, although we can clearly identify her as a woman, Britannia does not stand for a specific individual that existed and that should be celebrated in currency thanks to her contributions to the nation. Britannia is an imaginary, fictional, mythical creation grounded on the anthropomorphic strategy of bringing this concept to life using the figure of a woman.

The allegory of Britannia has been used since the times of the Roman Empire to refer to the British Islands. For some reason, the founders of the Bank of England thought Britannia would be a good symbol to use to define the Bank's identity with reference to some specific traits. One of those traits is solidity, a sense effect for which using an image connoting classicism and tapping into discourses of antiquity clearly contributes. The other is the national imprint, because the allegorical image used is the one that stands for British territory. Here, the selection of an iconographic element might have served the purpose of positioning the Bank of England as a *national* bank, and not just any other private bank. Following a strategy that produces a sense effect of a prolonged type of historical continuity, the Bank of England has maintained the image of Britannia in its seal (and logotype).

In ancient Rome, Britannia was usually depicted as a warrior. Her images were that of an armoured woman holding a shield and a spear, in an attitude that looked ready to engage in war. In the previous reverse design of the £2 coin (Figure 24), the depiction of Britannia wears a helmet and holds a trident instead of a spear. This image of Britannia differs from the one used in the seal of the Bank of England. In the seal, Britannia is sitting, she does not wear a helmet, the shield stands next to her, and she holds a spear and an olive branch, the latter being a conventional sign standing for peace. Hence, in holding it, Britannia looks friendly and inviting (vs. aggressive and challenging).

For banking purposes, such an image seems more adequate than one of an individual ready to engage in war: banking is a social activity based on institutions, understanding, respect, institutional reliability and collective trust. We can see how the same cultural unit – Britannia – which stands for another cultural unit – British national identity – can be brought to life in the plane of expression through two different types of images, which connote different types of social meanings. As we saw, these connoted social meanings are semantically related.

If we look at Britannia's shield, we can identify a cross that reminds us of the flag of England. Since the creation of the UK, depictions of Britannia have been modified to include the Union Flag in the shield as a way of relating the personification of the British Islands to UK's national identity as a whole, rather than simply the English part. However, the image the Bank of England still uses in the banknotes has the *English* flag, a choice that some might read as an exclusion of the other three nations that compose the UK. This is particularly interesting because, recently, the Bank of England updated its logotype and, in the new version, Britannia's shield includes the Union Flag. If banknote design was updated upon the change of reigning monarch, might it not have been appropriate to update Britannia's seal as well, with the purpose of including this more encompassing symbol, rather than the one currently used?

In the current pound sterling's banknotes, Britannia's presence is marginal. However, in the past it was used as the main design element of some banknotes: she was featured on British coins since 1672, and on banknotes since 1694 (de Heij, 2012). A good example of her presence in currency design is the front side of the £5 note of the B series (introduced in 1957 and withdrawn in 1967) and on the reverse of the £5 note of the C series (introduced in 1963 and withdrawn in 1973) (Figure 24).

According to David Blaazer (1999: 47), the £5 banknote of the B series, from 1957, is 'an orgy of nationalist symbolism', and he describes it as follows:

> The front of the note is dominated by a bust of helmeted Britannia at left, whose Aryan (Saxon) beauty and blonde curls could equally well have graced a note of the Third Reich. At the bottom centre an armoured, helmeted, and *haloed* St George skewers the dragon [...] On the back, a large lion holding a double-sided key (allegedly to secure and release the nation's treasure) stands on a plinth facing the watermark silhouette of Britannia.

In the reverse of the £5 note of the C series (1963), Britannia is depicted as less aggressive and war-ready, and hence more in line with what we see in the current seal of the Bank. This friendlier depiction shows how this allegory has been generally included in the designs of banknotes of the pound sterling.[4] Again, we can see how the same cultural unit can be depicted using different figurative strategies, and how the preference for one or other strategy of figurativization can depend on the circumstances of textual creation (the conditions of production), as well as on axiologization.

As used in the current designs of the pound sterling, the seal depicting Britannia contributes to the sense of the political community in three different ways. To begin with, it functions as a codified sign for the Bank of England, which is the public institution responsible for issuing banknotes in two of the UK's nations. This sense effect results from the logo of the Bank including this

Figure 24 Depictions of Britannia on the front side of the £5 note from the B series (1957), on the reverse of the £5 note from the C series (1963), and on the £2 coin replaced by one with the new design.
Source: Bank of England.

allegorical character in it. Moreover, the medal amounts to a certain continuity with previous series, all of which have usually included an image of Britannia, either as a main portrait or in the seal. Hence, there is a sense effect of a historical continuity of the political/national community. Finally, Britannia stands as a sign for British national identity thanks to cultural codification throughout history.

Britain is a political entity composed of four countries: England, Northern Ireland, Scotland and Wales. It is hard to bring these four countries to life *together* in figurative terms using images that these four nations can consider appropriate to identify them. The option of an allegoric image such as Britannia probably facilitates this challenge. However, it is not an option free of polemics, because Scots and Irish have their own personifications of the nation: Scotia and Hibernia. Together with Britannia, they form what Virginia Hewitt (1999: 99) calls 'a graceful triumvirate'. In fact, some old banknotes issued by Irish banks

Figure 25 Curvy design element including the coats of arms of the UK's four nations.
Source: Bank of England.

in the nineteenth century include images of these three women sitting together, where Britannia seems to be the eldest of them, in a sort of mother–daughters relationship (Blaazer, 2002: 14–15).

Another strategy for bringing British national identity to life in visual terms as one that is composed of four national identities is using the official emblems of the four constitutive nations. This is done on the front side of each banknote, through a design element located above the depiction of the Bank's building. There, we see an elegant, curvy shape that rhymes with the curves of the typeface used to stylize 'Bank of England' and 'Pounds', and which includes the four national coats of arms on it, one for each of the UK's constituent nations (Figure 25). Thanks to cultural competence, we can recognize these symbolic signs as referring to the nations.

Similarly, the new design of the £2 coin takes the design previously used in the £1 one, which consists of four flowers, conventionally associated with these four nations: the rose (England), the thistle (Scotland), the shamrock (Northern Ireland) and the daffodil (Wales) (Figure 26). The substitution of Britannia from the higher-value coin with these four national symbols is certainly meaningful.

The four UK nations are reunited and coexist under the political form of the monarchy. This is the political form that justifies their union, and it is not surprising that the monarchy is used as a productive mechanism to design the pieces that compose the national currency system. The central position given to the reigning monarch in banknotes and coins seems to be an expression of this productive mechanism. So does the image of the crown located above the security window on banknotes, which works as an isotopy reinforcing the

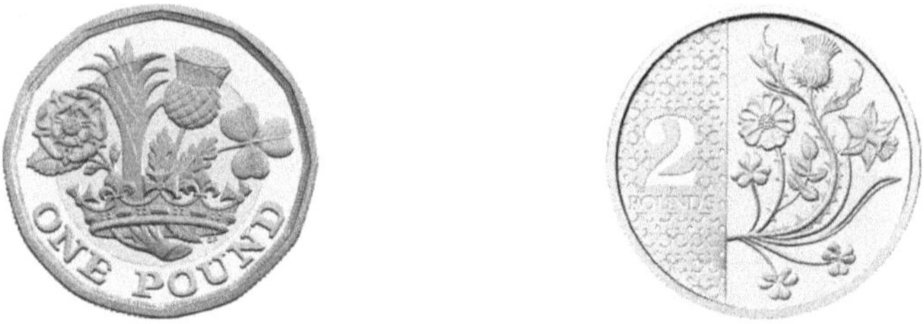

Figure 26 £1 coin from the previous series, and current £2 coin, both depicting the national flowers.
Source: Royal Mint.

Figure 27 £1 banknote from 1960, the first one including the portrait of the reigning monarch.
Source: Bank of England.

monarchical content, and the crown at the base of the four flowers in the old £1 coin (Figure 26).

According to Blaazer (1999), it was the inclusion of the monarch in banknotes of the pound sterling for the first time, in 1960, that sealed the national status of banknotes. In that banknote (Figure 27), we can identify some design elements that are visible in today's designs, such as the position of the Bank of England's name, the image of the queen (plus its location on the right side of the design), the seal including Britannia and the curvy shape that in the current designs reunites the four national coats of arms.

In that banknote, the queen is depicted wearing a crown. This is an ornamental element that, thanks to cultural codification based on historical custom, functions as a sign expressing the position of power held, as well as the institutional role of the monarchy. This is the standard sign probably almost anyone would use to express the idea of monarchy, for example, when playing a game such as *Pictionary*.

In line with this first appearance of the reigning monarch in the banknotes of the pound sterling, the queen also wears a crown in the notes of the G series, although it is a different crown than the one used in her 1960 portrait. The queen's profile portrait included on the front side of the previous coins also wore a crown, but it did not in the depictions of the queen in the Canadian dollar (in the C$20 note and in the previous series of coins). This decision might be meaningful and could evidence that the inclusion of the monarch in the Canadian dollar has a different meaning than its inclusion in the pound sterling.

Curiously, the portrait of King Charles III included in the new designs of the pound sterling banknotes and coins does not wear a crown or any other element functioning as a sign expressing the status of monarchy or his power position. What we see is the image of a man, and it is thanks to our cultural competence that we can make sense of his presence in the notes and coins. If this choice was deliberate, we can assume it to be meaningful thanks to the opposition between presence and absence of such signs. Perhaps the absence of them is seen by the enunciator as one that serves to construct less distance between the people and the ruler, who does not need to affirm his or her authority using such conventional – and why not, intimidating – signs. However, in interpretative terms, the most relevant point here is that someone unfamiliar with King Charles III – a tourist, for example – might not be able to read the royal role by looking at the portrait. In this sense, the presence of a crown would almost immediately activate an interpretation linked to monarchy.[5]

To sum up, we can argue that the front side of the current banknotes of the pound sterling is heavily loaded with signs that convey a national identity thanks to the mediation of the discourses of royalty and institutionalism. Regarding the latter, this is done thanks to the use of design elements that convey the identity of the Bank of England as a *national* institution. Therefore, instead of merely denoting the Bank *of England*, these signs connote a *national* institution that assures the legitimacy and credibility of the UK's *national* currency. This is the case even if the main figure chosen to express the bank's brand identity in the designs, Britannia, historically originates in discourses about *English* identity, and not necessarily *British* identity.[6]

However, in these banknotes, thanks to the inclusion of Britannia, there is also a mediation of an allegorical type of discourse whose sources are to be found in antiquity and its classicism. In fact, the image of Britannia was used during the British renaissance as a symbol to foster the idea of nation. Therefore, it does not come as a surprise that the Bank of England saw in this allegorical figure an appealing design element to construct in discourse its identity as the national bank.

If we now turn to the designs of the reverse of the current banknotes, we encounter a type of discursive construction that does not activate discourses of royalty and institutionalism, as the front designs do. Each of the four banknotes includes the portrait of a historical character that is unrelated to British monarchy. These characters are Winston Churchill, Jane Austen, Joseph Mallord William Turner and Alan Turing.

These four individuals clearly pertain to UK history, and as such, we can expect anyone in the country to know who they are. In using their portraits for currency design, we encounter a new encyclopaedic repertoire that we had not yet encountered in our analyses. So far, we found statesmen, monarchs, buildings, landscapes, animals, allegories, human activities and achievements. Here, we add a new portion of the semiosphere used in currency design: that of individuals prominent within collective memory thanks to their societal contributions. Specifically, the characters included in the current designs of the pound sterling were active in the fields of politics and ideas (Churchill), literature (Austen), painting (Turner) and science (Turing).

Whereas the front design of the four banknotes depicted the Bank of England's main building in the background, the backgrounds used in the reverses differ from note to note. Each of the portraits depicted on the reverses of the notes is presented over a different background image that can be thematically related to them.

In the £5 note, Winston Churchill's portrait appears over an image that combines a depiction of Westminster Palace, one side of the Nobel Prize medal and a book. These three items figurativize the double value and significance that this historical character has within the UK's collective memory. Above all, there is his identity as a statesman who successfully led the country in hard times of the Second World War. However, his winning of the Nobel Prize in Literature, in 1953, is also put forward in the banknote. Hence, we could say that, thanks to these design elements, Churchill is highlighted in currency not only as a statesman but also as an intellectual.

In the £10 note, the portrait of Georgian-era novelist Jane Austen appears over a background composed of two main images. On the one hand, a typical UK rural landscape, with a carriage that expresses a historical take and that is based on Godmersham Park, a property related to Austen's family. On the other, the drawing of a woman reading, which the knowledgeable viewer can easily relate to Elizabeth Bennet, a fictional character of the novel *Pride and Prejudice*, created by Austen.

In the £20 note, the portrait of painter J. M. W. Turner is located over a depiction of his painting 'The Fighting Temeraire'. Due to the nature of Turner's work, a specific image can be included to show his contribution to British culture, contrary to what happens with Churchill and Austen, for whom a collection of symbolic images had to be used to convey their relevance. In this sense, while we can recognize the image of the boat behind Turner's portrait as a mimetic copy of one of his paintings based on a strategy of iconism, in the case of Churchill and Austen, the images used in those designs mediate how we interpret the value attributed to these historical figures that grant them a place in the banknotes.

Finally, in the £50 note, the portrait of scientist Alan Turing appears over a background that seems quite complex compared to those of the previous notes. As is written in the Bank of England's website, this banknote features 'images of a matrix table and mathematical formula, ACE Pilot Machine, Binary code, Bombe technical drawings and technical drawings from the ACE Progress Report'.[7] Besides connoting the field of scientific research and innovation, the figure of Turing also connotes diversity and inclusion: Turing was legally hounded and punished for his homosexuality, and he eventually committed suicide for that reason. In 2013, he received a posthumous royal pardon following a government apology in 2009.

Besides the specific design elements used in the reverse of the banknotes that serve to signal the characters' merits and hence justify their relevance as to be included in national currency, each reverse includes their handwritten signature and a quote. The use of handwritten signatures is an interesting design choice, because it is not clear what value it might have in terms of the sense effects it produces. What would change if the handwritten signatures were not included in the designs? The answer to this question is different to that we could give to the question regarding the absence of the banking authorities' handwritten signatures, because these are a constitutive mark for the validity of banknotes as currency.

The quotes included in the banknotes serve to describe the discursive fields where these characters were active. In the case of Churchill, the quote used is 'I have nothing to offer but blood, toil, tears and sweat'. This is a quote from him from 1940, during wartime, which is open enough in terms of what it might mean as to allow multiple readings: on the one hand, it can be interpreted as expressing the commitment and trustworthiness a statesman is expected to have when serving their nation; on the other hand, it can be interpreted as a blunt and honest statement about what the UK citizenry could expect to experience under his wartime leadership. In either case, the quote activates a passional dimension linked to national identity.

The quote in Austen's note is 'I declare after all there is no enjoyment like reading!' It is taken from the novel *Pride and Prejudice* and refers to the pleasure of reading, which directly relates to the activity of writing (that upon which Austen is celebrated and included in the £10 note). In the case of Turner, the quote refers to the domain of painting and the visual arts: 'Light is therefore colour.' Finally, Turing's quote is: 'This is only a foretaste of what is to come and only the shadow of what is going to be,' in reference to the challenges of technological innovation.

These four historical characters were introduced in the designs of the G series, which started being produced in 2016. Before them, other historical characters considered relevant in terms of the UK's cultural memory were used in the reverse designs of banknotes. These included writers such as Charles Dickens and William Shakespeare, scientists and innovators like Michael Faraday, Isaac Newton, Charles Darwin, Christopher Wren and James Watt, a musician (Edward Elgar), a banker (John Houblon), an engineer (George Stephenson), a philosopher (Adam Smith) and social activists such as Florence Nightingale and Elizabeth Fry. In terms of geographical representativity, it is worth noticing that, from all these, only Adam Smith was non-English (he was a Scott).

As can be seen, the repertoire of portions of the semiosphere used throughout history and in the present in the UK to design currency is broad. In this sense, it differs from the strategies used in the US and Canadian dollars. When examining the pound sterling, we can see how there is not a single thematic selection including a specific differential trait (such as being a statesman, an artist, etc.) of prominent historical characters for them to be celebrated in currency. Therefore, if a new £200 banknote were issued, we could expect it to have the same design as the other banknotes on the front side, and the portrait of a prominent UK historical character, plus his or her signature, a quote and some visual elements expressing his or her field of action in the reverse. What we could not say with certainty is in which discursive field (literature, painting, politics, science, etc.) that character would have been active.

At this point, it is useful to introduce the concept of 'paradigmatic substitutions,' presented by de Saussure in *Course of General Linguistics*. For de Saussure, natural languages work based on two types of relationships: syntagmatic and paradigmatic. Whereas the former type sustains the relationship between signs that are actually used – such as when combining a subject with a verb and complements – the latter refers to possible substitutions between what we encounter in a text and what we could have encountered. As an example, a sentence such as 'My pet is a X' allows only a certain number of possibilities to replace that X. To begin with, we can expect the X to refer to an animal. Moreover, we can expect it to be a domesticated animal, such as a dog or a cat, but not a lion. The same occurs in currency design, where each cultural repertoire belonging to the national semiosphere functions as a paradigm from where those in charge of designing banknotes and coins can obtain elements to include in currency.

However, this selection is also limited by circumstantial constraints. Previously, we introduced Eliseo Verón's (1988) concept of 'conditions of production', which tries to leave aside a focus merely on the text as output and its internal articulations, and advocates for considering the sociohistorical conditions in which a text was produced. According to Verón, texts contain traces of enunciation that somehow give some hints about their context of creation. Before concluding the chapter, it is worth having a look at the conditions of production of the four visual texts that currently are part of the pound sterling as a visual system.

Nowadays, it is easy to find official texts explaining the procedure used to design currency. By examining these secondary texts (paratexts), we are considering texts that were enunciated by the same authority in charge of producing banknotes and coins. In this sense, these texts function as explanations that try to make the selection of design elements less arbitrary and more based on rational arguments. On the selection of characters that could be included in the reverse of the current banknotes of the pound sterling, the Bank of England writes:

> We want the characters who make it onto our banknotes to come from different backgrounds and fields. When selecting a new character, we take into account who has featured on notes in the past. This means that our choices can reflect the diversity of UK society. Of course, banknotes need to be universally accepted. We therefore look for UK characters who have made an important contribution to our society and culture through their innovation, leadership or values. We do not include fictional characters, or people who are still living (except the monarch on the front of the note). Finally, we need to have a suitable portrait of the person which will be easy to recognise.[8]

This approach, which is open and broad in the sense that it could include almost anyone belonging to the UK's public history, led to the establishment of an advisory committee. In the preparation of the current series, this committee discussed which characters could be included in the new designs.[9] All these conditions propose norms and legitimacy criteria, commonly agreed between participants, that shape currency design, excluding individuals that do not match them. The banknotes that finally get issued should reflect these productive principles, which are located at the discursive level and mediated by the act of enunciation that someone does to produce texts. Once more, we can see how textual analysis allows us to see the forces of discourse in action.

At the beginning of the chapter, we mentioned that contrary to what is the case in most national currencies, banknotes of the pound sterling with designs different than those we studied in this chapter circulate in some regions of the UK. This means that various designs for the same currency exist, depending on regional factors and institutional arrangements. This is something exceptional to the genre of currency design. Studying the design of banknotes and coins of the pound sterling issued by other entities allowed to do so in the UK, such as banks in Scotland and Northern Ireland, would require one chapter per country. Hence, we leave this task open for the future.

Before concluding, let us go back to the pound sterling's coins. On their front side, in every coin we encounter a profile portrait of the reigning monarch. With the passing of the queen, this design choice triggered a process of full redesign of the eight coins. On the border of the front side of the coins, surrounding the portrait of the reigning monarch, a verbal text is used, written in capital letters and composed of three elements: a year, the name of the monarch and an inscription. That inscription is 'DEI-GRA-REX-F.D.', in the case of King Charles III, and 'DEI-GRA-REG-FID.DEF', in the case of Queen Elizabeth II.

These inscriptions, which also change according to who the reigning monarch is since they are marked by gender, stand for the Latin expressions 'Dei Gratia Rex/Regina Fidei Defensor', which can be translated as 'By the Grace of God, King/Queen, Defender of Faith'. According to Jakob Dittmar (2009: 199), this sentence can be read as 'a reminder that the British monarch is also Head of the Anglican Church and, by extension, that the monarchy guarantees the observance of a specific set of Christian rules'. As was the case in the US dollar, in this national currency as well, religion serves as a discourse that intervenes in the discursive construction of the nation and the state, linking them to a more metaphysical type of discursivity.

To sum up, we can see how discourses of nationhood and statehood are conveyed differently than in the previous two currencies we studied. Here the figure of the reigning monarch, as an expression in the form of a specific individual of the political institution of monarchy, together with the identity of the Bank of England, serves as the basis for the design of UK banknotes, which are above all English banknotes with a pretension of recognition and acceptance in the whole UK territory. In the pound sterling's current designs, we can find a remanent of something that Blaazer (2002: 18) highlights in his historical work with UK currency: 'English patriotism was identical to Union patriotism, and the other nations of the Union were either to be carelessly subordinated, or simply disregarded.' Stabilized equivalences such as these are an interesting object of study for semioticians.

* * *

In this chapter, we studied the design of banknotes and coins of the British pound sterling. As we saw, both were recently updated because of the change of the reigning monarch, after Queen Elizabeth II's passing in 2022 and the accession of King Charles III. This event impacted the official texts of the British nation, such as currency and the coat of arms, which were restyled. In the chapter, our study of how currency design draws on the semiosphere and its contents was expanded: we identified new portions of the semiosphere used to be featured in banknotes and coins.

Different from the cases of the US and Canadian dollars, the UK had a relevant colonial past. Therefore, banknotes and coins produced in the metropolis circulated in contexts that were not that of their origin. For semioticians, it would be interesting to study not only how these designs travelled from the British Isles to other geographies, as some scholars have done (Hewitt, 1999), but also what Verón would call the 'conditions of recognition', that is, the specific interpretations triggered by the sociohistorical circumstances where these designs circulate. However, since our focus in the book is limited to study the designs used in banknotes and coins with current circulation in the countries we chose, we will not do it here.

7

Swiss Franc

In this chapter, we remain in the European continent and travel from the British Islands to continental Europe and, more precisely, to its Alpine heart, to study the design of the banknotes and coins of the Swiss franc. As we shall see in what follows, studying Switzerland's national currency will help us confront different design strategies than those we have encountered so far. Hence, this chapter should mean a further step in our journey, not limited to just studying a new currency but proceeding with identifying new productive mechanisms sustaining currency design.

7.1 Context

Switzerland is said to be one of the eldest European nations: it was founded in 1291 as an alliance of three of its cantons. However, the Swiss state as we know it today, one with a much-celebrated federal form, dates from 1848, when a new constitution entered into force sustaining this type of political organization. In that constitution, it was established that the only institution allowed to issue money in the country was the federal government. Two years later, in 1850, a monetary reform introduced the Swiss franc as Switzerland's national currency (Baltensperge and Kugler, 2017).

Since then, the Swiss franc has been the official currency of Switzerland, a relatively small country characterized by its neutrality and that is an oasis at the geographical heart of the EU, a political entity to which it does not belong. Banknotes are issued and regulated by the Swiss National Bank, which is the only institution allowed to print banknotes of the Swiss national currency on behalf of the federal government. The first series of Swiss franc banknotes was issued in 1907.[1] The banknotes currently circulating belong to the ninth series and were released in 2016 following a creative process that took a decade.

Swissmint is responsible for creating the coins of this currency system, as well as special coins.[2]

In 2005, the Swiss National Bank opened a competition between graphic designers to come up with the visual texts to be used in the banknotes of the ninth series. In a press release,[3] we read some of the requirements the Bank instructed the participant designers should consider to create their proposals. There we read that the new designs should respond to the idea of 'Switzerland open to the world' as the basic theme. According to the press release,

> Switzerland is to be represented as an entirety, as a country open to the rest of the world and also as a meeting place for the world. The focus should not be on any individuals, inventions or achievements. Much rather, a basic attitude and its manifestations should be conveyed: Switzerland as a platform for dialogue, progress, humanitarian commitment, exciting experiences, creativity and the search for practical approaches to solutions within organisations.

This passage is relevant for several reasons. To begin with, it evidences a clear communicative intention sustaining the redesign project: there is a specific view or conception of Switzerland (and, particularly, of a 'basic attitude' ascribed to it) that should be communicated through the designs of banknotes. Here the visual texts are regarded as media that should communicate a specific message, and not only signify.

Besides, there is a focus set on the relationship of the country with the rest of the world, which somehow suggests that the proposed designs should be recognizable by inhabitants of Switzerland, but also by people not residing in the country and not using the notes in their daily operations. Here the role of the actor 'the world' is interesting, because the depiction of national identity will be shaped by the existence, and particularly the views, of that abstract and diffuse actor. In terms of its content, we can assume 'the world' to be defined as all that is not Switzerland.

Thirdly, there is a specific and conscious distancing from the strategy of using individuals, inventions and achievements for currency design. All these are cultural repertoires that we have encountered in our previous analyses. Specifically, the Bank was interested in not having famous personalities depicted in the new banknotes, as was the case in past series of the franc. If all these repertoires are left aside, what can graphic designers work with to enter the competition? What other local encyclopaedias and cultural repertoires could be used to design currency considering the standards of this specific discursive genre?

Finally, the quoted passage refers to 'a basic attitude and its manifestations' as those that should be conveyed in the new designs. How can an attitude be conveyed in visual texts? While visual elements based on a mimetic and iconic take of the material world are easier to handle with – let us think of the portraits, buildings and landscapes we encountered so far – attitudes cannot – because of their less figurative nature – be simply 'copied'; they must be *expressed* through the mediation of signs, which can be read and interpreted as standing for these attitudes. This poses a challenge for graphic designers, who need to identify in culture some codes containing visual signs and contents that readers can easily relate to specific attitudes.

All the issues listed in the previous paragraphs are interesting for semioticians. In the case we are presenting, the institution sustaining the enunciation of banknotes wanted to convey a specific view of the country it serves, and designers were tasked with crafting a limited set of visual texts than could convey that specific view of the country. The main challenge these designers had to deal with consisted in identifying visual elements that could lead readers to grasp that view.

Moreover, the press release establishes that 'it is envisaged that these topics will be dealt with through the lens of economics, education, research and development, human rights, tourism and recreation, culture and, lastly, sports'. Here we find a hint on how the general view about Switzerland underpinning the new series of banknotes could be approached in *thematic* terms, and not with a focus on individuals. These discourses (economic, educational, etc.) mediate in how that abstract view of the country as one open to the world should be thematized. As such, they help reduce, even if partially, the abstraction of the main attitude that should be communicated in the designs.

Finally, since, at the time of the competition, the Swiss franc's series had six banknotes, the Bank decided that six specific topics should be depicted, one per existing banknote. These topics are expressed in the form of activities: (1) negotiating and exchanging, (2) teaching and researching, (3) helping and mediating, (4) enjoying and relaxing, (5) creating and designing and (6) deciding and implementing. Two years after the competition was launched, the designs created by Manuela Pfunder were selected, even if her proposal came second in the competition.[4] In 2025, a design competition for a new banknote series was launched, so we can expect the current banknotes to be replaced in the upcoming years.

7.2 Banknotes and coins of the Swiss franc

Our corpus in this chapter is composed of six banknotes and seven coins. As we can notice in our accumulative work so far, there seems to be some regularity between currency systems regarding the number of banknotes and coins they

<table>
<tr><th>Value</th><th>Front</th><th>Reverse</th></tr>
<tr><td>Fr. 10</td><td></td><td></td></tr>
<tr><td>Fr. 20</td><td>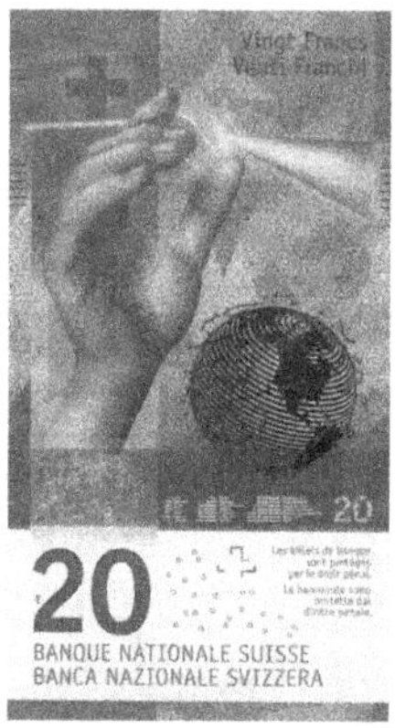</td><td></td></tr>
<tr><td>Fr. 50</td><td>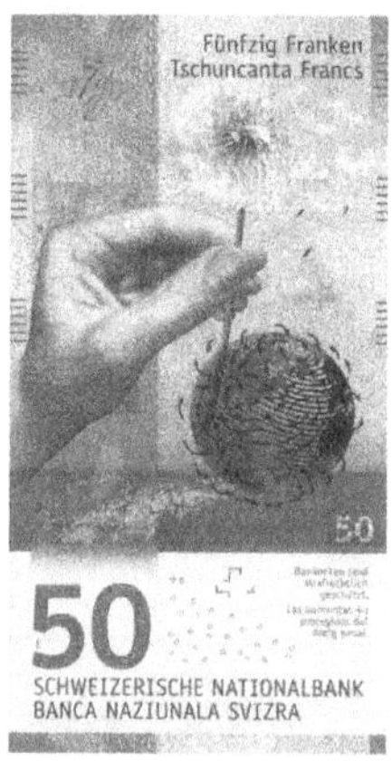</td><td></td></tr>
</table>

Fr. 100

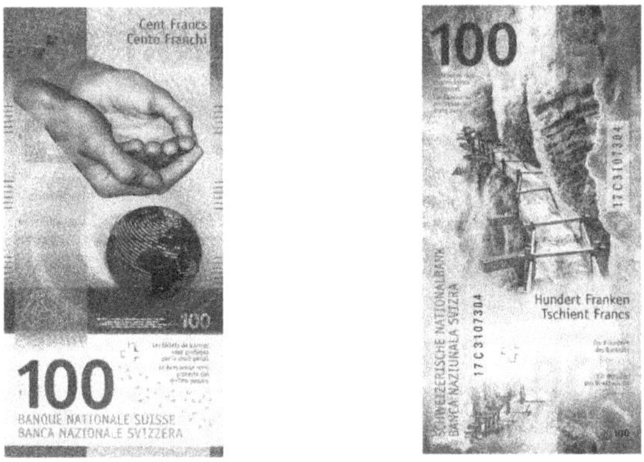

Fr. 200

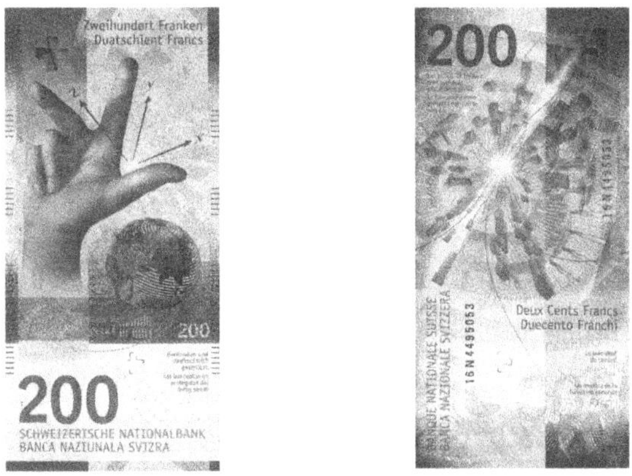

Fr. 1,000

Figure 28 The six banknotes of the Swiss franc from the ninth series.
Source: Swiss National Bank.

comprise. Figure 28 shows the six banknotes of the Swiss franc from the ninth series, which entered in circulation in 2016, and Figure 29, the seven coins currently used in Switzerland.

Table 7 lists the design elements we can identify in banknotes, and Table 8 does the same with coins. As we can see in the first of these tables, the complexity of the visual texts we encounter in the banknotes of the Swiss francs in terms of its design elements is higher than that of the currency systems studied before.

7.3 Analysis

In terms of format, layout and the overall features of the visual system, the current series of the Swiss franc are easily identifiable as being currency. This is the case even if this is the first currency system of the ones studied in the book whose banknotes are designed using a vertical layout.

This design option has been used for the Swiss franc since its previous series, in which both sides of each banknote were designed vertically. Previously, in the sixth series,[5] the front side of banknotes was designed horizontally, and the reverse, vertically. If we leave aside the new C$10 banknote, which announces an upcoming full vertical series, the Swiss franc is the only currency studied in this book that went for the full vertical option, that is, on both sides.

In terms of format and formal issues, size is used in this banknote system in a relation with economic value. As was the case with the banknotes of the British pound sterling, the banknotes of the Swiss franc grow in size as the nominal value does. Moreover, the six banknotes are clearly identifiable as part of the same family thanks to a few common visual elements that contribute to the sense effect of a continuous visual system to which all these units belong.

Despite this clear continuity existing between them, each banknote has its own identity. This occurs thanks to the use of colour and some types of elements that are common to the six notes, but that are modified from one to the other and, hence, appear to us as meaningful discontinuities. On the front, these elements are (1) the pair of hands located in the upper part, (2) the image of planet Earth located in the middle and (3) the lower space of the note including the denomination and some institutional information. Something similar occurs in the reverses, although the design elements in those designs are not always easy to relate with those included in the other banknotes of the system.

In terms of content, when looking at the current banknotes of the Swiss franc, we immediately identify the difference with the currencies we have studied so

Value	Front	Reverse
5 cents		
10 cents		
20 cents		
50 cents		
Fr. 1		
Fr. 2		
Fr. 5		

Figure 29 The seven coins of the Swiss franc.
Source: Swissmint.

Table 7 List of Distinctive Design Elements Identified in the Six Banknotes of the Swiss Franc.

Value	Front	Reverse
Fr. 10	A pair of hands holding a baton An image of planet Earth with the time zones A map of Switzerland highlighting the Swiss rail network An inscription with the country's longest railway tunnels and their distances Clocks on the background	Rail tracks going into a tunnel Watch's movement
Fr. 20	A hand holding a prism refracting light An image of planet Earth with star constellations A map of Switzerland highlighting night-time light emissions with circles An inscription with the distances between the Earth and a selection of celestial bodies A pattern with geometric shapes in the background	Light beaming a movie, outdoors Butterflies
Fr. 50	A hand holding a dandelion An image of planet Earth with arrows representing wind flows A map of Switzerland highlighting the Alps region, in Switzerland and beyond An inscription with the names of the main 4,000+ m peaks in the Swiss Alps Wind flow arrows in the background	Mountains from the Swiss Alps A paraglider
Fr. 100	A pair of hands holding and scooping up a liquid substance similar to water An image of planet Earth with isobars on it A map of Switzerland highlighting the waterflows and rivers flowing through Switzerland An inscription with the list of the longest Swiss rivers and their length	Water flowing alongside a vertical mountain though an irrigation channel
Fr. 200	A hand with three fingers stretched, doing a number three, with three arrows indicating three dimensions on it An image of planet Earth including the land masses during the late Cretaceous period A map of Switzerland highlighting the geological ages An inscription with a timeline showing the stages in the formation of the universe Figures that resemble atoms and particles in the background A model of the solar system	A depiction of a particle collision A particle collision map
Fr. 1,000	Two hands shaking hands An image of planet Earth with letters from the International Phonetic Alphabet A map of Switzerland highlighting language regions in Switzerland and its neighbouring countries An inscription including the names of all Swiss cantons	A depiction of the parliament in session from above A relation graph

Source: Author's own elaboration.

Table 8 List of Distinctive Design Elements Identified in the Seven Coins of the Swiss Franc.

Value	Front	Reverse
5 cents	Head of Libertas (Roman goddess of liberty) facing right, with braided hair tied with a ribbon and wearing a tiara	A wreath formed of two alpine rose springs with flowers tied with a ribbon below
10 cents		A wreath formed of two oak branches with acorns tied with a ribbon below
20 cents		A wreath formed of two alpine rose springs with flowers tied with a ribbon below
50 cents Fr. 1 Fr. 2	Depiction of Helvetia standing, wearing a toga, holding a spear in the right hand and supporting a shield with coat of arms of Switzerland in the left hand Twenty-three stars along the borders of the coin	A wreath formed of oak and alpine rose branches tied with a ribbon below
Fr. 5	A depiction of a herdsman, partially sided and wearing a hood	An image of the Swiss escutcheon surrounded with flower wreaths

Source: Author's own elaboration.

far. As explained above, this responds to an explicit strategy adopted by the Swiss National Bank – the institutional enunciator responsible for creating the visual texts – for the design of the series. These strategic lines can be found on its website, in line with the paratexts presented above:

> For the current series the SNB adopted an entirely new design approach – individuals are no longer depicted. Rather, each denomination depicts a typical Swiss characteristic, represented by means of a key motif. Each characteristic is illustrated with an activity, a location in Switzerland and other design elements. The theme of the current banknote series is 'The many facets of Switzerland'.[6]

This text evidences that the enunciator is aware of the novelty of the chosen approach, which we can read as one that is disruptive with regard to the genre's norms. Although these norms are not 'mandatory', they were stabilized throughout time based on custom and practice, becoming a standard. The paratexts show how there is a deliberate intention to deviate from the standard and innovate.

Perhaps the most salient trait of this approach is that it deliberately leaves aside individuals from currency design. As is customary in the discursive genre, the banknotes of the Swiss franc historically featured individuals. In the eighth series (that is, the previous one to that we are studying), these were architect Le Corbusier, composer Arthur Honegger, artists Sophie Taeuber-Arp and Alberto Giacometti, writer Charles-Ferdinand Ramuz and historian Jakob Burkhardt. In the sixth series (which was the circulating series before the eighth one was introduced), these were mathematician Leonhard Euler, architect Francesco Borromini and scientists Albrecht von Haller, August Forel, Horace-Bénédict de Saussure and Konrad Gessner.

As can be seen from this list, none of the historical characters included in the designs of previous banknotes and coins of the Swiss franc were related to politics or the state, as was the case in US dollar, the Canadian dollar and the British pound sterling.[7] As in the reverse designs of the pound sterling, in the two previous series to the current one of the Swiss franc, banknotes featured portraits of prominent Swiss people active in the fields of science and the arts.

Therefore, we can clearly see how discursive constructions of the national in currency design can be done with different focuses. One of them – obviously thanks to the conflation of the nation and the state that is customary in our world of national states – consists of focusing on political figures such as monarchs, presidents and prime ministers – in short, heads of state and government. These are specific individuals that throughout history occupied such roles and hence function semiotically as expressions of these institutions.

Another type of construction consists of highlighting the action of citizens (members of the nation) that did not occupy positions of institutional power but that nevertheless produced things (in a broad sense, achievements) that are praiseworthy, particularly in terms of the identity of the nation. This is what is in play when individuals active in the sciences and the arts are celebrated on currency: they function as semiotic resources carrying meanings linked to national grandeur, particularly in terms of what the citizens of that nation have achieved. Hence, their portraits used in currency design *denote* – they are supposed to stand for the depicted individual – but they also *connote*, since, to properly make sense of the portrait, we must consider that its presence in currency is granted not only by the individual's genius but also because of what that genius means in terms of national identity.

The analyses presented in the three previous chapters evidence how depicting individuals is a customary practice in the genre of currency design. In past editions of the Swiss franc, this was also the case. However, for the ninth series, the Swiss National Bank decided to explore a new territory, opening the field to creativity in a genre whose normative traits tend to be conservative. As we saw above, the main idea encountered to replace the customary use of individuals in currency design consists in focusing on a set of characteristics that are considered as somehow describing the Swiss as a nation.

This choice comes along with a series of interesting dynamics. To begin with, there is an interpretation that the Bank – or, to be more precise, the people working for the bank that are responsible for currency design – does about an alleged way of being of the Swiss. In semiotic terms, this occurs thanks to the establishment of relationships of difference regarding other ways of being, which are different from those that characterize the Swiss people. If the Swiss are A, B and C, that is because other national peoples are not A, not B and not C, or eventually they might have some of these traits but not all. Otherwise, the features A, B and C are not meaningful as differential traits to characterize a given national identity.

Moreover, just as phonetic traits allow us to classify sounds and distinguish the sound of /b/ from that of /p/, the Bank's idea seems to be that those characteristics, which are considered *typically* Swiss, can be listed and described. This discursive operation implies relating some specific traits with the alleged national character – the same process in action in (national) stereotyping.

Finally, there is the assumption that these characteristics can be brought to life and expressed visually. In writing, we can use words to express the defining features of a collective identity, and specifically those more abstract and complex such as attitudes. However, bringing this type of content to life figuratively through images that readers can interpret as conveying those desired messages is a different story, much more complex and challenging for the technical creators of those images. There is a difference in depicting visually a sport praised nationally (such as ice hockey in a previous series of the Canadian dollar) and an attitude or mindset.

In semiotic terms, the challenge for the designers that participated in the design contest of the current series of the Swiss franc were two. On the one hand, they had to understand the segmentation of the plane of content proposed by the Bank and be sure of properly understanding the set of characteristics that the Bank proposed as being typically Swiss. An incorrect grasping of this articulation of the plane of the content could lead to choosing an inappropriate strategy for the creation of the visual texts to be included in the banknotes.

On the other hand, the designers had to find *visual ways* of expressing these abstract national characteristics, so that what we see in the texts they created can be clearly and easily read as what they meant to express. This requires a profound familiarity with the semiosphere, both local and global (remember the references to 'the world' in the paratexts studied above), and identifying design elements that, thanks to cultural codification, can serve to express these characteristics figuratively, through specific units in the plane of expression that can be recognized and related to the contents that the enunciator wants to express.

In the Swiss National Bank's website, it is explained that these characteristics, defined as 'some of our country's many facets', are the following: (1) organizational talent, (2) creativity, (3) wealth of experiences, (4) humanitarian tradition, (5) scientific expertise and (6) communicative flair. There is a clear challenge for the designers to express these concepts using images. Hence, a specific semiotic effort needs to be made, so the reader can understand what he or she sees in the banknotes as referring to these concepts. In this sense, we can see in action a process of *translation* that goes from abstract concepts and ideas to specific repertoires that can be identified as referring to them, and that is characterized by the mediation – as steps in that translation process – by the motifs and themes proposed by the Bank.

To help in that process of translation, the Swiss National Bank recurred to a selection of semiotic repertoires – portions of the local encyclopaedia – that serve the purpose of figurativizing these abstract characteristics, that is, of rendering them identifiable through elements that we can recognize when looking at them. These repertoires are actions, places and objects (Table 9).

Table 9 Repertoires Used in the Designs of the Current Swiss Franc's Banknotes.

Value	Theme	Motif	Action	Place	Object
Fr. 10	Organizational talent	Time	Musical conduction	Train tunnel	Clock mechanism
Fr. 20	Creativity	Light	Light refraction	Urban outdoor cinema	Butterflies
Fr. 50	Wealth of experiences	Wind	Holding a flower	Mountain peak	Paraglide
Fr. 100	Humanitarian tradition	Water	Giving water	Mountain	Water conduction system
Fr. 200	Scientific expertise	Matter	Expressing dimension	Laboratory	Particles
Fr. 1,000	Communicative flair	Language	Greeting/ agreeing	Parliament	Relation graph

Source: Author's own elaboration.

The most interesting (or even relevant) column in Table 9 is the one of motif, because that is where we can find the conceptual modulation of the six selected themes. Even if the motifs still evidence a high degree of abstraction, they somehow delimit how – and, perhaps most importantly, drawing on which discursive domain – each of the characteristics to be communicated should be depicted. Then three major sets of design elements are used to bring those motives to life: actions, places and objects. These are easier to express using images and hence serve as semiotic resources to translate the conceptual motifs.

The hands used in the upper part of every banknote are the first major design element used to express the selected themes and motifs. These hands are not intrinsically valuable – that is, they are not the hands of a specific person that should be valued or venerated – but work as a semiotic resource that is both metonymic and symbolic. It is metonymic because the part is standing for the whole: hands stand for humans and what they do in terms of actions. They are symbolic because what they are doing stands for something else in a manner that evidences a strong degree of cultural convention.

The symbolic strategy used to express actions through hands doing things somehow opposes the strategy based on iconism that we identified as the one characterizing the banknotes studied in the previous chapters. There, what we saw were usually copies, using a mimetic type of representation, of existing individuals, buildings and landscapes. Even if the hands we see are based on a strategy of iconism – we do not find major artistic interventions or deviations from what we know a standard hand is and looks like – the sign does not stand for the hand we can identify as what it stands for, but for something else. To decodify that 'something else', a cultural competence is needed. Figure 30 shows the six hands used in the banknotes, so we can have a better view of the specific actions they are doing and how they might stand for the general themes proposed by the Bank.[8]

A second common element is featured on the front side of each banknote: the globe, standing for planet Earth, and with it 'the world'. Although, within the topological grid underpinning the six designs, the globe is always located in the same place, it rotates from banknote to banknote, so we manage to see throughout the series its entirety. The globe, which is slightly modified depending on the banknote's main motif, can be interpreted as a resource that is useful to depict Switzerland as a country that is aware of the world and connected with it. Moreover, showing the world in its entirety throughout the series can be read as a strategy used to express that it is a world that Switzerland sees and recognizes in its entirety. As expressed on the Swiss National Bank's

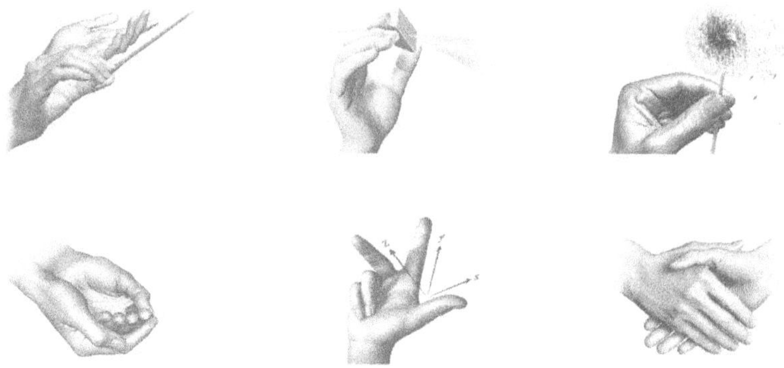

Figure 30 Depictions of hands included in the banknotes of the ninth series of the Swiss franc.

Source: Swiss National Bank (www.snb.ch/en/the-snb/mandates-goals/cash/new-banknotes/design/design-elements).

website, 'the shimmering globe reflects how Switzerland sees itself as part of an interconnected world'.[9] Let us not forget that the abstract actor 'the world', not in sense of the Earth but of global communities excluding the Swiss, were specifically referred to in the description of what currency design should express. In this sense, this abstract actor is also present, through a standard symbol, in the designs of the series.

The front designs of the six banknotes also include more direct references to Switzerland as a country, that is, as a political entity grounded on a territory that is delimited by specific boundaries and that can be clearly located on a map. These are the depictions of the country that we find on the security strip. In each banknote, the strip is modified depending on the key motif sustaining its design. The banknotes of this series also include a list related to the key motif. Finally, as a symbol of Switzerland, we find the cross included in the Swiss flag, a symbol that, in semiotic terms, works as the maple leaves did in the Canadian dollar: thanks to a stabilization of meaning throughout time, this sign can be easily related to the country.

The reverses of the notes relate thematically to the front designs. However, this relationship is not evident, as it could be in cases where we find an artist on the front of the banknote and his or her work on the reverse. In this case, this relationship is mediated by the key motifs: time, light, wind, water, matter and language.

The design of the Fr. 10 note is based on the motif of *time* and should convey the characteristic of *organizational talent*. How do these two semantic units relate to each other? What situations, stories, objects and practices can be used to express this relationship visually? The first evident association of time with a specific practice or object is the one existing with clocks. This object is particularly relevant in the case of Switzerland, because it serves to connote some stereotypical characteristics defined in national terms, such as precision, planning, punctuality and a meticulous handle of time. In this banknote, time is expressed using a cultural codification: on the front, we encounter the world's time zones and small clocks used as background; on the reverse, we encounter the mechanism of a clock. All these signs function isotopically.

However, in that note, there are two other interesting codifications of the motif of time. The first of them is musical tempo, expressed through the hands holding a baton, an action that stands for musical conduction. An orchestra conductor is above all a master of time, that is, someone who can guide a group of musicians to play coordinately. Although the relationship between motif and sign is recognizable, it is not as evident as the one the motif has with the imagery revolving around clocks and time zones.

The second not-so-evident codification of the motif of time is the world of trains and railroads, as expressed in three design elements included in the note: the railways entering a tunnel, the map of Switzerland featuring the railway lines and a list with the names of the country's longest tunnels. With the purpose of exemplifying how language and meaning work, Ferdinand de Saussure (1959: 108) saw in the domain of trains a good comparison:

> The linguistic mechanism is geared to differences and identities, the former being only the counterpart of the latter. Everywhere then, the problem of identities appears; moreover, it blends partially with the problem of entities and units [...] This characteristic stands out if we draw some comparisons with facts taken from outside speech. For instance, we speak of the identity of two '8:25 p.m. Geneva-to-Paris' trains that leave at twenty-four hour intervals. We feel that it is the same train each day, yet everything – the locomotive, coaches, personnel – is probably different.

How does the railway system relate to the motif of time? There does not seem to be an evident relationship between the two semantic universes. However, in the Swiss case (and others, like the German – at least in stereotypical terms), there is the mediation of national character as a discursive force: it is widely 'known' (or, better, believed) that, in normal circumstances, transport systems in

Switzerland are extremely and exceptionally precise and always on time. Thanks to the mediation of this social imaginary, the national train and railway system can connote organizational talent through the motif of time. We can see all the discursive forces that are involved in this process of equivalence.

The Fr. 20 banknote features the motif of light. The hand holds a prism, which refracts light. The image of the Earth is depicted with some abstract drawings on it, meant to stand for star constellations. Since stars are made of light, they seem a legitimate semiotic resource to express this motif. The map of Switzerland we encounter in this note includes some marks that stand for light emissions at night. The list next to the map comprises distances between the Earth and specific star constellations.

The geometrical shapes used as background on the front side might remind us of the shapes or figures we see through a kaleidoscope, also operating thanks to light. On the reverse, we find butterflies, a codified symbol of beauty (partially thanks to colour), together with a depiction of people gathering around a cinema screen on a public and open space. In that situation, the projection of the movie is possible thanks to light. All the design elements we identified serve the purpose of bringing the key motif to life in figurative terms and, as such, to be recognized by the reader. Moreover, we can also see how some of the resources used in this note are culturally related to the theme of creativity, which is the one attributed to this banknote.

The theme of the Fr. 50 note is wealth of experiences, and the chosen motif, wind. The role of the hand here is interesting, because the action it is supposed to stand for is not easy to describe using words. We can recognize a hand holding a dandelion, as well as what is happening in the image: the pleasure associated with letting the wind (either natural or created using our mouth) to break it apart and letting a part of it to be carried away. Moreover, in this note, arrows are used as culturally codified signs to express the wind's direction. Here we encounter them on the globe and in the background of the front side. The activity of paragliding is another resource used as an expression of what the wind can do since this sport depends on wind.

Since the wind is a natural element, the domain of nature is also used in this banknote to express the motif, most notably a few mountain peaks, which define the identity of Switzerland in geographical terms, as an Alpine country. Anne-Marie Thiesse (2000) claims that a nation can be expressed using a specific landscape, as we saw in the case of Canada. For Thiesse, this is the case because, during the nineteenth century, a codification of nature in national terms occurred, particularly in the work of writers. About Switzerland, Thiesse (2000: 57) writes that Swiss territory is small when compared to the vast territories of the countries surrounding it, and that its 'prodigious and sparkling peaks' serve to illustrate this identity. Since mountain peaks are characterized by the presence of wind, they serve as a semiotic resource, originating in the realm of nature, to convey the motif of wind, as well as the theme of wealth of experiences sustaining the design of this note. The theme of the new banknote series for which a design competition was organized in 2025 is 'Switzerland and its altitudes', and it aims to reflect 'the diversity of life at the various altitudes'.

The Fr. 100 note uses the motif of water, which should express the characteristic of humanitarian tradition. Design elements that serve to figurativize this motif are the hands holding water, the map of Switzerland including its rivers, the list of rivers and their lengths next to the map and the irrigation system depicted on the back of the note. Besides the hands scooping up water, which can be interpreted as a gesture of helping someone in need, it is not very clear that the banknote expresses the characteristic of humanitarian tradition, as was the case with creativity in the Fr. 20 note.

The motif of the Fr. 200 note is matter, as a means of expressing scientific expertise. In the note, we find design elements that convey science in a conventional manner, using visual models that we immediately relate to the world of atoms and particles, as well as the solar system. These visual models serve as signs codified in culture to express the natural sciences. Moreover, the diagram included over the main hand evidences a typical and conventional representation of science, with a chart including the variables X, Y and Z. References to mass and science are also visible in the globe, which includes marks standing for the land masses during the late Cretaceous period, the map of Switzerland highlighting the geological ages and a timeline showing the stages in the formation of the universe. On the reverse, the depiction of a particle detector and a particle collision serve to produce a more contemporary and less conventional take of the scientific domain, as was the case in some of the reverse designs of the current series of the Canadian dollar, with space tools and medical innovation.

Finally, the Fr. 1,000 banknote uses the motif of language to express the characteristic of communicative flair. This is perhaps the most abstract of the six banknotes that compose the system, probably because the characteristic and motif it should express is polysemous. The two shaking hands express agreement and partnership, which at first sight do not have an evident relationship with language or communication. However, agreement and partnership stand for forms of mutual understanding, and language and communication serve this purpose as well. A similar function will be that of bridges on the euro banknotes, as we will see in Chapter 11. In the background of the front, there are letters, and on the globe, there are signs belonging to the International Phonetic Alphabet, which stand for the sounds we use when speaking any natural language. Contrasting the signs covering the globe in the other notes, here there is not a clear definition of what those signs might be standing for when related to the specific areas of the world.

In this note, the map of Switzerland highlights the four linguistic areas that characterize this multilingual country where French, German, Italian and Romansch are official languages. In fact, every banknote includes the denomination in these four languages. On the reverse, we encounter a depiction of the parliament, which functions as a symbol of dialogue, negotiation and communication through language use. Whereas, in the case of US and Canadian dollars, the parliament was present using *the building* (that is, an object belonging to the domain of architectural heritage), here the focus is set on parliamentarian activity, without any focus on material heritage. The note also features a relation graph, a mathematical figure that serves to express connection between nodes, standing for communication, although in a more technical and less human sense.

To sum up, the six banknotes of the Swiss franc currently circulating tell a story of Switzerland that does not include any prominent characters, neither from the domain of politics nor from that of science and arts. Neither does it include buildings, specific landscapes or historical moments and events. The story we encounter in these six banknotes is based on a discourse of national identity mediated by *ways of doing*. Moreover, even if some of these ways of doing originate in past times, what we encounter in these notes is a repertoire of very contemporary actions, all of them *located in the present time*. This as well is an innovation for the standards governing currency design as a genre, which tends to focus *on the past*. As we argued in Chapter 6, this focalization in the past might serve as a discursive strategy to draw on while at the same time constructing a collective memory defined in national terms which grew throughout time, and that, thanks to sedimentation and stabilization, shaped the national identity being expressed. In the current series of the Swiss franc, the strategy is different: the message is not so much about how the Swiss arrived to be the nation they are but about how they live, as a differential way of understanding Swiss national identity compared to other national identities.

Something different occurs when examining the coins of the Swiss franc. In them, we find a different story, not evidencing a direct relation with that of banknotes. On the front, coins feature three different characters – two women and a man. However, contrary to most of the portraits encountered in the coins studied so far, none of these three characters depict real individuals, that is, who actually existed. As was the case with Britannia in the pound sterling, in the Swiss franc we also encounter a resource to allegorical discourse to produce sense and construct the nation.

The lower-denomination coins have a profile depiction of a woman, which in formal terms reminds us of the depictions of the reigning monarch in the coins of the pound sterling and the Canadian dollar. The woman we encounter here is wearing a sort of crown, where we read the inscription 'LIBERTAS'. Thanks to the proximity between the word and the character, we can read the former as an anchorage and read the inscription as the name of that character. Hence, the woman we see is Libertas, the personification of an ancient Roman deity: the goddess of liberty. In Chapter 4, when studying US dollar's coins, we saw that every coin includes the inscription 'Liberty' in it. In old coins of the US dollar, a similar anthropological depiction of Liberty as a woman was used already in 1793.[10]

However, the most interesting allegorical figure used in the Swiss franc is Helvetia, which is featured in the coins of 50 cents, Fr. 1 and Fr. 2. There we see a full image of Helvetia, in the form of a standing woman, wearing a togue and holding a shield and a spear. Despite some minor differences, this depiction of Helvetia is similar to Britannia's studied in Chapter 6. This makes sense, since both are personifications of the nation and, as such, originated in a similar time and were shaped by similar discourses. Just like the depiction of Britannia had a design element linked to the nation in the shield, we can expect a design element expressing Swiss identity to be present in the depiction of Helvetia. In fact, this is precisely the semiotic function of the cross included in her shield.

Helvetia has been an object of scholarly interest (Kreis, 1991; Maissen, 2001; Haver, 2013; Müller, 2024; Jürg and Dubach, 1998). According to Haver (2013: 274), it is one of the national symbols frequently used during the period of national construction following the federal constitution from 1848. Then, Helvetia fulfilled the role that similar anthropomorphic allegories did in other nations, such as Marianne in France, Germania in Germany, Italia turrita in Italy, Hispania in Spain, Britannia in Great Britain and Columbia in the United States. Therefore, we could propose a common epochal productive matrix sustaining the discursive efforts to bring nations to life in visual texts, which still lives today.

The figure of Helvetia was first included in Swiss currency in the first national series of the franc, issued in 1907 (Figure 31). The depiction of Helvetia included in that series was similar to the one used in the current coins of the Swiss franc.

Therefore, we can see how the current designs of the Swiss franc feature two different visions of the nation. On the one hand, there is a focalization in the

Figure 31 Fr. 100 from the first series of the Swiss franc, from 1907.
Source: Swiss National Bank.

present and in the activities that make Switzerland what it is when defined in terms of the forms of life we encounter in the country. In sociocultural semiotics, the concept of 'forms of life' is used as an analytical category to encompass signs, texts, objects, practices and strategies into broader signifying conglomerates (Fontanille, 2008, 2015; Perusset, 2020). In the current designs of the Swiss franc, we identify a discursive construction aimed at presenting the form of life considered to be 'typically Swiss', at least in the eyes of the institutional enunciator in charge of overseeing currency design. This form of life is composed of six characteristics, and they are expressed through the mediation of specific motives, which we can identify thanks to hands expressing actions, places and objects.

On the other hand, when considering the designs used in coins, we found a discourse focused on the past, and particularly, a past that seems quite distant from our age: that of antiquity. Even if Helvetia is a personification of the Swiss nation and, as such, is very much a product of discourses that were hegemonic in the nineteenth century, the productive matrix sustaining this character is based on styles and visual elements that easily bring us to an ancient past, probably as a way of locating the origins of the nation in immemorial times, as is normally the case (Smith, 2004).

* * *

In this chapter, we examined the Swiss franc. Compared to the analyses presented in the three previous chapters, we could see how, in its ninth series, the Swiss national currency has an innovative approach to the standards governing currency design as a discursive genre. As such, if – when studying the US dollar, the Canadian dollar and the pound sterling – we got used to encountering individuals and buildings, among other design elements, the current designs of the Swiss franc mean an expansion of the possible discursive strategies to use to design currency. This shows how national identity can be thematized in discourse using several resources, and not a limited set. Chapter 8 should shed more light on the various and diverse strategies that can be used for this purpose.

8

Brazilian Real

In this chapter, our analytical journey takes us back to the American continent, but now to it South. Here, and in the following two chapters, we study the currencies of three South American countries, starting with Brazil. As was the case when working with the previous currencies, our study of the Brazilian real should expand our understanding of the semiotics of currency design. Specifically, we aim to identify some innovations when comparing the design of this national currency with those studied so far in the previous chapters. However, as shall be seen, several of the discursive strategies and contents sustaining those currencies are also present in the current designs of the Brazilian real.

8.1 Context

The real was introduced in Brazil as the country's official currency in 1994, to replace the cruzeiro real. This substitution was implemented by the Central Bank of Brazil, an institution created in 1965. It was based on economic reasons related to macroeconomic indicators. In fact, when the real was introduced in 1994, the cruzeiro real had only been in circulation for ten months. The first banknotes were created in 1835 by the Treasury Department. Since 1942, the country had eight different currencies, whose names revolved mainly around the lexemes 'cruzeiro' and 'cruzado', modified with adjectives such as 'novo' (new), 'segundo' (second) or 'real' (royal).

The Brazilian real takes its name from the currency that was used prior to 1942. We could interpret this move as supported by a *restorative* discursive strategy, that is, one aimed at rescuing a tradition of (relative) stability prior to the proliferation of currencies that was common in Brazil during the decades of the mid-twentieth century. While some scholars have studied the real (Costa, 2011; Fernandes, 2008), they have not used a semiotic perspective.

As we shall see in this chapter, the recovery of an old name to designate the new currency implies an interesting contradiction between two discursive universes. This is the case because this choice reintroduces a reference to the discourse of royalty and monarchy – in this context, 'real' stands for 'royal', although it could also be interpreted as standing for 'real' – in a monetary system sustained by the idea and the values of republicanism, which replaced those of monarchy, as we shall see below.

As a final contextual remark, it is worth mentioning that, as a relatively young nation, the issue of national identity has been one of interest to several Brazilian intellectuals. The most well-known ideas about national identity are condensed in books and studies now considered classics, such as *Raízes do Brasil* by Sérgio Buarque de Holanda (1995), *O Povo Brasileiro* by Darcy Ribeiro (1995), *Brazil: An Interpretation* by Gilberto Freyre (2001) and many other texts. Using different perspectives within the social sciences and the humanities, these studies attempt to account for the nature of Brazilian identity both as a unit that can be characterized through a set of traits – and, therefore, distinguished from other national identities – but also, above all, as a process of historical construction and negotiation of sense between different actors.

8.2 Banknotes and coins of the Brazilian real

In this chapter, our corpus comprises the seven banknotes of the second family of the real (Figure 32), introduced in 2010 as an update of the original series, from 1994, due to security reasons. From these notes, the one of R$200 was not part of the original designs, but introduced only some years ago, in 2020. The coins currently circulating in the country are six, as shown in Figure 33.

Table 10 includes a description of the distinctive design elements featured on the banknotes, and Table 11 does the same with coins. When looking at them, remember how complex some of the equivalent tables presented in previous chapters were, so the iconographical simplicity of these designs can be properly grasped.

Value	Front	Reverse
R$2		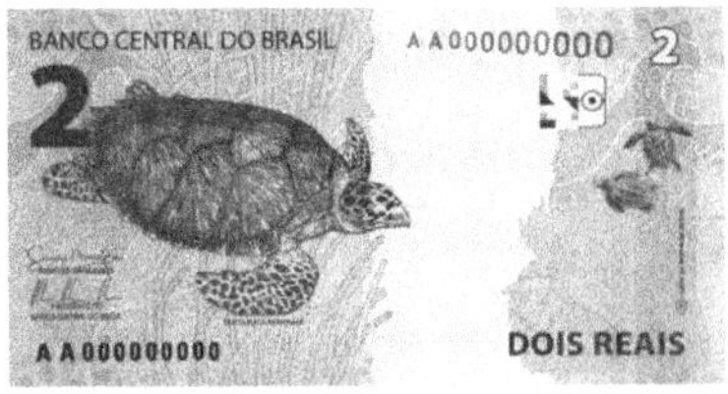
R$5		
R$10		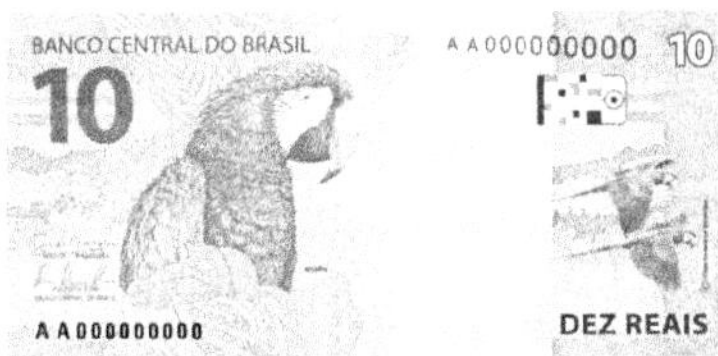
R$20		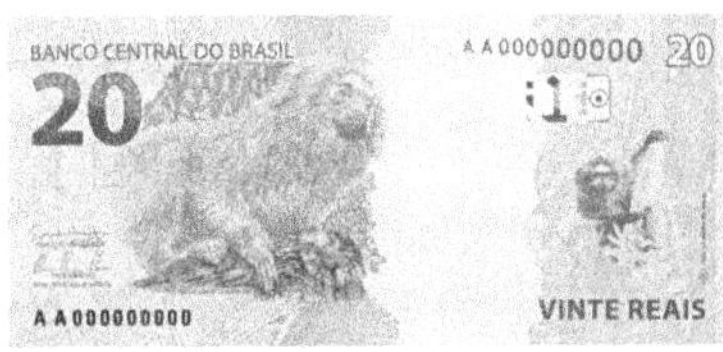
R$50		
R$100		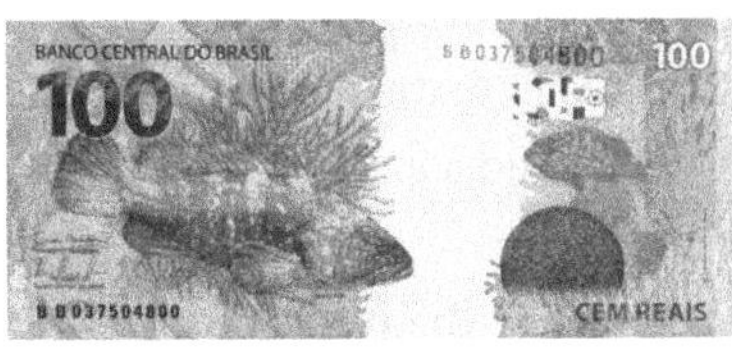

R$200

Figure 32 The seven banknotes of the Brazilian real from the 2010 series.
Source: Central Bank of Brazil.

8.3 Analysis

The first thing that stands out when looking at the banknotes is the absolute harmony that we encounter between the seven units of the system. This harmony in terms of visual unity is based on several elements. To begin with, the seven notes have an almost identical design on the front side, with the same main figure, except for a few design elements that serve to give each banknote its own identity. According to what we have encountered so far in our analytical journey, this repetition of the main figure seems to be exceptional to the discursive genre of currency design. Usually each banknote has a different figure depicted on it, as a strategy to allow a clear distinction from the other notes of the system. This was the case in the US dollar, the Canadian dollars and the Swiss franc.

The British pound sterling was an exception to this principle, and we saw how this decision might be based on the primacy of the monarchy in the design elements used in that currency. Something similar occurs with the banknotes of the Brazilian real, but with some differences. As we saw, the design of the pound sterling is dependent on facts and events of the political world. Hence, when the reigning monarch changes, so does the portrait featured on the banknotes. This depends on the nature of the type of character depicted on the banknote. As we shall see here, this is not the case in the Brazilian real.

A second aspect that contributes to an effect of unity in the Brazilian real as a visual system is sustained through colour. The seven banknotes are harmonious in terms of their colouring. Moreover, the colours change gradually – at least between the R$2 and R$50 notes – unlike what happens in other currencies, such as the Canadian dollar, the Swiss franc and the euro. In these systems, the change of colour from one banknote to the next seems more arbitrary and not based on the composition of the colour spectrum, which changes gradually.

A third element that contributes to creating the effect of a unitary visual system is the design of the reverse. There we find an easily identifiable production

Value	Front	Reverse
1 cent		
5 cents		
10 cents		
25 cents		
50 cents		
1 real		

Figure 33 The six coins of the Brazilian real currently circulating.
Source: Central Bank of Brazil.

Table 10 List of Distinctive Design Elements Identified in the Seven Banknotes of the Brazilian Real.

<table>
<tr><th>Value</th><th>Front</th><th>Reverse</th></tr>
<tr><td>R$2</td><td rowspan="7">Effigy of the Republic</td><td>A water turtle (Tartaruga marinha)</td></tr>
<tr><td>R$5</td><td>A heron (Garça)</td></tr>
<tr><td>R$10</td><td>A macaw (Arará)</td></tr>
<tr><td>R$20</td><td>A golden lion titi monkey (Mico-leão dourado)</td></tr>
<tr><td>R$50</td><td>A jaguar (Onça-pintada)</td></tr>
<tr><td>R$100</td><td>A grouper (Garoupa)</td></tr>
<tr><td>R$200</td><td>A maned wolf (Lobo-guará)</td></tr>
</table>

Source: Author's own elaboration.

Table 11 List of Distinctive Design Elements Identified in the Six Coins of the Brazilian Real.

<table>
<tr><th>Value</th><th>Front</th><th>Reverse</th></tr>
<tr><td>1 cent</td><td>A portrait of Pedro Alvares Cabral and a maritime vessel</td><td rowspan="5">The nominal value of the coin, expressed in numbers
The figure located in the centre of the Brazilian flag
The Southern Cross constellation</td></tr>
<tr><td>5 cents</td><td>A portrait of Joaquim José da Silva Xavier</td></tr>
<tr><td>10 cents</td><td>A portrait of Dom Pedro I</td></tr>
<tr><td>25 cents</td><td>A portrait of Manuel Deodoro da Fonseca</td></tr>
<tr><td>50 cents</td><td>A portrait of José Maria da Silva Paranhos Junior</td></tr>
<tr><td>R$1</td><td>Effigy of the Republic</td><td>The nominal value of the coin, expressed in numbers
The figure located in the centre of the Brazilian flag
The Southern Cross constellation
An indigenous graphism on the outer golden ring (marajoara)</td></tr>
</table>

Source: Author's own elaboration.

matrix based on a specific cultural repertoire: each banknote includes an animal. Moreover, all these animals are somehow *exotic*, and hence could be considered as being featured on currency because they are *native* of Brazil or, more specifically, of the Brazilian territory – water, land and air – and hence of the Brazilian nation.

Finally, a fourth element that fosters visual integration between the seven units is related to format: banknote sizes grow in their length – and some in height, from 6.5 to 7 cm – as the nominal value does, as was the case with the pound sterling. As we have seen, not every currency system uses this strategy to differentiate banknotes, but when one does, there is a progressive relationship moving from the pair /low/–/small/ to the one /high/–/big/. However, the new R$200 note defies this logic: the new note is smaller than R$100 (7×15.6 cm), with a size of 6.5×14.2 cm, the same dimensions of the R$20 note.

Based on these elements, we can see how the Brazilian real is harmonious as a banknote system. In this sense, it contrasts with the heterogeneity and lack of systematization that we encounter in other South American currency systems, such as Paraguay's guaraní, which is comprised of banknotes from series created in different times of history and with no apparent relationship between them in terms of design or iconographic content.

Something similar occurs with the coins, which also feature traits that allow us easily to identify them as part of the same series. The six coins have an anthropomorphic character on their front sides. On the cent coins, we encounter historical characters, whereas on the R$1 coin we encounter the effigy of the Republic, that is, the same character used in banknotes. On the reverse, each coin includes their nominal value expressed in a number, together with a series of diagonal stripes, the spherical symbol that is part of the Brazilian flag, and a depiction of the Southern Cross constellation. When looking at the coins, the production matrix can be easily identified, although the colours vary between them. Moreover, the R$1 coin has a golden ring around it, which distinguishes it from the other coins.

In visual terms, the banknotes also have certain elements that help to create the sense effect of a visual system. At the same time, these elements allow each of the units to have its own identity. The first element – not particularly relevant for us – is the set of marks – stripes – located on the front side of the banknotes, in the lower right-hand corner. A second element – of greater interest for semioticians – is the stripe used on the front side, at the left (Figure 34), which seems to have been included as a mere ornament.

With two exceptions – the R$50 and R$100 notes – each banknote includes this ornamental form, which is coloured using a more intense tone of the same colour used to give each note its own chromatic identity. This design element is similar in the five notes where it was included, but it differs from note to note in the type of plant it is made of. Since this seems to be an element used for the visual continuity of the series, it is curious that the two banknotes containing the

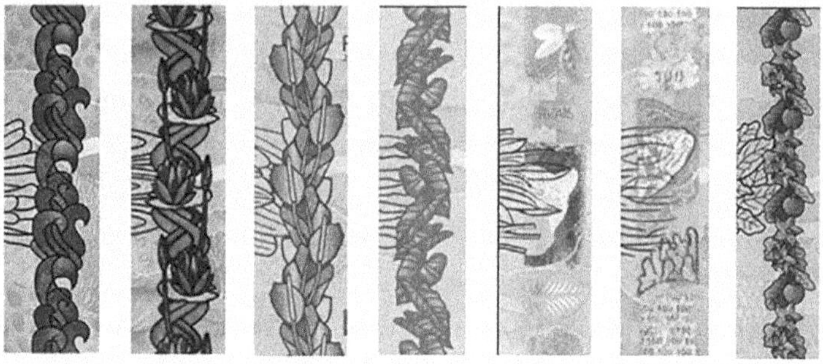

Figure 34 Ornamental stripes included in the banknotes of the Brazilian real.
Source: Author's own elaboration.

highest values up to 2020 – the year when the R$200 banknote was introduced – evidence a discontinuity regarding the presence of this element, because the R$200 note also includes it. However, those two notes include a specific plant, on the left, in the middle of the frame, which varies from note to note.

The fact that this distinctive stripe is made of plants – an element belonging to the domain of nature – could be interpreted as establishing an isotopic relationship – that is, a reiteration of units located in the plane of content – with what we find on the reverse of the banknotes. There we encounter a set of elements belonging to the natural-animal domain, which gains its meaning thanks to the existing opposition with the domain of the cultural-human, as we saw when studying the Canadian dollar. Moreover, those plants could be read as isotopic with the habitats of the animals depicted on the reverse, with the exception of those featured in R$200, which are the fruits that the maned wolf eats.[1] In either case, there is a relationship between the plant and the animal featured on the note.

Moreover, the ornamental strip made of plants is not straight but has an undulation or curvature. Analysing the discursivity of *malandragem* and *ginga*, two concepts frequently used to make sense of the Brazilian form of life, Paolo Demuru (2015: 8) proposes that the curve functions as a translation, in the eidetic dimension – that is, the dimension of forms and shapes – of these concepts. Hence, the curve would function as a 'highly significant plastic trait, which rhymes with the elasticity and flexibility of Brazilians in everyday life, reinforcing it' (Demuru, 2015: 8, my translation). This is a plastic trait highly praised in Brazilian design, for example, in touristic logotypes and brands. As Demuru further develops, the curve is 'a synthesis of national style and character. The curve of rivers and hills, of the dribbling of Garrincha and Romario, of the sea waves, of the floating step of *sambistas* and *capoeiristas*. Senna's curve and Niemeyer's curve. The same curve of the *malandro* who *ginga* in life' (2015: 11, my translation).

This ornamental strip is an addition made to the second series of the real, introduced in 2010. Leaving it aside, all the banknotes of the series are almost identical to those of the first series, introduced in 1994, except that the design and material used were updated. Moreover, while the front side of the first series of the real was designed using a horizontal format and the reverse a vertical orientation, the new series are designed horizontally on both sides.

When the design update occurred, the R$1 note from the original series was eliminated. In the current series, we can find it as a coin only. In 2020, the R$200 note was added. With the elimination of the R$1 note from the 1994 series, the image of the hummingbird (*beija-flor*) that was featured on its reverse was lost. However, the effigy of the Republic, which was and still is included on all the banknotes of the series, was also featured (Figure 35).

The creation of the R$200 note is relevant to our semiotic perspective because it serves as evidence to validate the creative matrix we can postulate when looking at the design of a given currency system. When looking at that note, we can see

Figure 35 Banknote of R$1 from the 1994 series, including a hummingbird on the reverse.
Source: Central Bank of Brazil.

how it clearly aligns with the homogeneity of the productive matrix that we have identified as underlying the designs used to decorate the real's banknotes.

In this sense, considering the designs used in the existing banknotes, we could expect that a new, higher-value banknote would retain the elements that are characteristic and defining of the semiotic system. These are the effigy of the Republic on the front; a new colour – distinct from the others already used, but harmonious with them; a depiction of a native animal on the back; and the inclusion of the ornamental strip on the front. Except for the (unexpected) size reduction, the R$200 note confirms all the predictions, and hence functions as evidence of how this note was designed using the same productive matrix underpinning the series.

In previous chapters, we referred to the distinction between the poles of the natural-animal and the cultural-human, and we mentioned it again in this chapter. For semioticians, this is a purely analytical distinction, not an ontological one. Some, such as Claudio Paolucci (2021a: 5), argue that 'the distinction between nature and culture is misleading, and it must be abandoned when it comes to defining what semiotics is and what it does'. While Greimas (1983, 1986) argued that nature and culture are only poles of a semantic continuum and, therefore, effects of sense, Marrone (2012: 20, my translation) claims that semioticians should conceive of nature as a sense effect, that is, 'as what appears as such due to a series of social and cultural processes that have generated such habits, customs and codes'.

This is precisely what occurs in the designs we encounter on banknotes and coins that are grounded in a repertoire based on nature. In our analysis, we deliberately maintain the opposition between nature and culture because it serves as an interpretative lens to identify two main paths when choosing currency iconography. On the one hand, we can assume that the enunciator of the texts intends to construct the idea of the nation drawing on natural resources such as territory, flora and fauna. Here the geographical space that is read through the lens of the nation and the national community is crucial, because what we encounter in banknotes and coins relates to it and the dynamics that occur within that specific territory. When this strategy is employed for currency design, we will encounter animals, landscapes, protected areas and parks, and plants, among other resources, that belong to the domain of nature.

On the other hand, it is common to encounter in currency design the recourse to the cultural-human pole. As we saw, this pole tends to be the most frequently used strategy for currency design, probably as a means to model cultural memory around specific human characters and achievements such as buildings, events and innovations. Within semiotics, speaking of 'culture' in this sense is inaccurate, but above all this refers to human action and agency, which has the capacity to manipulate and transform the geographical space and the natural resources.

When the cultural-human pole is used for currency design, in banknotes and coins we will find historical characters such as military men and women; former presidents, prime ministers and monarchs; creators of cultural products; popular heroes and so on, as well as specific historical events regarded as relevant in the construction of the nation, such as those related to independence, the creation of the flag, armed conflicts and military campaigns and so on. Moreover, we can also encounter relevant works and achievements, which can range from literary texts to works of civil engineering.

If we look at the design elements that we encounter on the Brazilian banknotes and coins, we could argue that banknotes are the material support for a double mythification. The first mythification is that of the Brazilian territory, together with its flora and fauna. Something similar was in play in the old designs of the Canadian dollar, where the Canadian territory was depicted as pristine and idyllic, untouched by humans. In the Brazilian real, the mythification of the Brazilian territory occurs in terms not only of fauna, through the inclusion of native animals considered in danger of extinction, but also of flora, because these animals do not appear out of context but inhabit landscapes that were included in the designs representing the environments they usually inhabit. Due to their diversity, these landscapes serve to depict the Brazilian territory as one characterized by diversity.

The seven animals included in the repertoire used in the designs of the reverse belong to the domains of water, land and air, which cover nature in its three standard reigns. However, some of these animals are not exclusive to the Brazilian territory. The jaguar, for example, is also found in other South American countries. In fact, as we will see in Chapter 10, this animal was used in a recent series of the Argentine peso as a design element as well. Besides, all these animals are somehow exotic,[2] perhaps in a semiotic attempt to construct an image of Brazil as a natural, tropical and hence exotic nation to be explored and enjoyed.[3]

In addition, the second type of mythification evidenced on the Brazilian banknotes is that of the republic, both as a concept and as a formal organization of the Brazilian state. The figure that dominates the iconography of the Brazilian real is the effigy of the Republic (with capital letter because here we consider it to function as the proper name of the anthropomorphic figure that we see portraited). The centrality given to this figure is already evident in its repetition on each of the seven banknotes of the series, together with its positioning on the front side of each note. Something similar occurred with the portrait of the reigning monarch on the banknotes of the pound sterling.

As was the case with Britannia and Helvetia, the depiction of the Republic we encounter in the banknotes of the Brazilian real is anthropomorphic, taking the form of a woman's head with a crown of laurels and a Phrygian cap. This depiction seems to be based on a bust (a sculpture), and not on an image of a real person. This is something we had not encountered so far in our journey through the genre of currency design: whenever we encountered mimetic or iconic depictions on banknotes and coins, they were usually a *second* copy, that is, a copy of a painting or photograph that was itself a mimetic copy of an individual. In the Brazilian real, we encounter what seems to be a mimetic copy of a bust, which is not necessarily mimetic, albeit it is clearly figurative since we can identify it as being a bust.

On a second layer of sense, this depiction conveys a flair of antique classicism, as did the depictions of Britannia and Helvetia as women wearing togas and carrying elements that connote a distant and classic past, as in representations of Greek and Roman goddesses. The mediation of such a social imaginary adds an extra layer of sense to the discursive intention of mythifying the idea of the republic on currency as one that defines Brazilian national identity. As argued above, this mythification of the republic is double – both as a political concept and as an organizational form of the Brazilian state.

The discourse of republicanism is fundamental in Brazil because it is linked to the country's independence in the nineteenth-century post-Empire period. The effigy of the Republic we encounter on Brazilian banknotes emerges from this social discourse and, as such, stands for it. The depiction of the Republic in the form of a woman began to be used in Brazil at the end of the nineteenth century, in the context of debates regarding what configuration the post-imperial state should take (Murilo de Carvalho, 1990). Since November 1889, when Brazil adopted the formal republican organization, the figure we encounter in the seven banknotes and the R$1 coin began to be used in different circles and contexts as a symbol expressing that political form.

The decision to include the effigy of the Republic in the designs of the Brazilian real is interesting for us because it serves to see the circulation of social discourses in action. This was a dimension of semiosis highlighted by Verón (1988), who insisted that a gap exists between the conditions of production of a text and those of its consumption ('recognition', in Verón's terms).

In this sense, it should be noted that the effigy of the Republic is not a Brazilian creation. Historically, this anthropomorphic figure is based on discourses originating in the French revolutionary period, which travelled to America and, in doing so, also to Brazil. Therefore, the effigy that we encounter in Brazilian currency draws on and updates a series of pre-existing discourses, meanings and social imaginaries, which are used to construct a specific image of Brazilian national identity in a context different from that of its origin (Murilo de Carvalho, 1990: 75–96).

The depiction of the Republic that we encounter in the current series of the Brazilian real was taken from one of the banknotes of a previous series: that of 200 cruzados novos (Figure 36). Issued in 1989, this banknote was meant to commemorate the centenary of the declaration of the Brazilian republic. Then this note became 200 cruzeiros, first with a stamp assigning it a new value and then with a new printing, issued in 1990.

The depiction that we encounter on this banknote is exactly the same as the one on the current banknotes of the real. The difference is that, whereas in the 1989 series the effigy was *just another figure in* the visual system, now it is *its central figure*. As such, it evidences a higher degree of axiologization, which is expressed in the decision to repeat the figure in every banknote, as was the case with the reigning monarch in the pound sterling.

However, as a cultural unit, the effigy of the Republic had already appeared before in Brazilian currency. For example, it was used on the 1 cruzeiro banknote, from 1970, albeit with a different design (Figure 37). That depiction evidences a different figurativization strategy used to bring the concept of the republic to life. As argued in previous chapters, figurativization strategies consist in the articulation of the plane of expression so that an abstract unit, located

Figure 36 Front of the 200 cruzados novos banknote, including the effigy of the Republic.

Source: Central Bank of Brazil.

Figure 37 Banknote of 1 cruzeiro, from 1970, including a depiction of the Republic.
Source: Central Bank of Brazil.

on the plane of content, is expressed in a way so readers can interpret it as an expression of that specific content, thanks to a resemblance with elements of the natural world, such as a woman. In this banknote, the effigy of the republic is depicted using a profile portrait and surrounded by a circle, a design strategy that resembles that of coins and medals. In previous chapters, we saw how it is usual to encounter profile portraits on coins. In fact, when looking at Figure 37, we could think that the main design element of the banknote is a coin depicting the effigy of the Republic.

When looking at the current Brazilian banknotes and at the 1970s one, we can recognize both depictions as standing for the same content. Even if the depictions are different, our recognition occurs thanks to some signs, particularly two: on the one hand, the Phrygian cap the figure is wearing (on this regard, let us recall here what we argued about the crown in the pound sterling notes); on the other hand, the fact that the figure is a woman. Regarding this second trait, it is interesting to think what visual traits help us to identify the figure we see as a woman, and even question if such traits exist, or if we read the image as referring to a woman thanks to the cultural competence we have.

In this sense, the crown of plants – probably laurels – that the effigy of the Republic wears in the depiction used in the Brazilian real is not a necessary element to recognize it. As a matter of fact, it is absent from the depiction in the 1970s 1 cruzeiro banknote. Therefore, we could assume that, in the figure used in the current banknotes, this extra sign was included as a design element to express ancient classicism, as it has been widely used in depictions of this type grounded in discourses and imagery from Renaissance and Neoclassicism. With it, currency iconography gains connotations of tradition and roots in a distant past.

That which probably strikes the most about the design of the current series of the Brazilian real is the choice of including as the central figure an effigy representing an abstract concept. As we saw in the previous chapters – and as we shall see in the upcoming ones – currency design tends to be anchored in real individuals such as rulers, artists, scientists and so on. In Brazilian currency, this was the case in the past, as can be seen in Figure 38, which depicts two banknotes with portraits of Machado de Assis and Mário de Andrade, two well-known and very much celebrated Brazilian writers.

The banknotes of the current Brazilian real depict an allegorical figure, and hence some semiotic mechanisms already discussed when studying Britannia (Chapter 6) and Helvetia (Chapter 7) are also at play here. However, the strategy of including allegories in currency design is not original to the Brazilian real but was used in the past. We can specifically identify it in the cent banknotes of the cruzeiro novo, used in the 1970s.

In the four banknotes depicted in Figure 39, we encounter anthropomorphic representations of four abstract concepts: national unity (in the 10 cent note), the golden law (in the 50 cent note), national culture (in the 100 cent note) and the opening of the ports (in the 500 cent note). Moreover, when looking at those older notes, we can also identify some design elements – particularly related to overall style of the note – that remind us of those used in US dollars and previous designs of the Canadian dollar.

Figure 38 Banknote of 1,000 cruzados, with a portrait of Machado de Assis, and banknote of 500,000 cruzeiros, with a portrait of Mário de Andrade.

Source: Central Bank of Brazil.

Figure 39 Front designs of the 4 cent banknotes of the cruzeiro novo.
Source: Central Bank of Brazil.

Although the Republic is not part of the selection of abstract concepts featured through allegories in the series of banknotes depicted in Figure 39, we can see in action the allegory-based discursive strategy that is at the base of the current banknotes' design. This strategy consists of using anthropomorphic figures to stand for abstract concepts. As such, it is a strategy defined thanks to an opposition with the option of using specific characters from local history and activity.

As mentioned above, the option for using the effigy of the Republic in currency design has its roots in a discursivity that originated in Europe, specifically that linked to the rhetoric of the French Revolution. Despite its origins in a different continent than the American, it is a social discourse with a strong circulation in the transatlantic Lusophone semiotic space. In fact, the symbol of the Republic was also used at the beginning of the twentieth century in Portugal, when the monarchy fell in 1910. Hence, if the king of Portugal was a man, the Republic is now a woman, in an inversion of gender that might be meaningful in the attempts to renew discourses about the nation and who rules it.

The iconography used on the front of the current banknotes evidences a discursive strategy that figurativizes an abstract concept through an effigy. As we have seen, this image is depicted with some traits that serve to connote classicism and, with it, tradition and the antique past. Therefore, it seems plausible to speak of a recourse to mythification, which consolidates republicanism as a core component of Brazilian national discursivity thanks to the mediation of discourses of classicism. But also of modernity: although the political form of the republic was created in ancient times, its modern form is a European product.

The combination of classical traits such as the laurel wreath with modern ones such as the Phrygian cap taps onto these two social discourses and imaginaries.

In the designs on the reverse of the banknotes, we encounter a different universe, clearly linked to Brazil's territory and the biodiversity that characterizes it due to its enormous extension. These are fundamental themes in the discourse on national identity in Brazil and are taken up, for example, in Brazil's modernist literature. A good example is the novel *Macunaíma, o herói sem nenhum caráter* (*Macunaíma, the Hero without Character*), written by Mário de Andrade and published in 1928, in which the main character, usually interpreted by critics as a symbol of the Brazilian people, is often surrounded by exotic animals, most of them native to the Brazilian rainforest.

The diversity associated with Brazil's vast territory is a central theme in the discourse on Brazilian national identity, whether in terms of macro-regions – northeast, north, south and so on – or of specific spaces, such as the Amazon rainforest, the *sertões*, the *serras* (or *planaltos*) and so on. It also has been functioning, since the European discovery of the territory that is now Brazilian, as a source of mythifying idealization, usually in the form of Eden (Buarque de Holanda, 2000).

According to Sérgio Buarque de Holanda (2000: ix), the reliance on nature as the main norm for aesthetic, ethical, behavioural and social organizational patterns was very characteristic of Romanticism. However, this social discourse can be traced back to the Renaissance. As the author suggests, the first settlers of South America were 'attracted by the hope of finding in their conquests a paradise made of worldly wealth and heavenly beatitude, which would be offered to them without demanding further work, as a free gift' (Buarque de Holanda, 2000: xviii, my translation). Hence, we can see echoes of this discursivity in the visual strategy based on mythifying nature.

Regarding coins, all the designs of the current series are new. They replaced the designs used in the first series of the real, which was highly unified in terms of the productive matrix sustaining them. On one side, coins featured a depiction of the Republic; on the other, they had the economic value only. Moreover, while our analysis of the banknotes shows a universe devoid of human beings, action and work, humans are featured on the coins.

As Table 11 shows, the list of historical characters depicted on the coins is made up of five men, all of them linked to the Brazilian state, as was the case in the banknotes of the US and Canadian dollars and coins. Some of them were already depicted in Brazilian currency since 1942, when the cruzeiro was introduced as the national currency. The inclusion of these men is innovative regarding the first coins of the real, all of which included the effigy of the Republic as their main iconographic element, as banknotes did and still do.

Hence, the current coins include the only real individuals depicted in Brazilian national currency. These are Pedro Álvares Cabral, the Portuguese navigator who discovered Brazil in 1500; Joaquim José da Silva Xavier, known as 'Tiradentes', a major figure of Brazilian independence from Portuguese rule who was publicly assassinated and became a national martyr; Dom Pedro I, who proclaimed independence in 1822; Manuel Deodoro da Fonseca, responsible of proclaiming the republic and Brazil's first constitutional president, between 1889 and 1891; and José Maria da Silva Paranhos Junior, a Brazilian diplomat and historian considered a symbol of Brazil's republican diplomacy. Whereas other currency systems might have used historical characters as these as the main figures to decorate each of the banknotes, in the current Brazilian real they are depicted in coins.

Finally, the effigy of the Republic is also included on the R$1 coin, establishing a link between the coin system and the banknotes. Hence, we can see how the semiotic system that we encounter in the Brazilian real is based on a clearly identifiable productive matrix. This matrix is characterized by certain features that give unity and continuity to the system as a set of interrelated units. The front of the banknotes is dominated by the effigy of the Republic, without any visual variation from one note to the other. On the reverse, a native animal is depicted in its habitat. In this sense, the recent introduction of the R$200 banknote confirms the production matrix underpinning design. It is therefore to be expected that, if higher denominations of the real are added to the system, this creative pattern will be maintained.

In this way, the current Brazilian banknotes function as the material support for a double mythification. On the one hand, they mythify the Republic, an abstract political concept that is considered central to the nation's identity; on the other, they mythify Brazilian territory through the fauna and flora that can be encountered on it. As we have seen in this chapter, these design choices are rooted in pre-existing social discourses, which circulate in the Brazilian semiosphere and, here, are used to project a specific image of Brazilian national identity.

As for the coins, they function as the material support for another type of discursive construction, in this case more clearly linked with statehood. In the coins, we encounter not only the few human characters depicted in the currency system but also the spherical symbol included in the country's flag, one of the key symbols of the national state. The selection of historical figures is limited exclusively to individuals related to the formation of the Brazilian state, and not to other fields of society such as the arts and sciences.

To conclude, it would be interesting to highlight some issues relating to the discursive matrix that we identified in this chapter. We could argue that this matrix highlights aspects of Brazilian identity that are somehow in tension with other existing discourses regarding what it means to be Brazilian. A first discourse on Brazilianness, currently hegemonic due to its stereotypical functionality, is related to living the good life and the everyday practices it entails such as dancing, enjoying music, the carnival, spending time on the beach and practising sports. Nothing of this stereotype, generally linked to what has been identified as the lifeform of *malangragem* (Candido, 1970; Demuru, 2015), appears in the construction of Brazilian identity that we encounter in the national currency.

In this sense, while Demuru proposes that *malangradem* is characterized by the distinctive traits of sinuosity, informality, improvisation, cunning, creativity and flexibility, the semantic universe that we encounter in the banknotes and coins of the real is completely different, and much more official, formal, rigid, classical and devoid of specific lifestyles that could be identified as 'typically' Brazilian. This seems in order since the discourse that we encounter in currency design is an *official* type of discourse, while stereotypes and social imaginaries linked to specific ways of life tend to circulate in informal spaces.

Moreover, the iconography used to design the Brazilian real also shows a tension between the discourse of royalty and that of the republic. Thus, there seems to be a coexistence of two visions of Brazil's political organization. On the one hand, there is the monarchy, associated with the pre-republican past but still used in the name of the national currency. On the other, there is the republic, which is dominant in the iconography of the currency system. Was the decision to call the new coin 'real' (royal) consciously taken, or was it based on an attempt to propose a cultural 'forgetting' of the weak cruzados and cruzeiros through a return to square one, that is, through recovering the currency used from the colonial period, until 1942? It is at least striking that the central figure used in the design of the real is the effigy of the Republic.

In a book published in the context of the commemoration of the 100 years of the Brazilian republic – that is, some years before the introduction of the real as Brazil's official currency – José Murilo de Carvalho offers an interesting reading of republicanism and its symbols. As de Carvalho (1990: 141, my translation) writes,

> The efforts of the republican trends that tried to expand the legitimacy of the new regime beyond the limited borders in which it was confined by the victorious current failed. They were unable to create a popular republican imaginary. In the aspects in which they had some success, this was due to compromises with

> the imperial tradition or with religious values. The effort made was not enough to break the barrier created by the absence of popular participation in the implementation of the new regime. Without roots in the collective experience, the republican symbology fell into the void, as was particularly the case of the feminine allegory.

Murilo de Carvalho identifies a lack of republican identity due to a tension between the divergent visions of the republic – liberal, Jacobin, positivist – that coexisted during the twentieth century in Brazil. Hence, the choice to use the effigy of the Republic as the main figure of the real may be read as an attempt of official discourse to reinforce this social imaginary, giving it a visibility on objects of material culture that circulate in everyday contexts. In this sense, given the informality and flexibility connoted by the curve, which is a design element probably highly recognized by the Brazilian public as a plastic element 'of their own', we encounter the formality and rigidity connoted by the classic bust of the Republic.

Finally, another focus of discursive tension can be identified between the poles of nature and culture. This is a tension already identified by Buarque de Holanda (1995: 31, my translation) in *Raízes do Brasil*, when he writes that 'the dominant fact and richest in consequences' in the origins of Brazilian society was 'the attempt to implant European culture in a vast territory, endowed with natural conditions, if not adverse, then largely foreign to its millenary tradition'. The tension between nature and culture has been strongly linked to the social imaginary of Brazil since its origins, and what we see in the banknotes of the real is not too distant from it: while European culture is condensed in the effigy of the Republic (a sign standing for it), the Brazilian territory is expressed through natural elements such as fauna and, to a lesser degree, flora.

* * *

In this chapter, we began our journey through South America, studying the design of the current series of the Brazilian real, introduced in 1994 and redesigned in 2010. In the analysis, we identified how the poles of nature and culture can be used in a complementary manner to express ideas about the nation and project a specific image of it. As we will see in the two chapters that follow, this is a strategy commonly used in South American currencies, even if the centrality given to each domain differs from system to system. Moreover, we saw how different social discourses relating to apparently diverse themes (monarchy and republicanism) can coexist, and how they can be used to reinforce specific images of the nation through the political system it adopts.

9

Uruguayan Peso

In this chapter, we continue our analytical journey through South America and study the Uruguayan peso, the official currency in Uruguay. As we shall see, the banknotes of this national currency include as its main design elements portraits of historical characters that were creators of high – or highbrow – culture, such as music, painting, literature and ideas. Therefore, they convey a specific image of the nation mediated by cultural practice, and specifically by a clear idea of culture.

However, the most recent designs used for the coins of the currency system feature four animals considered autochthonous to the country. In this sense, studying this national currency will allow us to see the semantic opposition between culture and nature in action. Moreover, it will also enable us to approach the dichotomy between the urban and the rural that characterizes national discourses and the social imaginary in Uruguay since its origins as a nation.

9.1 Context

The Uruguayan peso has been the official currency in Uruguay since 1993, when it was introduced to replace the *nuevos pesos* (new pesos), the official national currency since 1975, due to macroeconomic reasons. The Uruguayan peso is regulated by the Central Bank of Uruguay (Banco Central del Uruguay), an institution created in 1967.

The Uruguayan peso circulates only in the Uruguayan territory, although the dollar is also accepted in the country for specific types of economic transactions and specific types of goods, normally of a high price and/or imported. In recent years, the two banknotes of lower economic value – that is, $20 and $50 – were redesigned using polymer. In the change from the cotton-based fabric to polymer, the previous designs were maintained, but new security features were included, such as a translucid oval window, similar to that we encounter on the Canadian dollar and the pound sterling, and the size of the note was slightly reduced.

9.2 Banknotes and coins of the Uruguayan peso

In this chapter, our corpus is composed of seven banknotes (Figure 40) and four coins (Figure 42). Those seven banknotes currently circulate in Uruguay. However, we will also consider two notes (Figure 41) that stopped production in 2008 since they lost purchasing power. These two notes show a clear systemic relationship with the banknotes currently in circulation, both in visual and discursive terms. Therefore, analysing them will help us to strengthen the argument regarding the discursive matrix sustaining the visual texts that we encounter in this national currency.

A special $50 banknote was created in 2017 as a commemorative edition, to celebrate the 50th anniversary of the Central Bank of Uruguay. Although this note still circulates in the country, we deliberately exclude it from the corpus because it is clearly not part of the usual currency system.

From all the banknotes, the one with the highest denomination – $2,000 – was created later in time, in 2003. As was the case with the Brazilian R$200 note, which also was added later to the system, we can see how this banknote is fully consistent with the design and discursive matrix used for the Uruguayan peso since the 1990s.

In addition to the banknotes, Uruguay's monetary system has currently four coins of standard circulation (Figure 42), plus a special edition of a $50 coin, which also will be left out of the analysis since it is clearly divergent from the standard series. In the past, there were cent coins, but they are not produced anymore. Hence, this is the first currency system that does not have denominations below the full unit.

In terms of the design elements used for banknotes and coins, we see how each material support is assigned with a specific encyclopaedic repertoire: while in banknotes we encounter humans and a discursive universe related to culture and human action (Table 12), in coins we encounter animals and a symbol of the state (Table 13).

9.3 Analysis

In the present case, instead of beginning by studying the banknotes, as we did in the previous chapters, let us begin with the coins. In terms of their format, the four coins have different sizes following a logic that we already are familiar with: as the

Value **Front** **Reverse**

$20

$50

$100

$200

$500

$1,000

$2,000

Figure 40 The seven banknotes of the current series of the Uruguayan peso.
Source: Central Bank of Uruguay.

Value | **Front** | **Reverse**

$5

$10

Figure 41 The two withdrawn banknotes of the current series of the Uruguayan peso.
Source: Central Bank of Uruguay.

Value | **Front** | **Reverse**

$1

$2

$5

$10

Figure 42 The four coins of the current series of the Uruguayan peso.
Source: Central Bank of Uruguay.

Table 12 List of Distinctive Design Elements Identified in the Nine Banknotes of the Uruguayan Peso.

Value	Front	Reverse
$5	A portrait of Joaquín Torres García	A depiction of Torres García's painting 'Pintura constructiva 1943'
	A painter's palette with brushes in the middle, three geometrical figures with volume (sphere, cube, pyramid) and two pencils, surrounded by a wreath of laurels	
$10	A portrait of Eduardo Acevedo Vásquez	A depiction of the building of the Faculty for Agronomy
	An open book, surrounded by a wreath of laurels	
$20	A portrait of Juan Zorrilla de San Martín	An allegory of *Leyenda Patria*, with a very short excerpt of the manuscript of *Tabaré*, signed by Zorrilla de San Martín
	A writing feather, an inkwell and a papyrus (blank on the front side and written on the reverse), surrounded by a wreath of laurels	
$50	A portrait of José Pedro Varela	A depiction of a sculptural monument honouring José Pedro Varela, located on a square in Montevideo
	An open book (blank on the front side, written on the reverse) with a faced-sun rising behind it, surrounded by a wreath of laurels	
$100	A portrait of Eduardo Fabini	A musical allegory depicting a naked young man, seated in profile, playing a pan flute in a bucolic landscape
	A lyre and a trumpet, with a score with musical notes behind it, surrounded by a wreath of laurels	
$200	A portrait of Pedro Figari	A depiction of Figari's painting 'Baile antiguo'
	Painter's palette with brushes in the middle and blank parchment behind it, surrounded by a wreath of laurels	
$500	A portrait of Alfredo Vásquez Acevedo	A depiction of Universidad de la República's main building
	An open book (blank on the front side, written on the reverse) with a faced-sun rising behind it, surrounded by a wreath of laurels	

Value	Front	Reverse
$1,000	A portrait of Juana de Ibarbourou	Eight books with titles matching those published by de Ibarbourou – *Chico Carlo, Raíz salvaje, El cántaro fresco, Perdida, Las lenguas de diamante, Loores de Nuestra Señora, Estampas de la Biblia* y *La rosa de los vientos* – with a depiction of La Palma de Juana (Juana's Palm tree), a commemorative palm tree located in Montevideo. A short, handwritten text, dated 8 September 1924, signed by the poet and titled *El Cazador* (The Hunter). The text reads: 'Porque yo no sé alzarme de este suelo / donde tengo mis hijos y mi casa, / hermano Calibán, detengo el vuelo / del pájaro que pasa.' (Because I do not know how to rise from this ground / where I have my children and my home, / brother Caliban, I stop the flight / of the passing bird.)
	An amphora with a rose at the base, surrounded by a wreath of laurels	
$2,000	A portrait of Dámaso Antonio Larrañaga	A depiction of the National Library of Uruguay and the date of its foundation: 26 May 1816
	A bird and a microscope, surrounded by a wreath of laurels	

Source: Author's own elaboration.

Table 13 List of Distinctive Design Elements Identified in the Four Coins of the Uruguayan Peso.

Value	Front	Reverse
$1	A depiction of an armadillo (*mulita*)	Uruguay's coat of arms surrounded by an inscription including the country's official name
$2	A depiction of a capibara (*carpincho*)	
$5	A depiction of a rhea (*ñandú*)	
$10	A depiction of a jaguar (*puma*)	

Source: Author's own elaboration.

economic value grows, so does the size of the coin. This does not happen with the banknotes of the current Uruguayan peso, even if the new emissions of $20 and $50 using polymer are smaller than the rest of notes of the system.

Three of the four coins are gold-coloured, while one combines gold and silver, similar to the R$1 coin studied in Chapter 8, and the €1 and €2 coins we will study in Chapter 11. In this sense, the $1, $2 and $5 coins are easily recognizable as part of the same system, whereas the $10 coin is visually different. In terms of format, this difference is visible in two of its traits. On the one hand, the colour combination used for it deviates from the one used on the remaining coins. On the other hand, the position of the depicted animal and the economic value – a topological issue – is also different. This difference might be explained considering that the design of the puma used in the current $10 coin is based on the design of an old Uruguayan coin, from 1936. However, despite these differences of format and layout, the design elements we encounter in the four coins belong to the same encyclopaedic repertoire: on one side, there is the country's coat of arm (a classic symbol of the national state), whereas on the other, there is a single animal.

The format and layout of the banknotes presented in Figures 40 and 41 presents us with nine pieces of paper with the same size (even if the new $20 and $50 notes, created using polymer, are smaller). These nine banknotes are easily recognizable as part of the same visual system thanks to a number of design elements, which are above all topological and relate to the positioning of design elements on the banknote's surface.

Besides the economic value expressed both in number and words, the marks granting notes with legal validity, the silhouette of the country's territory, the symbols of the nation and the security and validity features – such as the serial number, a watermark and so on – the banknotes feature portraits of historical characters active in the domain of culture, an encyclopaedic repertoire that we mentioned in previous chapters, but which we only encountered partially on the designs of the pound sterling. In the Uruguayan peso, this repertoire is the one chosen for banknote design.

Probably unknown to the reader, the characters featuring on the Uruguayan banknotes (eight men and a woman) were active in the domain of culture, and specifically in the fields of pictorial art (Joaquín Torres García and Pedro Figari), literature (Juan Zorrilla de San Martín and Juana de Ibarbourou), music (Eduardo Fabini) and the intellectual field with a close relation with education (Eduardo Acevedo Vásquez, José Pedro Varela, Alfredo Vásquez Acevedo and Dámaso Antonio Larrañaga).

As can be seen, the domains of action of the individuals depicted on the Uruguayan peso's banknotes relate to a traditional and classical conception of culture and cultural activity, that is, as a specific type of production. If these characters are featured on the banknotes of the national currency, it is because of their professions and the products of their action. The selection of characters does not include any creators of works of what we could refer to as 'popular culture', that is, a type of artistic creation originating in popular practice and traditions, such as *candombe*, carnival or other types of folklore, both urban and rural. Rather, on the banknotes we encounter creators of what we could call 'high culture', that is, a type of culture that is not accessible to anyone but which requires specific competences to be consumed. This is a type of cultural production characterized by its being strongly urban, enlightened and – of particular interest for our analysis – usually influenced by foreign – above all, European – trends, movements and works.

In our previous analyses, we did encounter a few portraits of historical characters active in the domain of culture and the arts, such as Jane Austen and J. M. W. Turner, on the reverse designs of the pound sterling. Moreover, we mentioned that in previous series of the Swiss franc, a discursive matrix similar to the one we encounter on the current Uruguayan peso's banknotes was used, featuring artists and scientists. However, it was withdrawn, and these characters removed. In the case of the pound sterling, we also saw how the state was represented on banknotes through a number of institutional symbols, such as the reigning monarch, a depiction of the building of the Bank of England, the inclusion of the coats of arms of the four UK nations and the allegory of Britannia.

In the current Uruguayan peso banknotes, only characters representing the encyclopaedic repertoire of creators of culture are featured, with an absolute absence of figures belonging to the institutional sphere, such as former presidents and statesmen. In this regard, the most intriguing absence is that of José Gervasio Artigas, a historical character central to the local nineteenth century's politics and considered the national hero – the *prócer*, in Spanish – thanks to how his actions led to Uruguay's independence.

Whereas Artigas was featured through portraits in the design of banknotes of the old nuevos pesos (that is, the currency preceding the current one) and in the design of the previous coins (Figure 43), his portrait was removed from the current designs. In those pieces, he was depicted using profile portraits, as was

Figure 43 Portraits of José G. Artigas on an old banknote and an old coin.
Source: Central Bank of Uruguay.

common on coins (US dollar, Canadian dollar, pound sterling, Swiss franc) but not on banknotes. Interestingly, the recent addition to the portraits depicted on the Uruguayan peso banknotes, notably the $2,000 note, is via a profile portrait – a type of depiction not encountered yet on the banknotes studied in the book.

According to Roberto Ares Pons (2020: 15, my translation), 'in the origins of peoples, there is generally a personality around whom the factors that determine the emergence of a collectivity are nucleated'. Moreover, he writes that, 'as time goes by, this individual is transfigured, the fabric of the legend covers him, and he becomes the archetype, the paragon, the sublimated imago that illuminates the collective unconscious'. In other words, there is a process of mythification around such historical characters, in which they are invested with connotations and meanings located on a level that transcends the merely referential and denotative function of semiosis.

Therefore, 'Artigas' ceases being the surname of an individual and is used to designate a mythologized social discourse, manipulable according to the intentionality of the social actor who resorts to it to generate senses within the public sphere.[1] In the case of Uruguay, Artigas is the historical figure around which discourses associated with the Uruguayan nation have been articulated.[2]

As is the case with other South and Latin American countries, the mythification of an individual (in this case, José G. Artigas) as the national hero can be encountered in various material expressions of official discourse. For example, every office of the state and every classroom in Uruguay invariably has a painted portrait of him. Moreover, his birthdate – 19 June – is one of Uruguay's national yearly holidays. In this sense, for a Uruguayan citizen, encountering his portrait on banknotes and coins was not a surprise since they are products the state creates as the main institutional enunciator. If there is a personality cult in the country around a specific individual, and this cult is evidenced in various materials and spaces, encountering his portrait on currency seems natural. What evokes surprise is not encountering any trait of this historical character on the current notes and coins, especially knowing that he was once featured on both.

The choice for historical characters linked to the field of cultural action is less problematic regarding the connotations these people might activate, and hence regarding the political debate on who should be featured on banknotes and coins. In Chapter 10, we will study the Argentine peso and see how including historical characters from the political domain can be a cause of debate, disagreement and discursive struggle. Although the selection of producers of traditional cultural works such as books, poems, music, paintings, education and so on that we encounter on the current banknotes of the Uruguayan peso could in principle also be a source of disagreement – for example, in terms of the type of cultural action depicted, gender parity, who is left aside or what type of national cultural canon is being constructed – this cultural repertoire seems less problematic than the political one, even if the characters featured on banknotes can be linked, either formally or loosely, to one of the two Uruguayan traditional political parties, in a balanced relationship.[3]

The current banknotes of Uruguay's currency delineate an idea of Uruguayan national culture anchored in the field of an erudite and complex cultural production, that is, as a set of artistic, literary, musical and intellectual works. The *national* character of this (high/highbrow) culture is based on the nationality of the individuals depicted on banknotes. This is the case because, besides being great creators of culture such as literary works, paintings, musical pieces, libraries, the national – and public – educational system and so on, these individuals were *indisputably* Uruguayans. This means that they can hardly be claimed by other national states as belonging to their imagined community (even if Vásquez Acevedo was born in Buenos Aires, albeit naturalized as Uruguayan).

The following substitution test serves to evidence the discursive strategy used for the selection of the historical characters included on the Uruguayan banknotes. Would it have been acceptable for writer Juan Zorrilla de San Martín to be replaced by Isidore Ducasse, also known as Count de Lautréamont, a world-known writer who was born in Uruguay but to French parents and whose work was created in French? The inclusion of a figure such as Ducasse on the Uruguayan currency would certainly contribute to the expression of a content in terms of erudite culture. However, it would perhaps not be so evident in terms of expressing a content in terms of *national* culture. This is the case even if courses of Uruguayan literature usually include Lautréamont in the contents that are taught (usually using Spanish translations).

Of the nine characters that we encounter on the Uruguayan banknotes, eight are men. Poet Juana de Ibarbourou is the sole woman featured on currency. As we saw in the previous chapters, current discourses linked to specific social movements intend to achieve a greater representation of women on state products. Hence, we could argue that this gender imbalance would hardly have been accepted if the banknotes had been designed in the last couple of years, and not in the 1990s. In addition to the fact that hegemonic social norms in that decade still accepted gender unbalance without much questioning, Uruguay's scholarly and urban cultural production was for most of its history associated mainly with male figures. Only in recent decades, efforts began to be made for women to have more visibility in public discourse. Issues such as this show how currency design is dependent on time and space, and how banknotes and coins function as indexes of specific socio-historical circumstances.

In this sense, the design of banknotes and coins can be a cause for debate regarding the criteria sustaining it. Besides, since currency systems are composed of a few units, the repertoire of characters that can be included in currency design is limited. In some cases, a selection of images and symbols that a specific social actor considers biased can generate demands for a more equitable and inclusive integration of a plurality of events and personalities in the textualization of the shared history, as was the case with the campaign demanding Harriet Tubman to be included in the US$20 banknote. In this sense, the list of characters featured on the front sides of the current Uruguayan banknotes seems to be a safer choice.

However, even when selecting a less problematic encyclopaedic repertoire for currency design as is the case of writers, artists, musicians and educators, questions can arise challenging that choice. Some questions are: Why were only creators producing a type of erudite and urban culture selected? What does this selection connote about the type of cultural production the state celebrates and cherishes? Why were design elements expressing a type of popular and, specifically, rural culture not included in currency design as part of cultural production? What was the criterion to choose the specific characters that are featured on banknotes, and not others?

All these questions serve to highlight the challenges linked to the broad and polysemous concept of 'culture' (Williams, 1976) but also to evidence some of the dominant connotations that are associated to cultural practice. A more anthropological sense of culture would include, following UNESCO (1982), 'the set of distinctive spiritual, material, intellectual and emotional features of society or a social group, that encompasses, not only art and literature, but lifestyles, ways of living together, value systems, traditions, and beliefs'. The characters featured on Uruguayan banknotes serve to express a more restricted sense of culture, normally measured through the capacity of producing high-quality works that can transcend time and, eventually, become classics and, as such, part of the national canon.

This is what we encounter in the designs of the Uruguayan banknotes. The focus is set above all on art and literature, which UNESCO clearly sees as only a part of culture. The writers, painters, musicians and intellectuals depicted in these banknotes are creators of such type of culture, and this constructs a specific take about what culture and cultural activity are. It is a serious, erudite and formal type of culture, which the state can celebrate.

This seriousness and formality are reinforced in the facial expression of the characters featured on the notes, who do not express any emotion that we can easily recognize (Moreno Barreneche, 2025). Could we imagine portraits in which these individuals are depicted laughing, as is often the case with photographs in our time? The only hint of joy could be said to be on Juana de Ibarbourou's lips, whose visual articulation can be read as a smile. The rest of her face, however, does not match this interpretation, such as the arching of her eyebrows. What's more, some of the characters appear to be frowning.

The lack of emotionality – or, more precisely, the choice to include neutral, serious faces, without any kind of emotion to identify the individuals portrayed as human beings who feel – may function as a semiotic resource to reinforce the sense effect linked to formality, which, as we have seen, is a transversal one in the design of banknotes and coins. This transversality of formality arises from the very nature of the discursive genre, which is one created by the state in an enunciative praxis that implies a high degree of formality since it is one that creates texts that express *official* discourse. Moreover, formality is also reinforced by the type of attire the portrayed characters wear (as evidenced by the collar). The combination of elements such as formal attire and the neutral facial expression functions as an expression of formality.

Moreover, each banknote includes both on the front and the reverse a small image, surrounded by a wreath of laurel. That image stands as an expression of the domain of cultural activity in which the portrayed character was active. In the two banknotes depicting painters ($5 and $200), that small figure consists of a painter's palette, plus some other design elements that reinforce this creative domain. In the banknote that depicts a musician ($100), the small icon features a lyre and a trumpet together and a score with musical notes. The banknote depicting an intellectual that was also a natural scientist ($2,000) includes a bird and a microscope in that small image, while those depicting intellectuals linked to education ($10, $50 and $500) consist of a book, a conventional symbol that stands for learning and education. Finally, the notes depicting writers of poetic texts ($20 and $1,000) include different elements: a feather used to write, an inkwell and a papyrus on the $20 note, and an amphora with a rose at its base on the $1,000 note. In every case, the wreath of laurels surrounding the domain-related image elevates it thanks to the associations stabilized in the culture of wreath of laurels with classicism, tradition and greatness.

As pointed out in the previous chapters, it is common for the discursive genre of currency design to include on the front and reverse design elements that are related. On the reverse of each banknote of the Uruguayan peso, we encounter design elements that relate to the character depicted on its front. Specifically, each banknote features at least one work – in a broad sense, as the output of someone's activity, even if the output does not have an evident material nature – produced by that character, such as a literary text, a painting or an educational institution.

However, multiple strategies are used to figurativize the designs included on the reverses. We can identify four. The first one consists of using works produced by the historical characters included on the front of each banknote, such as the fragment of the epic poem *Tabaré*, a verse from one of de Ibarbourou's poems and one painting by Torres García and one by Figari on the $20, $1,000, $5 and $200 banknotes, respectively.

A second strategy consists of using design elements that function as signs of the intellectual work of the portrayed characters, such as the central building of the University of the Republic, the National Library and the Faculty of Agronomy, included on the $500, $2,000 and $10 banknotes, respectively. These buildings were included not because they are intrinsically valuable or were built by these men (as would be the case when portraying a celebrated architect) but because they stand for the achievements of these characters in the intellectual field. Specifically, these buildings relate to the development of education, science and academia in the country. In this sense, they differ from the type of buildings we encountered on the banknotes of the US dollar, the Canadian dollar and the pound sterling, which were buildings directly expressing the state identity since they stood for it as an institution. Here these buildings, which are public – that is, owned by the state, also serve to express the state but differently.

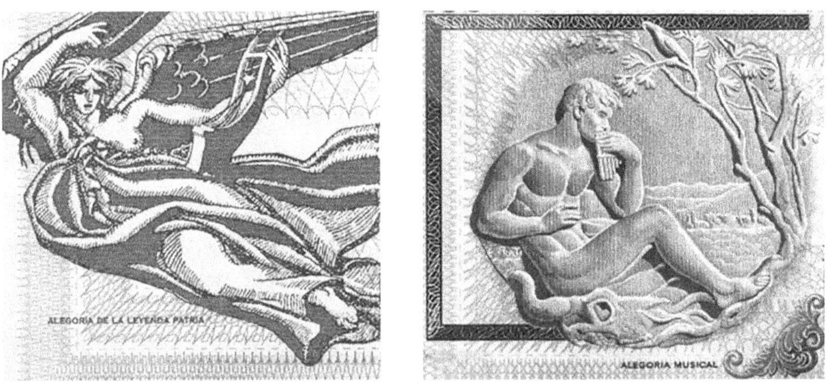

Figure 44 The two allegories depicted on the current Uruguayan banknotes.
Source: Central Bank of Uruguay.

A third strategy consists of using allegories (Figure 44), as was the case with Britannia, Helvetia and the effigy of the Republic that we studied in previous chapters. In the current Uruguayan banknotes, the reverse of the $20 note features a female figure, depicted with some traits that remind us of the images of female characters we encountered in previous chapters: she wears a toga, carries a musical instrument that looks like a lyra, is winged and is showing a breast. As the anchorage text located next to it indicates, it is an allegory of the *Leyenda Patria*, a concept we could translate as 'Patriotic Legend', a long epic poem written by Zorrilla de San Martín in the late nineteenth century.

The reverse of the $100 note depicts a musical allegory, consisting of a naked young man seated in profile, playing a pan flute and located in a bucolic landscape. In this case as well, the type of depiction connotes an ancient past, distant from the social realm inhabited by the portrayed characters. Therefore, we could argue that using allegories to express contents that might be harder to convey in figurative terms is done through the mediation of discourses of antiquity and classicism. These discourses are based on a figurative strategy, consisting of using allegories. These semiotic resources are used to express contents that are abstract in nature, using figures one can easily recognize in denotative terms (we identify what we are seeing), but whose connotations are not given, but depend on cultural competence. The allegories we encounter on these banknotes are isotopic with the wreath of laurels surrounding the small domain-related figure included in each note, because these also connote antiquity, classicism and tradition.

Finally, as a fourth strategy to express in figurative terms the contents related to the work of the character portrayed on the front side of each note, the notes of $50 and $1,000 include on the reverse depictions not of the works of the characters but of monuments celebrating the characters. While in the former we encounter a monument dedicated to José Pedro Varela located on a square in Montevideo, Uruguay's capital city, in the latter we encounter a palm tree honouring Juana de Ibarbourou, also located in Montevideo.

The different strategies used to articulate the visual dimension with the purpose of expressing specific contents respond to the nature of the type of cultural production the historical characters chosen to decorate banknotes did. Moreover, these strategies also depend on the material nature of currency. Hence, while a painting and a poem can be easily printed on banknotes mimetically, that is, copying the original works and depicting them *as they are* – based on a strategy of iconism, with a high degree of figurativity – works of an intangible nature such as musical pieces and intellectual achievements cannot be represented on paper in an iconic/mimetic manner. Therefore, they must be expressed using other types of textual strategies, such as *indexes* and *symbols*.

This is the case with the cultural contributions of Larrañaga, Varela, Vásquez Acevedo and Acevedo Vásquez, which were of intellectual nature, and that of Fabini, who produced musical compositions. The physical characteristics of the material support used for currency design prevent expressing in a mimetic manner the immaterial nature of the works of these creators of culture. Therefore, it is necessary to use a figurative strategy in which a sign or text is used either in an indexical way, where a sign stands for something by being its cause or consequence, such as smoke indexically expressing fire, or in a symbolic way, that is, based on a high degree of cultural codification and convention, such as a white pigeon expressing the concept of peace. These textual strategies are necessary to express contents of this type, since it is not possible to include depictions of the works themselves to express the nature of the work of the historical character.

As for the coins, all the designs from the previous series portrayed on their reverse the profile of José G. Artigas. Moreover, with the exception of one design (Figure 43), all the coins also featured the inscription of the country's full official name: 'República Oriental del Uruguay'. On the front, those coins included the economic value expressed both in numbers and words. The design of the four coins of our corpus, introduced gradually since 2011, replaced those design elements with depictions of animals, whereas on the reverse, they include the national coat of arms, accompanied by the inscription of the full name of the country.

The coat of arms is the only common element featured on banknotes and coins, and it is the only design element included in every single piece of currency. When we studied the US dollar, we saw that the only common element to banknotes and coins was the inscription 'In God We Trust'. The difference of sense between a design element grounded on religious discourse and one grounded on statehood is relevant, for it contributes to producing a different sense effect. In fact, the only presence of religion on Uruguayan banknotes and coins is sort of hidden: besides being an intellectual and natural scientist, Dámaso Antonio Larrañaga was a priest. Since Uruguay is a secular republic since 1917, it makes sense that currency does not feature explicit religious contents.

The four animals depicted on the coins are interesting, because they are part of the social imaginary of the Uruguayan local fauna, albeit not as the most common or evident animals. Whereas a cow and a horse are featured on the national coat of arms, other animals such as sheep and pigs are also commonly seen in the Uruguayan territory and, as such, are part of the Uruguayan landscape and, hence, function as indexical signs of it. However, the animals chosen to be featured on the coins are not these common ones but some that function as more exotic, perhaps because they are harder to encounter. Moreover, these are animals that cannot be found in other geographical areas besides the south of the American continent and, as such, function as differential traits to characterize Uruguayan identity. We can see how another type of strategy – not so much based on the animals that are easily found in the Uruguayan territory but those that are considered as special – is used. This was also the case in the banknotes of the Brazilian real, and will be the case in the Argentine peso, the focus of Chapter 10.

In any case, as with the animals included in an old series as well as coins of the Canadian dollar, in the pound sterling and on the notes of the Brazilian real, these four animals serve to express national identity through the mediation of a discourse of nature, with a focus on fauna (and not flora, as in other cases). Therefore, in the coin system, we encounter the rural component that is so characteristic of Uruguay as a nation in terms of its territory and the practices shaped by it. It is in the four coins that we encounter this discursive universe, in a currency system that has a strong cultural, intellectual and hence urban character.

To sum up, we can see how the discursive strategy behind the creation of banknotes and coins of the Uruguayan peso appears to be similar. Each of the two material supports customary of currency design is allocated a specific portion of the local encyclopaedia: banknotes for historical characters active in the cultural field, and coins for specimens of autochthonous fauna. Based on this selection and classification of productive matrixes according to different cultural repertoires, the specific characters and animals were chosen.

With regard to what the images featured on banknotes and coins of the Uruguayan peso might stand for, we identify two different strategies. In the case of banknotes, the iconographic elements depicted stand for a specific and individualized human being; in the case of coins, the animals we see stand for a type. This means that the portrait of Juana de Ibarbourou on the $1,000 banknote stands for the historical person called Juana de Ibarbourou. However, the capybara we encounter on the $2 coin stands for the capybara *as a class*, and not a specific or particular capybara that the state decides to celebrate on currency. The distinction between type and token introduced in a previous chapter also serves to make sense of this logic.

Like in the previous chapters, the strategy we identified in this chapter as sustaining Uruguayan currency design allows us to postulate possible designs for future pieces. Hence, the day a $20 coin is created, we can expect its iconography to include an autochthonous animal regarded as typically Uruguayan, such as the teru-teru (which is used, for example, to identify Uruguay's national rugby team). Similarly, the day a $5,000 note is created, we can expect another historical character from the Uruguayan erudite cultural sphere to be portrayed on it. Or not, because the choice of characters to be portrayed on banknotes depends on the governing authority. Therefore, depending on its political ideology, the governing authority might choose to broaden the repertoire of characters, for example, including creators of popular and folkloric culture, representatives of minorities (for example, indigenous), or people who fought for their rights and social inclusion. In any case, the opposition between urban/rural and cultural/natural should still be present in currency design, at least according to the design pattern currently used.

As we saw in the cases of the US dollar, the Canadian dollar, the pound sterling and the coins of the Brazilian real, it is common for a currency system to depict individuals that are praised by the state, usually thanks to the political roles they occupied. The Uruguayan case is interesting in this sense, because at some point it was deliberately decided on the pole of enunciation to stop constructing the national semiosphere through the use of political and military figures on banknotes and coins – as we saw in the case of Artigas – and instead it was decided to adorn currency with writers, painters, musicians, intellectuals and, more recently, autochthonous animals. These two local encyclopaedias are unrelated with the historical construction of the nation in political-administrative terms, as was the case with the US dollar, to mention a contrastive example. Moreover, what is axiologized in positive terms here are two repertoires that are not evidently or directly related with the national state: animals and producers of cultural works. However, as we argued in this chapter, they function as discursive fields that mediate in constructing an image of the state.

Some possible interpretative lines can be found in studies and essays on the construction of the Uruguayan nation and its identity (Achugar and Caetano, 1992; Caetano, 2010; Hentschke, 2012). For example, in a geographical region where the dichotomy between the concepts of civilization and barbarism has been historically relevant to make sense of how history should develop (Aguerre, 2022; Olaya, 2007; Urdapilleta-Muñoz and Núñez-Villavicencio, 2014), the selection of historical characters that produced an erudite – and hence restricted, considering UNESCO's definition – type of culture as those that merit being depicted and celebrated on banknotes could be interpreted as an attempt to delineate a specific national profile, clearly located on the pole of civilization. In fact, a famous quote of Artigas from 1816 – when Uruguay was still not an independent country – during the opening celebration of the National Library was 'sean los orientales tan ilustrados como valientes', which could be translated as: 'Let the Orientals be as enlightened as they are brave.'[4]

Hence, such an iconographic choice would gain its value thanks to an opposition to the pole of barbarism, especially when we consider that in Uruguay – as in many other countries of the continent – high culture was produced in the city, which generally was literate and cosmopolitan (Hentschke, 2012). In this sense, a correspondence could be established between the city and civilization, in line with Raymond Williams's (1973: 1) proposal about the 'powerful feelings' the idea of the city has gathered since classical times and throughout history as a space of 'learning, communication, light'.

* * *

In this chapter, we studied the design of the current banknotes and coins of the Uruguayan peso, which we assume to be a currency our international reader is unfamiliar with – contrary to those studied in the previous chapters. In this study, we saw how the semantic opposition between the poles of nature and culture can be clearly seen in action in this currency system, assigning one of them to each material support of those used as currency.

In the previous chapters, we saw how the pole of culture was brought to life in different ways, for example, through human agency and action. In the designs of the Uruguayan peso, we encountered historical characters that were active in the field of high/highbrow, erudite culture, understood in a restricted way as only a portion of all possible cultural action. In this sense, only producers of a specific type of literature, music, paintings and ideas were depicted on currency, leaving aside others related to the domain of popular and rural areas.

All the characters featured on the Uruguayan peso's banknotes were chosen under the government of the so-called 'traditional' political parties. In 2005, the left accessed government for the first time, and at the time of writing this book, it is still the ruling coalition. If new banknotes were to be created, either as a replacement of the current series or as additional denominations, how would discourses of the left mediate in the selection of characters? This question remains open, but points out to the discursive forces that might shape currency design, in what could become a contest or struggle over the sense of the nation, as we shall see in Chapter 10.

10

Argentine Peso

In this chapter, we study our third and last South American national currency: the Argentine peso. While this currency is similar in its current and past designs to some of those we have studied in the previous chapters, it should serve us to see how currency design can be the object of political – and hence discursive – disputes regarding the ways of constructing and modelling national identity, namely, when the ruling party changes, and so do ideologies regarding the nation. Specifically, we shall see how the designs of the three different series of banknotes that currently circulate in Argentina are based in different discursive matrixes and include design elements that express different encyclopaedias, all of them useful to convey an idea of national identity.

10.1 Context

The Argentine peso was introduced in 1992 as the replacement of the austral, which was the country's previous official currency. The peso is regulated by the Central Bank of Argentina (Banco Central de la República Argentina), which is the country's monetary authority. Currently three different series of banknotes circulate in the country, each with its own defining traits as a visual system distinguishable from the others. The second series of banknotes was introduced in 2016 and the third one in 2022. Therefore, our case study in this chapter constitutes a clear exception to what is customary in terms of the currency that is valid in a specific country at a specific time. Here we can see a residual series of banknotes coexisting with an emergent one, plus the one stabilized.

Over the past decades, Argentina has experienced political, social and economic challenges that have led to a weakening of its economy, including the Argentine peso. As a result, banknotes of lower values stopped being printed, and new ones were created to adjust the currency system and its units that are part of it to economic reality. Until 2017, the highest banknote circulating in the country was $100. In November 2024, the Central Bank of Argentina launched the $20,000 banknote.

In 2022, the national government led by former president Alberto Fernández made public the designs that would be used for a new series of the Argentine peso banknotes. These would depict national 'heroes' and 'heroines' and gradually replace the designs introduced in 2016, which featured autochthonous animals on them. Considering how currency design developed in the country, the 2016 series constituted an iconographical disruption to how the peso banknotes had historically been designed, usually depicting statesmen on them.

A press release published in May 2022 on the government's official website, with the title 'Heroines and Heroes of Our History Return to Illustrate the Argentine Peso Banknotes', stated that the historical characters that had been selected to feature on the new banknotes 'mark the return of historical personalities to paper money, recovering the memory and recognition of national heroines and heroes who forged our country'.[1]

The use of nouns 'heroines' and 'heroes' in the text to refer to the historical characters that would be depicted on the new banknotes is enlightening, because this lexical choice reflects a positive axiologization of individuals who, according to the institutional enunciator, merit being celebrated in currency design. As argued previously, although we can assume anything depicted on currency to be positively valued by the entity responsible for creating the designs, the choice of words 'heroes' and 'heroines' to refer to them evidences the mediation of axiologization, particularly thanks to the intervention in the discursive matrix sustaining currency design of the mythification that is usually involved in discourses of heroism. This discursive mediation is evidenced not in the designs themselves but in paratexts such as the name given to the new series and the press release.

Moreover, the press release uses a plural pronoun when referring to the country: as argued, the heroes and heroines to be depicted are those 'who forged *our* country'. We can see how the idea of a collective actor – us – defined in national and patriotic terms seems to justify the encyclopedic repertoire that was chosen for the new design of currency. Using this plural possessive pronoun, the governmental enunciator creates a sense effect of a collective national identity, including both the nation and the citizenry.[2]

Before introducing the corpus, a relevant contextual note is necessary regarding political and partisan struggles in the country, as well as the so-called gap (*grieta*) between two political halves. The designs introduced in 2022 were created and made public by the government headed by Alberto Fernández, a politician associated with the Argentinean left. In fact, Cristina Fernández de Kirchner was vice president during Fernández's mandate. These designs were deliberately created to replace those from 2016, which were created during the government of Mauricio Macri, a politician associated with the right. Considering this information, the decision to redesign currency can be an expression of a political strategy, especially when reading the press release.

However, some of the new series' final designs were created during the government of Javier Milei, the libertarian outsider elected as president in November 2023, of whom Macri is a coalition partner. As we shall see below, some of the planned designs that Fernández introduced in 2022 were ultimately replaced, albeit respecting the overall visual elements that make them part of the same visual series.

Considering this contextual information, we could approach the designs of the newest series of the Argentine peso as the manifestation of a political and partisan dispute at the level of social discursivity, and particularly over the encyclopaedic repertoires that should be celebrated on currency. This dispute regards the meaning and sense of the nation, together with the question of which local encyclopaedias are more adequate for the state to use in the discursive construction of the nation. In this sense, in the context of the political dispute that is hegemonic in Argentina, national currency became another space of dispute between these forces.

10.2 Banknotes and coins of the Argentine peso

Studying the design of Argentinean currency with a focus on those banknotes and coins currently circulating is not a simple task. Given that three series of notes circulate in the country (Figure 45), all three of them should be included as part of our corpus. Therefore, if, as argued in the previous chapters, each series of a currency can be considered a semiotic system, we will be analysing three different semiotic systems. As we will see, even if these three systems are expressions of the same institution – the Argentine peso – each of them has its own systemic identity and its own differential traits.

The first series of banknotes that we will study here is the classic one (Figure 46). The notes from that series were designed at the end of 1990s and are very similar in appearance to those of the first series of the peso, as was the case

Figure 45 Some of the different banknotes currently circulating in Argentina.
Source: Photograph taken by the author in February 2024.

of the 2010 update of the Brazilian real series from 1994. Each of the banknotes of the classic series depicts one historical character on its front side.

Although the \$2 and \$5 banknotes were withdrawn from circulation in 2018 and 2020, respectively, due to depreciation, they clearly belong to this semiotic system in terms of their design. As we did when studying the Uruguayan peso, we will include these two notes in our analysis as well. Hence, the classic series is composed of six banknotes, four of which still circulate.

The second series of our corpus was introduced in 2016. Breaking the tradition of depicting statesmen on currency, this series – called 'Fauna autóctona' (Autochthonous fauna) – depicts an animal on the front side of each note (Figure 47). Due to depreciation, the new series did not create a new design for the \$10 banknote, and it created three new units: \$200, \$500 and \$1,000. In terms of units, from the previous system it maintained \$20, \$50 and \$100.

Finally, the third series (Figure 48) comprises – for the time being – only four banknotes: \$1,000, \$2,000, \$10,000 and \$20,000. In these series, two of the designs announced in 2022 were actually printed, whereas the other two notes feature newly created designs, unplanned when the series was announced. Once again due to depreciation, in this series the notes of \$20 and \$50 were removed,

Value	Front	Reverse
$2		
$5		
$10		
$20		
$50		
$100		

Figure 46 The six banknotes of the classic series of the Argentine peso.
Source: Central Bank of Argentina.

Value	Front	Reverse
$20	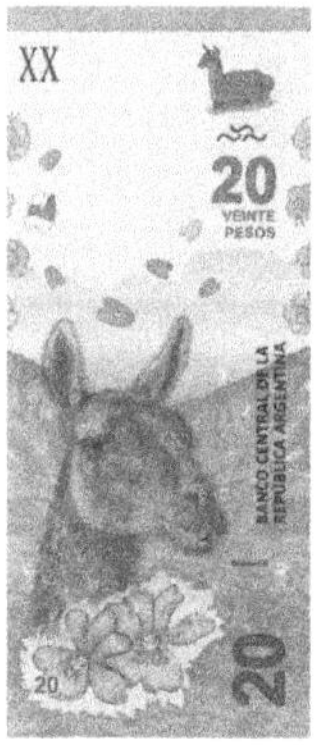	
$50		
$100	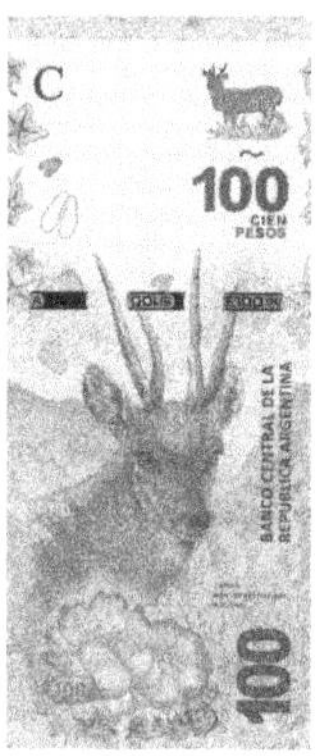	

$200

$500

$1,000

Figure 47 The six banknotes of the 'Fauna autóctona' series of the Argentine peso.
Source: Central Bank of Argentina.

Value	Front	Reverse
\$1,000		
\$2,000		
\$10,000		
\$20,000		

Figure 48 The four banknotes of the newest series of the Argentine peso.
Source: Central Bank of Argentina.

and new ones – \$10,000 and \$20,000 – were created. As a matter of fact, the current design of the \$10,000 note was presented in 2022 as that to be used for the \$500 note.

Regarding coins, the latest designs – introduced in 2018 – feature autochthonous trees and their flowers: the former on the reverse and the latter on the front (Figure 49). These coins are the medium to express a discourse of nature, in line with the banknotes featuring animals. However, coins from the previous series still circulate in Argentina.

Our corpus in this chapter is therefore composed of three series of banknotes, which in visual terms are three different semiotic systems, even if they serve to express the same economic and hence institutional system. This makes of Argentina's currency the most complex we will study in the book.

Value	Front	Reverse
$1		
$2		
$5		
$10		

Figure 49 The four coins of the newest series of the Argentine peso.
Source: Central Bank of Argentina.

Tables 14, 15 and 16 list the distinctive design elements identified in each of the series of banknotes, and Table 17 lists the same for coins.

Before proceeding with the analysis, and for the sake of a complete picture of the context where these banknotes circulate, Figure 50 shows the four original designs the national government made public in 2022. As stated above, only two of them were used. We will come back to them in the analysis.

10.3 Analysis

Our analytical corpus is composed of sixteen banknotes, organized into three different visual systems, and four coins. Thanks to the characteristics of format, layout and content, we can recognize and distinguish each system from the others, even if the classic and the newest have some family resemblance, above all in terms

Table 14 List of Distinctive Design Elements Identified in the Six Classic Banknotes of the Argentine Peso.

Value	Front	Reverse
$2	A portrait of Bartolomé Mitre A handwritten text on the background The depiction of the inner gates of a colonial-style house	A depiction of the façade of Mitre Museum A written summary of Mitre's biography An icon with the initials 'BM', stylized and surrounded by a strip with the name 'Bartolomé Mitre'
$5	A portrait of José de San Martín A handwritten text on the background A depiction of the 'Abrazo de Maipú' painting by Pedro Subercaseaux	A depiction of the monument Cerro de la Gloria (Glory Hill) located in the city of Mendoza A written summary of San Martín's biography An icon with a military man playing a trumpet
$10	A portrait of Manuel Belgrano A handwritten text on the background A depiction of 'La Patria Embanderada', part of the Monumento a la Bandera (Monument to the Flag)	A depiction of the Monument to the Flag with the city of Rosario in the background A written summary of Belgrano's biography An icon with a drum and a wreath of laurels
$20	A portrait of Juan Manuel de Rosas A handwritten text on the background A depiction of a portrait painting of Manuela de Rosas by Prilidiano Pueyrredón	A depiction of the Combate de la Vuelta de Obligado, a historical battle A written summary of Rosas's biography An icon with two crossed military trophies
$50	A portrait of Domingo Faustino Sarmiento A handwritten text on the background A depiction of a scene where a man wearing a suit teaches something to people wearing rural clothing	A depiction of the Casa de Gobierno (House of Government) A written summary of Sarmiento's biography An old sea vessel A group of people wearing traditional clothing An old locomotive An icon including a feather, an inkwell and a written papyrus with the title 'EL PROGRESO' (Progress)
$100	A portrait of Julio Argentino Roca A handwritten text on the background An image depicting a port, a vessel and a sun	A depiction of the painting 'La Conquista del Desierto' by Juan Manuel Blanes A written summary of Roca's biography An icon with a sword over a set of written papers

Source: Author's own elaboration.

Table 15 List of Distinctive Design Elements Identified in the Six Banknotes of the 'Fauna Autóctona' Series of the Argentine Peso.

Value	Front	Reverse
$20	A portrait of a *guanaco*	A depiction of the Patagonian steppe (Estepa Patagónica)
$50	A portrait of an Andean condor (*cóndor andino*)	A depiction of the Cerro Aconcagua (Aconcagua Hill)
$100	A portrait of a *taruca*	A depiction of the Famantina range (Cordón de Famantina)
$200	A portrait of a southern right whale (*ballena franca austral*)	A depiction of a marine habitat (Hábitat marino)
$500	A portrait of a southern jaguar (*yaguareté*)	A depiction of the Yungas rainforest (Selva de Yungas)
$1,000	A portrait of a *hornero*	A depiction of the Pampean plain (Llanura Pampeana)

Source: Author's own elaboration.

Table 16 List of Distinctive Design Elements Identified in the Four Banknotes of the Newest Series of the Argentine Peso.

Value	Front	Reverse
$1,000	A portrait of José Francisco de San Martín An icon depicting a torch	A depiction of the historical event 'Cruce de los Andes' (Andes crossing), 17 January 1817
$2,000	Portraits of Ramón Carrillo y Cecilia Grierson An icon depicting a medical shield	A depiction of the building of the National Institute for Microbiology 'Carlos G. Malbrán', with a written description of the institute
$10,000	Portraits of María Remedios del Valle y Manuel Belgrano An icon depicting a sun	A depiction of the historical event 'Jura a la Bandera' from 27 February 1812
$20,000	A portrait of Juan Bautista Alberdi An icon depicting a book	A depiction of Juan Bautista Alberdi's birth house

Source: Author's own elaboration.

of content. Even if there are visual discontinuities between these three systems, they are coexisting expressions of the same currency system. This means that the fourteen banknotes in circulation – remember that two from the classic series were withdrawn – have validity and value, regardless of their specific design.

Table 17 List of Distinctive Design Elements Identified in the Newest Series of the Argentine Peso Coins.

Value	Front	Reverse
$1	A *jacarandá* flower	*Jacarandá* tree
$2	A *palo borracho* flower	*Palo borracho* tree
$5	An *arrayán* flower	*Arrayán* tree
$10	A *caldén* flower	*Calden* tree

Source: Author's own elaboration.

Figure 50 The four designs announced in May 2022 for the banknotes of the Argentine peso.

Source: Central Bank of Argentina.

Colour is used to achieve a sense effect of continuity between the three systems. Despite the notorious differences existing between the three systems, the colours assigned to each banknote were maintained from one series to the other, and so was banknote identity – even if partially. This means that a banknote created as part of a series using a specific colour has the same colour in the upcoming series, such as the $1,000 note of the animal series, which was created using orange, a colour that was maintained in the newest series for that note. The banknotes featuring animals also maintained the colours of the classic notes. The designs announced in 2022 (Figure 50), which finally were not printed, also respected the colours of the previous two series.

In terms of format and layout, there is a discontinuity between the three series. While the classic and the newest series are fully horizontal, the banknotes featuring animals use the front side vertically and the reverse horizontally. According to the website of the Central Bank of Argentina, the vertical choice means 'an invitation to look at banknotes in a different way and a new way of raising awareness of environmental preservation'.[3]

This statement shows how format and layout can also be used to signify and express specific contents. Even if this series respected the colours used in the previous one to give each banknote a distinctive identity within the system, a double discontinuity was established, regarding both content and format/layout. This discontinuity could signify, for instance, when read as a visual strategy used to challenge the past and as an attempt to refound the currency system in terms of its iconography.

The hypothesis of an attempt to refound and displace the official discourse of the nation expressed in currency design seems justified considering the political struggle introduced above. The institutional enunciator that created the new designs was Argentina's national government on behalf of the national state. However, here the state did not act as a pure and abstract entity, but its act of enunciation was clearly influenced by the will and intentions of those who held power at the time.

In this sense, we see how political intentionality and specific motivations originating in the contest over meaning in the political field can shape currency design (Moreno Barreneche, 2023b: 59–80). It was a specific group of people ruling the country who, perhaps as a way of challenging the status quo, decided to replace the heroes and historical events featured on the classic banknotes with animals and their habitats, as well as to break with the customary horizontal design, opting for a vertical design on the front side of the banknotes. Years later, after that group lost power, a different group of people, from another political affiliation, decided to reinstate the heroes, the historical episodes and the monuments, as was the tradition in the country.

We will begin our analysis working with the six banknotes of the series featuring animals. As argued above, its creation can be read as an attempt by the ruling government to propose a new discursive strategy in an effort to construct a specific idea of the Argentinean nation. In addition to the economic value, the name of the Central Bank, official signatures, security features and some national symbols, the thematic content depicted on these banknotes draws on a discourse of nature, specifically grounded on animals, flowers and habitats considered autochthonous of Argentina, and hence distinctive of national identity through the mediation of territory. This is a type of discourse that we encountered in previous currencies, and which we also encounter in the four current coins of the Argentine peso.

Moreover, the six banknotes include a silhouette of the Argentinean territory on the reverse. This design element was also present in the banknotes of the Uruguayan peso, but the type of depiction we encounter in these two systems is different. In the Argentine peso, the map of the continental part of Argentina – actually what anyone would imagine when thinking of Argentina as a geographical unit – includes a smaller version of the map next to it, also portraying the portion of Argentinean territory in Antarctica. This map is usually referred to as a 'bicontinental map' (Benedetti and Eguren Zambrano, 2025). In a series of banknotes and coins strongly based on discourses of nature, territory, flora and fauna, the accuracy of geographical elements seems more relevant than when used on banknotes in which the discursive matrix is above all cultural and human.

In the two previous chapters, we saw that the coins of the Uruguayan peso and the banknotes of the Brazilian real also include animals. Moreover, we saw how those animals had the differential trait of being regarded as autochthonous and hence distinctive from that country, and not standard animals we could encounter anywhere, such as horses, cows and sheep. The selection of animals we encounter in this series of Argentine peso responds to the same principle: all the animals belong to species that serve to construct the idea of an Argentinean identity drawing on the domain of nature. Even if humans would not live in the territory, thanks to the geography and nature of the Argentinean territory, we could distinguish it from other national territories.

This would not be possible if the animals depicted were cows, horses and sheep: although these animals might help people to identify with Argentina and its nature, the same could happen with Uruguay and Brazil, where these animals are also abundant, as in many countries located in other geographical regions, and even continents. In this sense, as we saw in Chapter 9, even if Uruguay's coat of arms includes a cow and a horse, it is not surprising that the animals featured on the coins of the Uruguayan peso are less common than these and tend to be more exotic. Something similar occurs with the animals featured on the Argentine peso.

Nevertheless, the *guanaco*, the Andean condor and the *hornero* are animals frequently used for the purpose of national discourses in other South American countries. Chile and Peru, which share the Andes mountain range with Argentina, also have condors and *guanacos* in their territories, while in Uruguay, the hornero is a common bird, even if in Argentina it is considered the national bird.[4] Why were these animals chosen and not others? What makes these animals distinctively Argentine in the eyes of the enunciator? Answers to these questions would evidence a recourse to a specific conception of the Argentinean nation with a focus on territory, landscape and nature, that is, independently of any human action.

Moreover, the selection of native animals and habitats included on these banknotes covers quite extensively the vast Argentinean territory and a large part of its geographical regions. These are the central region; the northwest; the Argentine sea, together with Antarctica and the islands of the South Atlantic; the Andean region; and the Patagonian steppe. In fact, a text shared by the Central Bank stated that 'with the choice of native fauna and Argentine regions, the BCRA [Central Bank of the Argentine Republic] seeks a meeting point in which all Argentineans can feel represented in the national currency'.[5]

The argument used by government representatives to support this discursive strategy was that animals and habitats were unlikely to generate controversy and political polemics, as Federico Sturzenegger, at the time head of the Central Bank, argued in a Twitter thread in May 2020:

- 'A series with themes of flora and fauna implied a greater geographical awareness. Both animals and trees represented the whole of the Argentine territory, which we believed reinforced the concept of federalism.'
- 'Replacing heroes with flora and fauna sought to emphasise the vitality of a society connected in a concrete way with its current and future problems. It implied looking to the future rather than to the past.'
- 'Finally, there was an intention to cut the gap [*grieta*]. Many countries have gone down that road. The euro, for example, buries centuries of conflict by depicting the history of architecture with non-existent buildings.'

- 'Banknotes had become increasingly polemic. For example, the 50-note featured Antonio Rivero, who had caused a riot in the Malvinas, killing his employers, but actually because they had been paid their wages in paper money and not in cash.'
- 'That is to say that this banknote had the figure of someone who had revealed himself, curiously enough, against [...] a banknote. A twist of magical realism, which had earned me a request from the National Academy of History to withdraw the banknote from circulation.'

In these tweets, we encounter another interesting idea: that natural diversity can serve to express and reinforce the concept of federalism. In such a form of political organization, the constituent members maintain a certain degree of autonomy and, with it, their own identity, as we saw in the case of UK's member nations when studying the pound sterling. Here the abstract concept of federalism is expressed by a thematic selection unrelated with the realms of politics and human action but using one that involves drawing on the features of the country's flora and fauna. Nevertheless, there is the intention in the pole of enunciation to express a specific content, and the configuration of the plane of expression depends on that intention.

Moreover, these tweets show how the thematic change – from historical/political characters to animals – was intended to 'cut the gap', that is, not to generate new antagonisms in an already very divided Argentinean public sphere. As Faustina de Gennaro (2016: 228) proposes, when looking at these banknotes, Argentinean identity is reduced to fauna and flora, and the differences that characterize Argentinean society were eradicated by erasing from history the national heroes such as the ones depicted in the previous series.[6] It should be noted that the characters depicted in that series express different political views, such as the liberal, the federalist and so on.

The design of the banknotes of this series of the Argentine peso arises from a discursive strategy aimed at proposing a change in the principles that govern currency design within the Argentinean semiosphere. Now banknotes should avoid political tension, favour federalism and celebrate Argentina's biodiversity. In the pole of enunciation, this was seen as possible by anchoring the iconography in the natural realm, with a strong focus on territory, fauna and flora, instead of using elements from the cultural domain, such as historical characters and historical-political events and monuments.

This discursive strategy evidently contrasts with those underlying the previous and posterior series of banknotes. The six classic banknotes are, at first sight, *prototypically* banknotes, not only because they are very similar to what we commonly find (or used to find) in currency design but also because that is how banknotes used to look like in Argentina throughout history. Even if we do not know who the portrayed individuals are, thanks to their inclusion on the design of national currency, we can assume that they are individuals relevant within official discourse, and this is the reason why they are depicted in this medium.

The six historical characters listed in Table 13 are part of what is identified as the Argentinean national state in the sense of a geographically anchored space that was built on the basis of political and military actions. In fact, the vast majority of the men depicted on those notes held positions of power in the state, either as presidents or as provincial governors. These six characters were chosen from a much wider repertoire of men considered notable, all of them part of the Argentinean collective memory. Hence, in paradigmatic terms, other relevant historical figures could have been included in banknotes since they were related to constructing the Argentinean national state as well.

The same principle is recovered in the newest series. In fact, the \$20,000 note, created in late 2024, and not as part of the designs announced in 2022, includes a portrait of Juan Bautista Alberdi, who clearly belongs to this cultural repertoire. Although he was not portrayed in any banknote of the classic series, he was included in past banknotes. As Faustina de Gennaro (2016: 229, my translation) claims, the classic series would seem to tell 'the story of the forgers of a Nation State, who coined a country on the basis of progress, civilization, the free trade model, centralism in decision-making reduced to a literate minority, and admiration for European trends'. Several design elements included in the banknotes of that series – the locomotive, the port, maritime vessels and so on – serve to express these discursive contents linked to modernity.

If we look at the reverse of the banknotes in the classic series, we encounter places and episodes with historical value. The characters depicted on the front side relate to them. Moreover, these episodes and places serve to express the process of building an independent and modern nation. However, the strategies used to represent these episodes differ between the notes. While in some the historical events that seem to justify the selection of the portrayed hero – such as the Combate de la Vuelta de Obligado led by Rosas, or the Conquest of the Desert led by Julio A. Roca – are represented in an iconic manner – we can *see* the historical event as if we were there – in others the reference to the event that justifies the inclusion of the historical character on the front is represented in a symbolic manner.

The \$10 note includes a portrait of Manuel Belgrano, the creator of the national flag. This creation is expressed by an image of the Monument to the

Flag (*Monumento a la Bandera*), a well-known monument located in the city of Rosario. On the $50 note, the historical importance of Domingo Faustino Sarmiento is symbolized through an image of the Pink House (*Casa Rosada*), the national government palace located in Buenos Aires, which Sarmiento during his term of office had painted in pink, from which it derives its name (Pink House). In turn, the heroism of José de San Martín is also symbolically represented on the $5 note through a depiction of the Cerro de la Gloria (Glory Hill), a monument located in San Martín Park in the city of Mendoza.

In terms of gender, the only woman depicted on the banknotes of the classic series is Manuela de Rosas, on the front side of the $20 note. Rosas's daughter is depicted next to him through a copy of a painting by Prilidiano Pueyrredón, from 1851. The almost complete absence of women in the series is relevant – and carries a meaning as well – and it is one of the aspects that were considered in the selection of historical characters to be included on the newest banknotes, as originally presented in 2022.

The banknotes in this third series, the newest, reintegrate the design strategy of depicting relevant historical characters, episodes and places that were used in the classic series. However, they also mean an innovation regarding currency design in Argentina: two of the banknotes announced in 2022 portrayed a single character – which, as demonstrated throughout the book, seems to be the standard of the discursive genre – whereas two portrayed *a pair*. When those notes were announced, a total of six historical characters would be present on the new banknotes, three men and three women, which would contribute to gender parity.

Nevertheless, as mentioned above, those announced designs were not fully respected when the new banknotes began to be produced. Only two of the notes that were actually printed as part of those series feature two characters, respecting gender parity. However, the newest note of $20,000, produced during Javier Milei's libertarian – and anti-gender discourse – government, went back to the generic standard, portraying only one man.

When the new notes were made public, in 2022, Argentina's Ministry of Culture argued that they 'include the representation of three women and three men, important and decisive figures in the construction of our country, who fought for independence, development, inclusion and the expansion of rights'.[7] With this statement, the legitimizing matrix for the inclusion of characters in the new series no longer seems to be based solely on the concepts of national independence and state-building, but on broader values such as inclusion and the expansion of rights.

We highlight this point because it is relevant to properly understand the discursive forces underpinning textual creation. Inclusion and the expansion of rights, among other topics, are constitutive of the political identity of the Latin American left, especially in Argentina, where Peronist and Kirchnerist movements have attempted to construct chains of equivalence between subaltern groups to give a new sense to the popular-national contents that characterize these movements (Grimson, 2019). In this way, the inclusion of women – one of them Black – evidences a certain imprint of the government in highlighting specific heroes and heroines in currency design beyond the characters considered classic and part of the historical canon. This selection was not free of controversy (Cigena, 2022).

The images included on the reverse of the four banknotes of the newest series also include places and events. However, at the time of their 2022 public presentation, they included only events. Only those that were created after that public announcement include the facades of buildings. Hence, we see how the new notes are based on the same discursive matrix than the one sustaining the classic ones. However, the treatment of events in this series (considering the notes originally planned and the ones finally printed) is different: here those events are clearly delimited by dates, indicating a day, a month and a year. The only exception, covering a period of time and not a specific date, is the *gaucho* campaign, dated 1814–25, that was planned to be included in the new $200 note. However, this design has not been used.

The $2,000 note, however, evidences a discontinuity with the chosen encyclopaedic repertoire. Even if gender parity is maintained in the front design, both the thematic field and the iconography on the reverse are different from the rest of the series. Regarding the former, this banknote includes two prominent figures in the field of medicine and health, who are described as 'pioneers of Argentinean public health'. Cecila Grieson was the first Argentinean female doctor, and Ramón Carrillo was the first minister of public health in the country – between 1949 and 1954. Even if Carrillo was a minister – and hence occupying a power position in the state – it would be hard to argue that he pertains to the same encyclopaedic repertoire as presidents and governors. The choice for people who contributed to the domain of health seems to leave aside the standard type of national heroes, which generally belong to the domains of politics.

Regarding iconography, the reverse of this note portrays the facade of the Malbrán Institute of Microbiology, which functions as a symbol of Argentinean quality and excellence in research, as a paragraph included next to the image describes – a design decision which is also a novelty within the system: 'The National Administration of Laboratories and Health Institute "Dr. Carlos G. Malbrán" is a decentralized Public Body, a national and regional reference in sanitary, scientific-technological, teaching and research matters, fundamental pillars of Public Health' (my translation).

Why resorting to the field of medicine, public health and microbiology for the iconography of the new $2,000 banknote, which at the time was the highest nominal value of the Argentine peso? Perhaps the Covid-19 pandemic and the many questionings that Alberto Fernández's government received regarding its management of the health crisis may have justified resourcing to this discursive field, which has little to do with the dominant one in the new series. Besides, the verbal text accompanying the Institute's facade highlights that this institute is both *national* and *public*, together with a reference to public health. This affirmation of public resources is also a political statement, quite typical of the Latin American left.

When studying the Canadian dollar, we saw how innovation can be used to convey an idea of national identity focused on the present, and not only on the past. In the $2,000 banknote, the strategy seems to be this one: as long as innovations were produced by Argentineans, they are valuable and useful to populate the social imaginary regarding Argentinean national identity in terms of what the Argentinean people can achieve. In this sense, the emphasis that the note puts on the Institute being a public organization seems also meaningful.

A final issue that seems relevant to our analysis relates to the concretization of the designs announced in 2022. In those designs, the purple $100 note included a portrait of Eva Duarte de Perón. Known as 'Evita', she was the spouse of Juan Domingo Perón, the politician at the source of Peronism. Evita is a figure widely celebrated by the Argentinean left – particularly by the national popular left – to

Figure 51 Commemorative $100 banknote featuring Eva Duarte de Perón (Evita).
Source: Central Bank of Argentina.

the point of having become a kind of myth within the Argentinean semiosphere (Navarro, 2013; Rosano, 2006; Sebreli, 2008).

As such, her portrait was featured on a commemorative $100 note marking the 60th anniversary of her death (Figure 51). This note was created during Cristina Fernández's government and featured Evita's portrait surrounded by a circular shape that reminds us of a halo, as used when depicting saints. This decision – which could be interpreted as a strategic use, by the then president, of the semiotic efficacy of Evita's figure and the connotations associated with her to re position her as a new Evita – was not free of controversy and criticism, as it meant an arbitrary cut with the type of historical figures portrayed on the banknotes of the Argentine peso, all of them figures linked to the state and to national institutionality because they all held public office, something Evita did not.

The banknotes announced in May 2022 by a left-wing government (in which Fernández de Kircher was vice president) not only retained this polemic figure from Argentinean history with clear political-ideological connotations but also maintained her in the new note corresponding to the same denomination where she already appeared. With this move, a banknote created to commemorate an event would have been 'mainstreamed', that is, turned into one of the four constitutive units of the banknote system.

Moreover, the new design maintained the purple colour that gave Evita's commemorative banknote an identity in chromatic terms, which interestingly is the colour currently associated with feminism and women's movements. Therefore, the $100 commemorative note depicting Evita could be made sense of in terms of an attempt by a specific government to leave a political-ideological imprint on national currency and also perhaps one of the triggers of the iconographic refoundation put forward by the upcoming government, in 2016, led by Mauricio Macri.

Hence, it is hard not to read Evita's presence on the $100 note announced in 2022 as based on a mode of semiotic production that aims to reconnect with the pre-Macri era while at the same time winking at Kirchnerism through one of its most salient icons, as well as to the rupture it brought about in the currency system with the creation of the special commemorative banknote portraying her.

While Evita's original banknote still circulates in Argentina, the one announced in 2022 never saw the light. Besides, in the context of Javier Milei's libertarian and anti-Kirchnerism government, we could assume that none of the upcoming banknotes will portray Evita, because it does not seem plausible for the government he leads to celebrate such a character with strong connotations of the left.

To sum up, in the Argentinean case, we can see how different strategies can be used by the state, depending on who holds government, to define currency iconography. Moreover, we see how the different design strategies relate. This relationship is not visible in the banknotes themselves – it is not an immanent feature of the visual texts analysed – but requires an awareness of the adversarial component that characterizes the Argentinean political field. Whereas in the banknotes of the many series of the Argentine peso we encounter similar things to what we encountered in the previously studied national currencies, here we also encounter a discursive clash that is not itself visible, but which requires a knowledge of the local semiosphere and its dynamics.

According to Eliseo Verón (1987), politics is a discursive field characterized by its *adversarial* nature, that is, one in which different projects compete to impose themselves as the dominant one. Hence, we could argue that the three series of banknotes studied in this chapter are related based on two different strategies that refer to the currency tradition in the country. On the one hand, there is a strategy of refoundation, that is, of creating something new and setting the counter to zero. This is the case with the series featuring autochthonous animals, which proposes the use of a new section of the local encyclopaedia, as opposed to what was the norm within the discursive genre in the country.

On the other hand, there is a strategy of restoration, as in the case of the banknotes announced in 2022, which proposed to recover what the banknotes featuring animals had erased and deleted from public discourse, even if that deletion was based on a declared goodwill. In fact, when presenting the new designs, Alberto Fernández argued that 'currency is a central instrument for us to remember who made the homeland in which we live'.[8] In this sense, although Fernández expressed that he did not see a problem in highlighting fauna on currency, he did see a problem in prioritizing fauna over other encyclopaedic repertoires, which he probably considered more central to the nation.

* * *

In this chapter, we studied the three series of banknotes of the Argentine peso currently circulating in the South American country. In the analysis, we saw how currency can function as a space for political and ideological disputes over the sense of the nation. As argued, a government can use different discursive strategies to this end. One of them involves including in currency characters, events, monuments and architectural heritage clearly located in the past. This is perhaps the standard in the discursive genre of currency design – we identified this productive matrix in previous chapters as well.

But there are also other possible strategies that can be used, such as the one sustaining the 'Fauna autóctona' series of the Argentine peso. This discursive matrix leaves aside the historical and human dimension in favour of using a local encyclopaedia linked to the geographical-natural dimension, and specifically space, by highlighting landscapes, habitats and animals. Moreover, the current coins highlight autochthonous flora as well. In the previous chapters, we saw how the strategy of drawing on nature was used in other currency systems. Even if such a strategy was used in a declared attempt to depoliticize currency design, it was nevertheless a source of political discourse, as evidenced in Alberto Fernández's speech when presenting the new designs in May 2022.

In any case, the main conclusion of the analysis presented in the chapter is that currency can be a relevant and pertinent means to account for certain visions and senses of the nation, as well as for their political-ideological dispute. As such, it can function as a textual entry point to political discourse.

11

The Euro

In each of the previous chapters, we studied a national currency. The adjective 'national' is used to make clear that the banknotes and coins we studied were dependent on national states. Therefore, in our analyses we tried to relate the design elements we encountered in currency with discourses and social imaginaries about the nation and the state. Although most currencies currently used in the world are national currencies – they depend on a specific national state and are valid within its territory – there are exceptions.

The euro is one of those exceptions. To conclude our journey through the semiotics of currency design, this chapter studies a supranational currency that is not dependent on a specific national state. The euro was created and is regulated by the EU and used by many states as their official currency. Although most of the countries that adopted the euro are members of the EU, others are not. In any case, the euro is a currency that transcends national boundaries and that serves to express discursive contents that are located not at a national but a supranational level. However, as we shall see, there is space for national discourses on this currency as well.

This final chapter should serve to illustrate how collective identities, cultural memory and heritage do not necessarily function at the national level only – as is customary in the discursive genre of currency design – but can also be supranational. Evidently, the discursive strategies used to decorate the banknotes and coins of such a currency will be different than those used for national currencies. This the case because, in cases such as the euro, specific semiotic efforts must be made on the pole of enunciation to construct a *supranational semiosphere* with which both individuals and collectives can identify, without giving up their national identification. This is the case of the banknotes and coins of the euro, as we shall see in this chapter.

11.1 Context

As the common currency to be used by the members of the EU, the euro came into existence in 1999. The EU's 1992 Treaty of Maastricht created the Economic and Monetary Union (EMU) and a single currency to be used in that context. Following these developments, the euro banknotes and coins were introduced on 1 January 2002.

The euro is regulated by the European Central Bank, and it was first introduced in Austria, Belgium, Finland, France, Germany, Greece, Ireland, Italy, Luxembourg, the Netherlands, Portugal and Spain. Gradually other countries adopted it as their official currency as well, the latest to join being Croatia, in 2023. In 2025, Bulgaria has announced it will adopt the euro, on 1 January 2026, replacing the national lev. Some countries, such as the UK, Denmark and Sweden, decided not to join the initiative when it entered into force and continued with their national currencies. Currently several member countries of the EU still do not use the euro.

According to the ECB's website, the euro is 'a beacon of stability and a symbol of European unity'.[1] As such, it has become one of the various symbols that serve to express – and, at the same time, construct – European identity (Fornäs, 2012; Mangiapane and Migliore, 2021). Non-EU countries such as Andorra, Monaco, San Marino and Montenegro also use the euro as their official currency.

Since the euro was created, its banknotes had two series, which in terms of design elements are quite similar. The first series were created in the 1990s by Austrian graphic designer Robert Kalina. The banknotes of the 'Europa' series – the second, newest series – maintain the same denominations, colours and other design elements of the first series. As the ECB's website puts it, the theme of the first series 'has been continued in the Europa series but has been given a fresh look and stronger colours'.

In 2025, a process to redesign the euro banknotes is underway. It was announced in December 2021. According to Christine Lagarde, president of the European Central Bank, 'after 20 years, it's time to review the look of our banknotes to make them more relatable to Europeans of all ages and backgrounds'.[2] In 2022, EU-citizens were offered the possibility of participating in the redesign process by choosing possible themes for the new banknotes. After a period of public consultation and voting, in November 2023 two themes were shortlisted: 'European culture: shared cultural spaces' and 'Rivers and birds: resilience in diversity'.[3] Moreover, specific motifs were also chosen for both themes, as shown in Tables 18 and 19, respectively. Based on this

Table 18 List of Distinctive Design Elements Relating to European Culture to Be Featured in a Possible Upcoming Series of the Euro Banknotes.

Value	Cultural activities and spaces	Front	Reverse
€5	Performing arts	Maria Callas	Street performers (music/dance/ theatre) entertaining passersby
€10	Music	Ludwig van Beethoven	A song festival with a choir of children and young adults singing
€20	University and schools	Marie Curie	A school or university with a female teacher and young students. There are notebooks and books on the tables.
€50	Libraries	Miguel de Cervantes	A library with some adults reading paper and digital books. A little boy and girl in front of a bookcase trying to get a book
€100	Museums and exhibitions	Leonardo da Vinci	Adults and children admiring some examples of street art, contemporary art and so on
€200	Public squares	Bertha von Suttner	A tree-covered square allowing people to come together, with adults and children talking, walking, playing and so on

Source: European Central Bank.

selection, in July 2025 a design competition was launched, so new designs can be chosen in 2026. Moreover, the possibility of creating a digital euro is being explored.[4]

The euro has been studied by several scholars (Fornäs, 2012; Sassatelli, 2017, 2021; Risse, 2003, 2011; Raento et al., 2004). This interest is probably a result of its supranational nature, which poses a challenge to national identities, as well as due to the effects it has on European integration. In this sense, according to Johan Fornäs (2012: 205), the euro is 'the final, most recent and also in many ways the most effective and important official European symbol'.

11.2 Banknotes and coins of the Euro

The current series of the euro – the 'Europa' series – comprise six banknotes (Figure 52). The previous series, designed in the 1990s and set in circulation in 2002,

Table 19 List of Distinctive Design Elements Relating to Rivers and Birds to Be Featured in a Possible Upcoming Series of the Euro Banknotes.

Value	Front	Reverse
€5	Mountain spring Wallcreeper next to a mountain landscape	European Parliament
€10	Waterfall Kingfisher in a waterfall or run pool	European Commission
€20	Confined river valley Bee-eater colony in a sand wall on the side of a large, confined river valley along a riverbank	European Central Bank
€50	Meandering river White stork flying over a meandering river in an unconfined river valley	Court of Justice of the European Union
€100	River mouth Avocet sweeping over the surface of a mud flat	European Council and Council of the European Union
€200	Seascape Northern gannet flying over big ocean waves	European Court of Auditors

Source: European Central Bank.

included a €500 banknote as well, which was not maintained in the new series. Upon a quick look at the notes, we see that they do not feature any depiction of humans, animals or places.[5] In this sense, we can see, following Monica Sassatelli (2021: 200), how 'the design or euro banknotes marks a radical departure from the norm'.

The euro coin system comprises eight denominations. As was the case of the currency systems studied so far, the coins are used for the lower values, and nominal values are not repeated in coins and banknotes. Moreover, some countries have already stopped using coins of lower values.

The euro coins are an interesting object of analysis because their reverses are several. In fact, for each country using the euro, there is a different reverse design of the eight coins of the system. This is the case because, for the sake of maintaining national identity (even if marginally), each country using the euro is allowed to create and include their own designs on the reverse.[6] As we shall see below, these designs tend to relate to nationhood and statehood.

Working with all the designs of coins would mean working with an enormous analytical corpus. In 2004, Pauliina Raento et al. (2004) conducted an analysis of the existing euro coins and drew some interesting conclusions, including a

Value	Front	Reverse
€5		
€10		
€20		
€50		
€100		
€200		

Figure 52 The six banknotes of the euro from the 'Europa' series.
Source: European Central Bank.

Value	Front	Value	Front
1 cent		2 cents	
5 cents		10 cents	
20 cents		50 cents	
€1		€2	

Figure 53 Front designs of the euro coins.
Source: European Commission's DG ECFIN.

mapping of the cultural repertoires used to design them. Even if, since then, some of the designs have changed, that paper is still useful nowadays. In our analysis, we will only illustrate our argument with specific examples of euro coins, without any pretension of exhaustivity. Figure 53 includes the common side (front side) of the eight current euro coins.

11.3 Analysis

In the previous chapters, we saw how throughout history the tendency has been for states to gain independence and sovereignty in economic terms by producing their own national currencies linked to the state territory. These currencies are regulated by the state and usually are valid only within its territory, with some exceptions such as the US dollar or the border regions.

The creation of the euro challenges this historical tendency and goes in the opposite direction: instead of more independence in economic terms, it prioritizes integration and unity as the result of the project of a European Single Market and the European Monetary Union (EMU). As Heinz Tschachler (2010: 4) argues, 'the introduction of the euro effectively undid many of the monetary standardizations that had been undertaken in the name of the nation'.

When looking at the six current banknotes of the euro, we do not encounter any design elements that could be read through the lenses of national identity or the cultural memory of the countries that are part of the EU. This is a deliberate design choice. To begin with, these banknotes circulate in all the states using the euro as their official currency. Therefore, their design cannot be limited in territorial or national terms to only one state. Moreover, European identity is a supranational type of identity, that is, one that encompasses smaller units – other identities – that are defined in national terms. These two identity levels – national and supranational – coexist.

Although European identity is not a national identity, it is still a territorial identity, that is, one grounded in a geographical entity – the European continent – that functions as a source of social discourses. As every collective identity, the European one is constructed not only narratively but also through oppositions to other identities. As Fornäs (2017: 8) argues, people use the words 'Europe' and 'Europeanness' to refer to 'a specific lifeform in contrast to African, Asian or American ways of life, including a set of habits, practices and identities'.

In fact, the major discursive efforts of the EU seem to be focused on making Europe as a continent, as a historical idea and as the Union to coincide. According to semiotician Franciscu Sedda (2021: 125), 'when we say Europe, very often, highly partial and imperfect conventional equivalences echo throughout that sign'. For instance, the word 'Europe' can be used indistinctly in everyday language to refer to the European continent – that is, a geographical entity whose Eastern boundaries have never been clearly set (Rossi, 2007; Diez, 2004; Mangiapane and Migliore, 2021) – but also the political Union – whose boundaries are clearly delimited based on legal norms and the agreement of its members – and to a broader cultural-historical unit of meaning that is linked to a common past (Walkenhorst, 2009; Rossi, 2007; Sedda, 2021).

As is the case with any collective identity, European identity must be constructed in discourse using specific signs and strategies. Therefore, differently than what we encountered in the cases studied in the previous chapters, the banknotes of the euro feature design elements that could in principle be accepted by anyone identifying with the nations that are part of the EU.

In the euro, this sense effect is implemented using a discursive strategy strongly based on symbolism. In each of the six banknotes, we encounter a common set of elements: windows, portals and bridges. These are different in each note and are depicted using a high degree of figurativity, as if they were copies of real windows, portals and bridges. Hence, we can easily recognize the depictions of what we see as standing for the things they stand, even if we cannot identify the actual things being depicted.

This is so because the depicted architectural elements are not referential – that is, they do not stand for any real window, portal or bridge that we can encounter in the world.[7] Here the three architectural elements used to decorate currency are not intrinsically valuable but were chosen thanks to the sedimented connotations they carry: they are symbols of openness, connection, union and cooperation, all pillars of any supranational identity, including the European one.

However, each banknote gains its identity thanks to the style of the three architectural elements portrayed. When looking at the styles of those architectural elements. we identify a historical progression that reflects a history that is imagined and depicted as common to all Europeans. This progression begins in the classical ancient times – on the €5 note – and gradually moves into the present through different historical cultural styles, ordered according to how they emerged and developed in the history of the European continent. These are Romanesque (€10), Gothic (€20), Renaissance (€50), Baroque and Rococo (€100), and nineteenth-century iron and glass architecture (€200).[8]

The €500 note as part of the first series of the euro was an example of contemporary twentieth-century architecture (Figure 54), but it was abandoned in the 'Europa' series. Interestingly, the type of architecture we encounter in the old €500 note resembles that of EU institutional buildings located in Brussels, Belgium, such as the Europa building – the seat of the European Council and

Figure 54 The €500 banknote from the first series of the euro.
Source: European Central Bank.

the Council of the European Union – and the Berlaymont – the headquarters of the European Commission.[9]

According to Monica Sassatelli (2021: 202), 'the euro tells a story about history, even progress' because it portrays 'seven "ages and styles", tracing what could have equally been criticised as an essentialist and teleological, unified, path to European progress'. This is an insightful thought, because what is highlighted here is a conception of Europe and European identity as a historical process, which can be traced through time and whose progression can be segmented in specific ages and styles.

In terms of systemic continuity, we encounter several elements that allow us to identify the six banknotes as part of the same visual system. Each banknote is characterized by a distinctive colour, which seems to be arbitrarily assigned. Size changes gradually and banknotes are bigger as the nominal value augments. The positioning of numbers and other design elements in the topological grid also conveys the idea of belonging to the same system.

In terms of the design elements used, besides the architectural elements that give each banknote its identity through the mediation of historical style, we find some common elements that express European identity. The first of them is the European flag, a symbol composed of twelve golden stars in a circular formation over a blue background. The flag was introduced in 1955 by the Assembly General of the Council of Europe and used by the EU since the Treaty of Maastricht, from 1992 (Mangiapane and Migliore, 2021: 15–26; Fornäs, 2012: 115–48).

As we saw in the previous chapters, although banknotes and coins usually include symbols that stand for the nation (for example, the maple leaf in the Canadian dollar), the country's flag is not a common design element to find on banknotes and coins. However, given the supranational nature of European identity, the process of emergence of new stable signs has still not achieved a stage of maturity. Although values are widely used to express the idea of European identity (Moreno Barreneche, 2023c), other non-official signs are not yet strong or stable enough to be used. This could explain why the EU flag is included on the front side of the notes: it functions as an interpretant to make sense of the political community the banknotes stand for.

The second element common to the six banknotes is the circle of stars that we encounter in the centre of the EU flag. These twelve stars do not stand for anything specific, such as member countries of the Union. Since these stars are a central element of the flag, they can be used for the purposes of expressing the political community, as was the case with the maple leaf on Canada's flag, or the spherical shape of Brazil's flag used in the design of coins of the real. The circle of stars is used both on the front and reverse of the euro banknotes, maintaining the circular arrangement, albeit not the golden colour of the stars. On the front side, the circle partially overlaps with the image of the window and portal. As we shall see below, the circle of stars is also present in the coin system.

The third element common to the six banknotes is the inclusion of the map of the European continent on the reverse. The map of Europe is present in the coin system as well. This reference to geography and the territorial dimension of identity is interesting for us because the map chosen is one of the continent, and not one of the countries that are part of the Union. In the map included on the notes, we see countries such as Iceland, Norway, Switzerland, Russia and Turkey – and even entire regions, such as the north of Africa – that neither are part of the Union nor use the euro as their official currency.

However, country boundaries were not included in the map. Here Europe is above all a continent, one where internal divisions are not meaningful. As Giuseppe Bettoni (2021: 77) argues, 'any geographical map conveys a discourse, and therefore constitutes an object of study which conveys visions, and fosters a sense of identity'. Since the idea of a European collective and supranational identity depends on the territorial dimension (if we speak of Europe as a meaningful unit, it is thanks to the existence of a segment of land designed as such), drawing on a map seems to be an appropriate discursive strategy to bring this identity to life in figurative terms, together with other symbols such as the flag and the design elements that compose this official symbol. We will come back to the map of the European continent below.

The final common element we encounter on the six banknotes is linguistic. Every note includes the denomination of the currency in three different alphabets: Latin, Hellenic and Cyrillic. The inclusion of Cyrillic was done on the 'Europa' series – previously, only Latin and Hellenic inscriptions were included, as evidenced in Figure 54. When Bulgaria joined the Union, Cyrillic became an alphabet relevant to the EU, and hence it was decided to include it in the design of the euro. Besides, in terms of language, the acronym of the ECB is shown in ten linguistic variants on the side of each banknote. In the original series, it was written only in five.

As was the case with Queen Elizabeth's passing, design choices like these are motivated by ongoing and open facts of the world, such as the accession of new countries to the Union. In this sense, design elements expressing European identity might vary as the European project does, for example, in terms of enlargement (Zielonka, 2002), or when a country decides to leave the Union. If, in the future, Georgia joins the EU, we might encounter Georgian scripts on the euro banknotes as well, since we can assume Georgian will probably become an official EU language.

Finally, each banknote of the 'Europa' series includes a security feature that is almost invisible without holding the note and looking at it carefully: a watermark and a hologram including a depiction of the mythological character Europa, in the form of a woman (Migliore, 2021). This mythological character is the only anthropomorphic – it would not be appropriate to refer to Europa as 'human' – element included in the design of the euro banknotes. As the ECB's website puts it, this figure 'adds a human touch to the notes and, of course, is the origin of the name of our continent'.[10] Once again, we encounter a personification in the form of a woman, as was the case with Britannia, Helvetia and the effigy of the Republic.

All the design elements listed in the previous paragraphs were deliberately chosen and included in the banknotes of the euro because they serve to express the European collective identity. Hence, they serve as semiotic resources to construct this supranational identity in figurative terms. According to Fornäs (2012: 210), 'the euro was installed as a materially effective mechanism that could simultaneously be designed in a symbolically striking way, in order to further strengthening identification of and with Europeanness'.

As a collective identity bounded to a specific geographical entity, European identity is an interesting social construct because it coexists with national identities. Someone can be German *and* European, that is, identify in national terms as belonging to Germany and, in supranational terms, to Europe. Identifying both as German and French is more difficult, although possible in specific cases. However, these cases are exceptional, since people tend to identify with *one* national identity. Therefore, every national identity in Europe – Austrian, Croatian, Portuguese and so on – coexists with the supranational European identity, in a relationship where the latter subsumes the former.

These different identity levels are activated depending on the alterity they encounter. Therefore, within the European semiosphere, Austrian identity might be a useful unit of meaning to distinguish oneself from German identity, while in a global context, European identity might work to distinguish oneself from African identity. In any case, we are dealing with units of meaning, located on the plane of content and segmented based on oppositions and differences that are expressed in a plane of expression.

Given the coexistence of European identity and national identities in the European continent, it is common to encounter expressions of both identities juxtaposed. As an example, we can mention official buildings located in Europe, where the country's national flag flies next to the EU flag, and even the regional or local flag (for example, that of a federal state). This is not the case with currency: the euro replaced national currencies, deleting the portion of national discourse that was expressed on banknotes and coins.

That is why supranational currencies mean a challenge to national currencies. In their paper on banknote design in Eastern Europe – published in 2001, before the euro started circulating – Unwin and Hewitt (2001: 1009) wrote in a footnote that 'it does seem likely in the long term that countries now aspiring to join the European Union will indeed lose their own currencies and banknotes'. This is what is happening, with the euro now being a continental currency. With national currencies lost, so were portions of national discourse.

When creating the designs to be used on the euro banknotes, a specific decision was made to avoid depicting historical characters and real buildings, to avoid possible clashes between European and national identities (Fornäs, 2012: 215). Therefore, what we encounter in the euro banknotes is a discourse strongly based on symbolism. As such, discourses of this type oppose the discourses based on iconism that we encountered in the currencies previously studied, perhaps except for the hands featured on the Swiss franc. In the currency systems studied in previous chapters, we encountered portraits of people, landscapes, animals, works of art, buildings and activities in a logic according to which what we saw on banknotes and coins resembles what is being depicted. First comes 'the world' and then design.

Something different occurs with the euro banknotes. Although these banknotes are figurative – as opposed to abstract – their designs are not based on a referential intention: the images we see should be recognized as standing for windows, portals and bridges, but there is not an enunciative intention of these signs to bring us to a specific reference other than the very idea of a window, a portal and a bridge and, above all, to what these architectural signs *connote*. In short, denotation is irrelevant, and what matters is connotation, because it is at this level where the meanings to be associated with Europe, the European identity and the euro are located.

Although banknotes are rich in terms of their design elements, the most interesting subsystem of the euro is its coins. As we saw above, there are eight nominal values. When looking at the front side of the coins, we can see how the eight designs are quite systemic in terms of how they look, specifically in terms of where the design elements are placed.

Only two elements are common to the eight coins. These are the inclusion of the map of the European continent and the twelve stars of the EU flag. While on the reverse the twelve stars are displayed in the standard circular shape, on the front sides they are not. However, there are still twelve stars, in this case connected by parallel lines. This is a design choice that highlights the value of this design element despite the different eidetic configuration.

In the current series of the euro coins, we encounter two versions of the map of Europe. In the first one, included in the coins of 10, 20 and 50 cents and of €1 and €2, the map depicts the European continent without any internal country boundaries, a depiction that is common to the map included on the reverse of the banknotes. As argued above, this type of depiction can be interpreted as an attempt to make Europe a unitary totality, without internal divisions.

The second map, used in the 1, 2 and 5 cent coins, places the European continent in the globe. This design includes significant portions of the African and Asian continents as well, presences that activate meanings of the European continent as one embedded on an interplay of continental identities. Here the internal fragmentation in terms of countries and nations does not seem to be relevant.

However, the map of Europe included in the designs of the original series of the 10, 20 and 50 cent coins depicted the European countries as clearly – and somewhat artificially – separated. In Figure 55, we easily identify the contours of Portugal, Spain, the UK, Ireland, France, Belgium, Luxembourg, Italy, the Netherlands, Germany, Denmark, Sweden, Finland and Greece. Each of these countries is separated from the rest, and if we recognize them, it is thanks to their shape, which is reinforced by the country's borders. In that map, countries that at the time were not part of the EU were deleted, such as Switzerland, Norway, Slovenia, Croatia, Montenegro and so on.

Figure 55 Original 50 cent euro coin with a map highlighting the borders of the EU countries.
Source: European Central Bank.

Hence, in the original design of coins, three different maps were used to express three different discourses about Europe (Raento et al. 2004: 934–7). According to Raento et al. (2004: 935), these three maps portray Europe as 'a natural, unified, and harmonious entity whose member countries enjoy an independent and equal status'. To do so, 'the EU's internal boundaries are underplayed, but the entity is clearly differentiated from areas outside the EU's carefully guarded external boundary'.

However, in the current designs, the map highlighting internal divisions was replaced by a unitary map of the European continent. This decision can be interpreted as a strategy to reinforce the semantic values of union and totality, which is what the EU – the enunciator creating the designs – probably wants to convey isotopically in currency. Instead of depicting Europe as a collection of individual nations, the preference is for the supranational construction, without any reference to the national dimension. When studying design decisions such as these, we can identify what Sassatelli (2021: 195) calls 'an all-encompassing dichotomy' between 'visions of Europe as unity and homogeneity versus visions of fragmentation and diversity'.

The choice for a unitary depiction that deletes internal borders is relevant in semiotic terms because it shows the tension that exists between visions and conceptions of Europe as a collection of nations and a type of European, cosmopolitan identity (Sassatelli, 2021: 195). Clearly, the enunciator creating the designs of banknotes and coins aims at expressing the second type of conception, and hence currency design becomes another tool to achieve that goal.

On the reverse of the coins, we encounter a vast discursive universe, linked to discourses of national identity. Each EU member state using the euro decides what to depict on that side of the coin. Even countries that are not members of the EU but that use the euro, such as Andorra, San Marino and the Vatican, have their own designs on the reverse. As we shall see below, the encyclopaedic repertoires used for this purpose are many, and we shall see how they are coherent with those we encountered in the previous chapters.

The freedom of design that countries have leads to a coexistence of different design strategies. Some countries use only one design in the reverse of the eight coins. Belgium, Luxembourg and the Netherlands chose to include a portrait of their respective reigning monarchs only. Estonia, a map of the country. Ireland, a depiction of the harp, its national symbol. Lithuania, a depiction of the country's national symbol: Vytis on a horseback and a sword. Other countries prefer to use different designs for each coin, while others group coins in three categories: (a) 1, 2 and 5 cents, (2) 10, 20 and 50 cents, (3) €1 and €2.

We could dedicate an entire book to the semiotics of the designs we encounter on the reverse of the euro coins. In a study now twenty years old, Raento et al. (2004) identified six categories of elements used on the reverse designs of the coins, which might overlap: (1) human figures; (2) cultural patrimony (architecture, arts and literature); (3) state heraldry; (4) artifacts; (5) nature; and (6) texts (verbal, written texts). We have encountered all these elements in our analyses as well. To simplify the work, we will only work with a handful of designs (Figure 56).

In terms of human figures – the first category identified by Raento et al. – we can see how the Austrian €1 coin depicts Wolfgang Amadeus Mozart, whereas

Figure 56 A selection of twenty-three reverses of the euro coins.
Source: European Commission's DG ECFIN.

the Belgian €2 euro coins portrays the reigning monarch. Although both portraits are based on real and existing human beings (and not a mythical figure or a personification), the reasons for their inclusion in currency are different. In this sense, the selection of Mozart's portrait by Austria is equivalent to Nikola Tesla's by Croatia, or Dante Alighieri's by Italy. Here the selection is based on the value that is attributed in national terms to the work of the person. Something different occurs with the reigning monarch, as we saw when studying the British pound sterling. In fact, the portrait of Belgium's King Phillipe replaced the portrait of his father, King Albert II, which was included in the previous series of the Belgian euro coins.

Besides portraits of real human beings, also anthropomorphic depictions are present on some of the reverses, such as in France's cent coins, which include two different representations of Marianne. Some coins also include anthropomorphic images of mythical characters: examples are the depictions of Venus on the Italian 10 cent coin, or of Europa sitting on a bull on the Greek €2 coin.

Regarding cultural patrimony – the second category identified by Raento et al. – we can see different strategies of figurativization used to bring this cultural repertoire to life in visual texts. For instance, Italy's 20 cent coin includes a depiction of a sculpture by Umberto Boccioni, and the €1 coin, one of Leonardo da Vinci's Vitruvian Man. These are two specific works of art that are mimetically reproduced on currency. In the euro coins, the category of cultural patrimony also takes the form of buildings, such as the depiction of the Brandenburg Tor in various German cent coins, Viennese buildings in Austrian coins or the Bratislava castle in some Slovakian euro coins.

In terms of state heraldry, all the Finnish cent coins include a depiction of the country's lion (its coat of arms). Portuguese coins include the seals of past monarchs. The Irish euro depicts the harp as a national symbol in the eight coins. The Latvian cent coins include two variations of the coat of arms: one small and one large. On the €1 and €2 coins, Malta includes the Maltese cross. We have encountered heraldry and state symbols in the previous analyses as well – they evidently constitute a standard of currency design since they express statehood in a direct manner.

In the previous analyses, we also encountered nature, specifically through flora and fauna. In the euro coins, we encounter a similar repertoire, above all focused on flowers, such as in some Austrian and German cent coins, which depict flowers that connote national identity (edelweiss and oak branch, respectively). However, animals are also depicted, such as in some Slovenian cent coins, which include a stork and horses.

Some other depictions include maps, such as in some Croatian and Estonian coins. Others, such as the newly created Croatian designs, include the depiction of a *kuna*, the animal whose name was used for the former national currency. Finally, one of the Greek euro coins depicts the stamp used for an ancient coin from the Hellenic world, depicting an owl.

As can be seen from this brief summary, the discursive repertoire we encounter on the reverse of the euro coins expresses a vast universe of meaning and sense. As such, it consists of a selection of cultural repertoires that are brought to life figuratively in visual texts that we can clearly read through the lenses of the nation and the state, mediated by both cultural memory and heritage (natural, cultural, material, intellectual). In this sense, the designs used for the euro coins are a good summary of our journey through currency design.

To sum up, we could argue that the two sides of the euro coins reflect in a clear manner the constitutive duality of Europeanness as a supranational identity: the one existing between the national and the supranational/European identities, together with the discourses around the EU and Europeanness. As such, the euro coins construct an idea of Europe in which the national sovereignty, cultural memory and projects are respected but embedded in a broader project: that of European integration, where country borders are deleted and the two identities coexist as two sides of the coin. This is a good reflection of the EU's motto: 'united in diversity'.

Finally, it is worth mentioning that an interesting fact regarding the euro coins is that, although those minted by a nation are expected to circulate more in that country, this is not a rule. Thanks to tourism and other types of mobility within the European territory, the iconography expressing the national identities of the countries that mint coins of the euro travels from one country to another. As a result, national signs of every EU member state can be found anywhere in Europe, forging a shared sense of community, such as the Erasmus programme does (Paolucci, 2021b). According to Fornäs (2012: 223), this can be interpreted as 'a tangible illustration of how Europe is both united and diverse'.

Conclusions

As mentioned in Chapter 1, the purpose of this book was to use a semiotic perspective to study currency design, with a focus on a selection of banknotes and coins currently circulating in the world in 2025. Our analytical journey has taken us from North America to Europe, then to South America and finally back to Europe, where we can find an example of a currency that is not national but supranational. As such, the research efforts presented throughout the book are an attempt to making a new contribution to the broader research quest of making sense of the world we inhabit and the sense-making and signification dynamics that characterize it.

As argued throughout the book, and specifically in Chapter 3, scholars have already seen the value and relevance of studying the design of banknotes and coins. However, up to this date, such approaches have not drawn on a specific semiotic perspective. As argued in Chapter 2, semiotics is a specific discipline, science or outlook within the social sciences that has its own methods and instruments to conduct the empirical analyses aimed at informing hypotheses and arguments regarding the functioning of meaning, signification, sense, discourse and culture. In the eight analytical chapters, we used semiotic theory, concepts, methods and instruments to study currency design as a discursive genre, with a focus on banknotes and coins as visual texts. This was done by drawing on a necessary interdisciplinary dialogue, particularly when trying to argue how the design elements featuring on currency relate to broader discourses and visions of the nation and the state.

In Chapter 1, we argued that our purpose in the book was to identify the discursive forces that underpin this enunciative praxis – or act of sign production – that the state is in charge of and ultimately responsible for. Throughout the book, we revisited this premise once and again, trying to identify the discursive forces that shape such an act of enunciation. It is out of question that banknotes and coins are products of the material culture whose designs depend on the decisions made by a specific institutional enunciator, which is the state. Throughout a discussion of previous scholarship and in the analytical chapters, we saw how the state, as an actor, tends to be defined in national terms, that is, as a national state, where the boundaries of the nation and those of the state coincide.

The analyses presented in the eight analytical chapters confirm how discourses revolving around the nation and the state are pervasive in the genre of currency design, even if the specific design elements activate different portions of the national semiosphere. Even in the case of a supranational currency such as the euro, similar efforts have been made to construct the idea of a collective identity linked to a political entity, which in that particular case is not national but supranational. However, the mechanisms used for the purpose of currency design are similar.

In the book, we saw how the iconography used in the design of banknotes and coins taps on and reproduces social meanings that are considered relevant in the public sphere of the countries – and political organizations, in the case of the EU – where they are used. Moreover, we tried to explain why these design elements produce effects of sense linked to the nation, the state and, more broadly, a community defined in political and/or cultural terms. Particularly, we were interested in how these design elements contribute to constructing a sense effect of community belonging.

As argued in Chapter 2, semiotics is a discipline that grows and advances when it is properly informed and sustained by empirical analyses. In this sense, the book tried to be as applied and as analytical as possible. In analytical terms, it should be clear how the eight currencies we studied are illustrative of the genre of currency design. More currencies – and, especially, from different geographical areas and even from past eras – could have been analysed. Since the world of currency is broad, and hundreds of corpora can be built, this task remains for future endeavours, either by the author or other researchers. As argued in Chapter 1, the eight currencies studied in the book should function as models that can inspire similar analyses of other currencies, both current and past.

Based on the commonalities we found in the currencies studied in the book, we can expect specific encyclopaedic repertoires to be found also on other currency systems, past, present or future. The current process of redesign of the euro banknotes is enlightening in this sense. The process has advanced as the writing of this book did, and at the time of the book going to press, two themes have been shortlisted, and motifs for each of them proposed. These motifs – 'European culture' and 'rivers and birds' – are 100 per cent aligned with the type of encyclopaedic contents we encountered in the currencies we worked with in the book.

In this sense, we could claim that the analysis of each of the selected currencies added something new to our project of developing a semiotic approach to currency design, for example, through the inclusion of a different type of design element or the use of a new discursive strategy. We began with a national currency telling a story of notable statesmen who constructed a great sovereign and independent nation and ended up studying a supranational currency in whose banknotes we encounter architectonical elements standing for ideas of community, dialogue and openness. In between, we saw how nature, institutions, allegories and different types of social domains were used for the purpose of community building.

In our analyses, we studied currency design synchronically. This means that our focus and interest were set on a specific moment of time, which is the present time. As mentioned above, so far, the author's research interests in the field of sociocultural semiotics have been mediated by the era we live in, as an effort to make sense of its sense-making dynamics. In the specific case of currency design, this means that we worked with currencies currently being used in the world, which still produce sense effects within the community of users.

This choice leaves aside two relevant issues. On the one hand, by focusing on the euro as the current currency of numerous European countries, we did not have access to discourses of the nation and the state in major countries of that continent, which were the pioneers in nation building. A deep dive into the currency systems used by EU countries in the past will certainly be a major contribution not only to the semiotics of currency design but also to the semiotics of national discourses, signs and identities.

Moreover, our synchronous approach focused on present currencies, leaving aside the historical dimension, which is always relevant to understand the functioning of the semiosphere in terms of cultural memory. Even if in our analyses we generally drew on past banknotes and coins to trace the design elements featured in those currently in use, tracing the changes of currency design and the semiotic resources used to decorate currency can only broaden our perspective and its exhaustivity. Such a diachronic perspective is necessary to fully grasp how the design of banknotes and coins serves to express and construct ideas of the nation. Moreover, it can allow to see how social discourses change over time and, with them, the standards of the discursive genre of currency design.

As mentioned in Chapter 1, a major hope we have for this book is that it can inspire and motivate researchers in the social sciences to study other currencies, both currently in use and from the past. Such a research line can only contribute to an interdisciplinary research programme grounded on a semiotic perspective.

Finally, it is worth repeating that the purpose of this book is double. On the one hand, it aims to contribute to the development of semiotic scholarship through the study of a specific discursive genre, which as we saw is strongly shaped by cultural conventions and practice. At the same time, it tries to make semiotics accessible to readers not necessarily familiar with the discipline. In this sense, a compromise had to be found between the level and detail of semiotic scholarship and the empirical work, so that anyone willing to read the book can do it successfully. I hope the final product is of quality and can satisfy readers from both groups.

In terms of semiotics' main categories, the reader should now be more or less convinced that banknotes and coins can be approached as texts. These texts are created by an institutional actor, which has specific intentions when creating them, linked to expressing contents that are relevant in terms of the nation and the state. In this act of enunciation, we can see the dynamics of discourse and culture at work: those texts express social discourses that circulate within the semiosphere and that are relevant to those involved in the process of signification, both as producers and as consumers.

For scholars interested in the functioning of discourse and culture, the question remains open regarding the encylopaedic repertoires that could be used for currency design. As seen throughout the book, a relatively stable set of repertoires is used for these purposes. However, could we expect to find in future banknotes of the Argentine peso portraits of popular idols such as Diego Maradona or Lionel Messi? In principle, this repertoire should not be excluded. To begin with, they are popularly praised. Moreover, they are celebrated by the state as national heroes since they contributed with their talent to Argentina's winning of international football competitions. Does the genre of currency design allow for the inclusion of such characters? What should change in the genre of currency design for this to be a valid option?

Some similar questions arise regarding elected heads of government. Would it be acceptable for an elected head of state, whose mandate is generally limited to four to five years, to include a depiction of him- or herself on banknotes and coins? What would be the line of what is acceptable or not? Questions like these relate directly to how societies make sense of specific practices such as currency design.

Also interesting for our semiotics of currency design would be to study the reception of design elements we encounter in currency, that is, how people actually feel about them, and how they contribute to construct a national imagined community. How do citizens receive and interpret these iconographic elements? How do they contribute to forging a sense of national identity and belonging? These questions remain open.

Another issue that remains open is the narrative construction of identity. In the analyses presented in the book we saw how series of banknotes somehow tell stories. The most prominent case is perhaps the US dollar, featuring heroes, institutional buildings and a specific historical moment on its banknotes. In the Canadian dollars, throughout history we see a story being told about the country. Regarding this point, a more detailed analysis of narrativity would be welcome, for example, drawing on Greimas's actantial model. All this remains to be done in future works.

Notes

Chapter 1

1 However, in the transition towards the hegemony of virtual money and the disappearance of cash that we are currently experiencing, the cashless tendency is still resistant in some countries such as Germany, where it is common to find shops that only take cash as a means of payment, and others where payments with card are only accepted above a specific amount. These different trends are a clear sign that we are living in a period of transition and cultural change where dominant, residual and emerging practices coexist.

2 On the process of redesign of the euro currently underway, cf. www.ecb.europa.eu/euro/banknotes/future_banknotes/redesign/html/index.en.html.

3 According to Turri (2014), during the nineteenth century, philosophers and economists usually worked in the domain of moral philosophy, which encompassed topics and issues that now belong distinctively to philosophy and economics, and that are now two distinct disciplines that originated in moral philosophy.

4 The origin of the listed elements in official discourse helps to understand why destroying or defacing public monuments can be approached as a semiotic practice aimed at challenging official history: attacking the text, what is being attacked is the discourse sustaining it and the sense attached to it.

5 I would like to thank Kristian Bankov for signalling the existence of a monograph in Bulgarian, written by Miroslav Dachev and titled *Семиотика на парите* (*Semiotics of Money*). Due to language reasons, I did not have access to reading this book.

Chapter 2

1 The inclusion of all these options as possibilities to refer to what semiotics is as a research venture is not random: it reflects some of the options to be found in the discussions about the nature of semiotics and semiotic research.

2 Along these, the name of American philosopher Charles S. Peirce is also notable within the discipline. However, his work on signs has been influential in a different semiotic tradition than the one we draw on here, which is the one stemming from European structural linguistics since we deem it more appropriate to study texts and

objects of material culture. For Peircean semiotics, cf. Traini (2006), Broden (2014), Santaella (2002) and Tiercelin (2002).

Chapter 3

1 In those cases where the relationship between the design elements included in the front and the reverse is not evident, the two sides of the banknote are nevertheless related, even if more abstractly, in the sense that we can expect whatever depicted on a banknote to be part of a semiosphere that has been segmented in national terms. This predictability is relevant in terms of the features of the discursive genre of currency design and allows for strategies of innovation and experimentation (which are clearly not common in the genre).
2 This is an interesting research topic that we will not address in the book. However, it would be very valuable to study how preferences for currency design elements in terms of format, fonts, iconography and so on can relate with the ideological definition of the government in charge of the state.
3 For Greimas (1989: 631), iconic systems are usually described as different from other sign systems 'because the recognizable relation they establish between the two modes of "reality" is not arbitrary but "motivated", because they presuppose a certain identity, total or partial, between the features and figures of the represented and the representing'.
4 The interesting question here is what sense is conveyed by the choice of this less iconic type of depiction. Perhaps the answer is based on the connotations of modernity and innovation that this type of depiction carries, as opposed to standard portraits, which can convey values of classicism and tradition. If we think of the representations and connotations associated with Dutch design in the social imaginary (for example, in the field of architecture), the choice for this innovative type of currency design could be read as a strategy to foster national identity in terms of innovation in design.

Chapter 4

1 For a chronology of the US dollar, cf. www.uscurrency.gov/history.
2 Cf. www.bep.gov/currency/history.
3 www.bep.gov/currency/currency-redesign.
4 www.usmint.gov/learn/coin-and-medal-programs/circulating-coins.
5 For the history of US coins, cf. www.usmint.gov/learn/history/us-circulating-coins.

6 According to the website uscurrency.gov, 'the United States government redesigns Federal Reserve notes primarily for security reasons: to stay ahead of counterfeiting threats and keep counterfeiting levels low. Because the $1 note is infrequently counterfeited, the government has no plans to redesign this note. In addition, there is a recurring provision in the annual Financial Services and General Government Appropriations Act that prohibits the redesign of the $1 note' (www.uscurrency.gov/sites/default/files/downloadable-materials/files/en/1-1963-present-features-en.pdf).

7 Cf. www.uscurrency.gov/history?period=2000s.

8 Many of the historical figures used in the current denominations were introduced in designs from 1914. Then, Lincoln, Grant and Franklin were introduced as the main figures of the $5, $50 and $100 notes, respectively. Hamilton was introduced in 1929. In the 1914 designs, the $10 note included a portrait of Andrew Jackson. In 1929, Jackson was moved to the $20 note, which before depicted Cleveland. The $2 note with the portrait of Jefferson was reintroduced in 1976, to mark Jefferson's 223rd anniversary. Before, his image was used in that note since 1918, and even in some designs of the same nominal value in the nineteenth century.

9 On this selection, Morris (1973: 2) writes:

> Why just these Seven? Indubitably a case could be made for Samuel Adams, James Wilson, John Dickinson, Robert Morris, Thomas Paine, Patrick Henry, George Mason, and perhaps half a dozen others whose contributions to the making or the winning of the Revolution were noteworthy. On one ground or another they have failed the triple tests of charismatic leadership, staying power, and constructive statesmanship that the Seven Founders chosen for this volume passed with flying colors [...] All the rest can be excluded on the ground that none filled the variety of high-level posts in state and nation that the Seven did, that none performed that amazing range of public services that stamp the Seven not only as indomitable but even exceptional in an age of versatility.

10 www.usmint.gov/learn/history/us-circulating-coins.

11 To learn more about the campaign, cf. www.womenon20s.org.

Chapter 5

1 Cf. www.bankofcanada.ca/banknotes/bank-note-series/vertical-series/our-next-20-bank-note.

2 Cf. www.bankofcanadamuseum.ca/complete-bank-note-series/2001-2006-canadian-journey-series.

3 Cf. www.bankofcanadamuseum.ca/complete-bank-note-series/1986-the-birds-of-canada-series.

4 Cf. www.bankofcanada.ca/banknotes/bank-note-series/vertical-series/our-next-20-bank-note.
5 An interesting consequence of considering past series is that we can see how depictions of the queen evolved, starting as a child and finally as an old woman. To see this evolution in coins, cf. www.mint.ca/en/discover/faces-of-the-monarch.
6 Cf. www.bankofcanadamuseum.ca/complete-bank-note-series/1954-canadian-landscape-series.
7 Cf. www.bankofcanadamuseum.ca/complete-bank-note-series/1954-canadian-landscape-series.
8 Cf. www.bankofcanadamuseum.ca/complete-bank-note-series/1986-the-birds-of-canada-series.
9 These four animals are the beaver, the caribou, the bear and the loon. The latter is depicted in the reverse of the C$1 coin and motivates the informal denomination of that coin as the 'loonie'. Using a morphological mechanism, some call the C$2 coin 'toonie', merging 'two' and 'loonie'.
10 To account for this type of collective identity, with Juan Manuel Montoro we proposed the category of 'geocultural identities'. These are cultural identities – as every identity is – but somehow grounded on the territorial dimension. Cf. Montoro and Moreno Barreneche (2021, 2024).
11 Cf. www.bankofcanadamuseum.ca/complete-bank-note-series/1969-1979-scenes-canada-series.
12 However, and curiously in a system where the banknotes are already differentiated by the portrait used in their fronts, the portrait of Queen Elizabeth II is used in three of the banknotes, two of which were later withdrawn, leaving her portrait as the main figure of the C$20 note only.
13 For the semiotics of war monuments and memorials, cf. Abousnnouga and Machin (2013).
14 Cf. www.bankofcanada.ca/banknotes/principles-bank-note-design/indigenous-advisory-circle.

Chapter 6

1 Cf. www.royalmint.com/corporate/circulating-coin/uk-currency/mintages/two-pounds.
2 Cf. www.royalmint.com/corporate/circulating-coin/uk-currency/mintages/two-pounds.
3 Although the elements that are part of the coat of arms are maintained, a new stylization is created upon the accession of a new monarch. Cf. www.gov.uk/government/news/new-coat-of-arms-artwork-unveiled.

4 For a historical timeline of pound sterling banknotes, cf. www.bankofengland.co.uk/banknotes/withdrawn-banknotes.
5 As the banknotes including the portrait of the queen did, the banknotes featuring King Charles III include the Royal Cypher, that is, the king's monogram, next to the portrait, combining the letters C and R. Although this is a sign expressing the institution of monarchy and standing for it, its meaning is less known than that of a crown.
6 On the relationship between Englishness and Britishness, cf. Kumar (2003).
7 www.bankofengland.co.uk/banknotes/polymer-50-pound-note.
8 www.bankofengland.co.uk/banknotes/banknote-characters.
9 For example, the minutes of the meetings that concluded with choosing Turner for the £20 note can be found here: www.bankofengland.co.uk/-/media/boe/files/banknotes/character-advisory-committee-minutes.pdf.

Chapter 7

1 Cf. www.snb.ch/en/the-snb/mandates-goals/cash/all-series/series-1#t10.
2 Cf. www.swissmint.ch/en.
3 www.snb.ch/en/publications/communication/press-releases/2005/pre_20050202.
4 The entries of the competition can be found here: www.snb.ch/en/the-snb/mandates-goals/cash/new-banknotes/project/results#.
5 The seventh series, produced in 1984, never entered in circulation. Cf. www.snb.ch/en/the-snb/mandates-goals/cash/all-series/series-7.
6 www.snb.ch/en/the-snb/mandates-goals/cash/new-banknotes/design/design-overview.
7 This could be explained based on Swiss political culture, which is strongly based on consensus since the country's origin and does not evidence a culture of personalization of politicians. In fact, the country does not have a standard head of state and government, but a collegium whose members rotate in power yearly.
8 In terms of sense and meaning, the opposition between /right/ and /left/ in the cases of presence of a single hand could be meaningful if this choice could be used to express some unit in the plane of content. However, in this particular case, it does not seem to be pertinent, just as the location of human figures of banknotes at the right or left of the designs, or where the profile of a character is looking at a coin design. This is a good example of how semioticians must identify relations and find arguments regarding their pertinence in terms of signification.
9 www.snb.ch/en/the-snb/mandates-goals/cash/new-banknotes/design/design-elements.

10 Cf. www.usmint.gov/learn/history/us-circulating-coins?srsltid=AfmBOooPjJWLmSH-VREHkXGNwPlouwVCXvOFJmjsNGzz0WAtj86DlWek.

Chapter 8

1 Cf. www.poder360.com.br/economia/nota-de-r-200-tem-flores-e-frutos-da-lobeira-que-compoem-dieta-do-lobo-guara.

2 We will come back to this issue in an upcoming chapter. For the time being, consider the sense effects of depicting a cow, horse, dog, sheep or cat on banknotes instead of the animals that are actually depicted.

3 As an example, 'Tropical Natural' is the name of the collection of artworks from various artists featured in the international arrival hall of Galeão airport in Rio de Janeiro. Cf. https://oglobo.globo.com/boa-viagem/veja-as-novas-pinturas-do-corredor-da-area-internacional-do-galeao-22871531.

Chapter 9

1 This was the case of the Uruguayan political party Cabildo Abierto, organized to compete in the 2019 national elections drawing heavily on the discourse of Artiguism (Moreno Barreneche, 2021).

2 For an interesting analysis of Artigas's face, cf. Leone (2019). For a semiotic analysis of Artigas and his discursive uses, cf. Atme and Andacht (2011).

3 An interesting case in this regard is the Chilean peso, the official currency of Chile. During the military dictatorship that ruled the country in the 1970s and 1980s, the government decided to feature poet Gabriela Mistral on one of the notes, leaving aside the other major name of Chilean literature: Pablo Neruda. Although the decision seemed to be justified by the fact that Mistral had been awarded a Nobel Prize in Literature, analysts claim that, since Neruda was a declared communist, the dictatorial regime would never celebrate him on currency. Cf. Venegas Cienfuegos (2018).

4 Here the noun 'Orientales' (Easterns) is used to refer to the Uruguayan people. Currently the country's official name is República Oriental del Uruguay, that is, the Republic to the East of the Uruguay river. While, at the time of Artigas's quote, Uruguay did not exist as an independent national state, the denomination of Uruguayans as Easterns (*orientales*) is still used.

Chapter 10

1 www.argentina.gob.ar/noticias/heroinas-y-heroes-de-nuestra-historia-vuelven-ilustrar-los-billetes-de-pesos-argentinos (my translation).
2 Semioticians and discourse analysts have argued how plural pronouns serve to model collective identities and actors in discourse (Verón, 1987; Fabbri, 2019; Scavino, 2020).
3 www.bcra.gob.ar/MediosPago/Nueva_familia_billetes.asp (my translation).
4 Cf. www.bcra.gob.ar/Noticias/Documental_Animales_Autoctonos.asp.
5 www.bcra.gob.ar/Noticias/Documental_Animales_Autoctonos.asp.
6 Despite the goodwill of avoiding new conflicts and proposing designs that could be accepted by anyone, the chosen animals also generated political controversy. As Sturzenegger points out in the tweet thread, 'before the 20-pesos note came out, the Chief of Staff [*Jefatura de Gabinete*] asked if we could backtrack, because there was a big lobby against the [...] guanaco. We said it was not possible. In Argentina, even animals can cause a gap'.
7 www.argentina.gob.ar/noticias/heroinas-y-heroes-de-nuestra-historia-vuelven-ilustrar-los-billetes-de-pesos-argentinos (my translation).
8 www.lanacion.com.ar/politica/el-lanzamiento-de-los-nuevos-billetes-en-vivo-nid23052022.

Chapter 11

1 www.ecb.europa.eu/euro/html/index.en.html.
2 www.ecb.europa.eu/euro/banknotes/future_banknotes/html/index.en.html.
3 Cf. www.ecb.europa.eu/euro/banknotes/future_banknotes/redesign/html/index.en.html#process.
4 Cf. www.ecb.europa.eu/euro/digital_euro/html/index.en.html.
5 As mentioned in the previous section, this will change in the upcoming years, since any of the two themes selected for the redesigns will forcefully introduce one of these design elements.
6 Cf. https://economy-finance.ec.europa.eu/euro/euro-coins-and-notes/euro-coins/national-sides-euro-coins_en.
7 Interestingly – and curiously – the town of Spijkenisse, in the Netherlands, recreated the bridges of the euro banknotes and created real functional bridges based on those portrayed there.
8 Cf. www.ecb.europa.eu/euro/banknotes/current/design/html/index.en.html.

9 If the theme of birds and rivers is finally chosen for the new designs of the euro banknotes, all these institutional buildings will be portrayed on the reverses, as indicated in Table 18.

10 www.ecb.europa.eu/euro/banknotes/current/html/index.en.html.

References

Abousnnouga, Gill, and Machin, David (2013). *The Language of War Monuments*. London: Bloomsbury.

Achugar, Hugo, and Caetano, Gerardo (1992). *Identidad uruguaya: ¿Mito, crisis o afirmación?* Montevideo: Trilce.

Aguerre, Lucía (2022). 'Civilización y barbarie en Sarmiento y Martí: continuidades y rupturas en la búsqueda del nuevo sujeto político'. *Ideas y Valores*, 180: 147–71.

Anderson, Benedict (1983). *Imagined Communities*. London: Verso.

Ares Pons, Roberto (2020). *Uruguay: ¿provincia o nación?* Montevideo: Biblioteca Artigas.

Aristotle (1998). *Politics*. Translated with introduction and notes by C. D. C. Reeve. Indianapolis: Hackett.

Atme, Martín, and Andacht, Fernando (2011). *El padre nuestro Artigas*. Montevideo: Estuario.

Baltensperge, Ernst, and Kugler, Peter (2017). *Swiss Monetary History since the Early 19th Century*. Cambridge: Cambridge University Press.

Bankov, Kristian (2019). 'From gold to futurity: A semiotic overview on trust, legal tender, and fiat money'. *Social Semiotics*, 29(3): 336–50.

Bankov, Kristian (2022). 'Exploring Saussure's analogy between linguistic and monetary signs'. *Language and Semiotic Studies*, 8(1): 114–22.

Barbieri, Daniele (2017). *Semiotica del fumetto*. Rome: Carocci.

Barreto Bogo, Marc; Migliore, Tiziana, and Paris, Orlando (2025). *Riscrivere le città. Semiotica della street art per le politiche sociali*. Rome: Carocci.

Barthes, Roland (1964). 'Rhétorique de l'image'. *Communications*, 4: 40–51.

Barthes, Roland (1977). *Image Music Text*. London: Fontana Press.

Basso Fossali, Pierluigi, and Dondero, Maria Giulia (2011). *Sémiotique de la photographie*. Limoges: Pulim.

Benedetti, Alejandro, and Eguren Zambrano, Lucas (2025). 'El mapa bicontinental como representación oficial del territorio de la República Argentina'. *Boletín geográfico*, 47: 1–30.

Benveniste, Émile (1966). *Problèmes de linguistique générale, I*. Paris: Gallimard.

Benveniste, Émile (1974). *Problèmes de linguistique générale, II*. Paris: Gallimard.

Bernd, Zilá (2018). 'Redéfinir l'identité canadienne en termes de communautés de mémoire'. *Études Canadiennes*, 83: 133–45.

Bettoni, Giuseppe (2021). 'Geopolitics and images: From images to discourse', in Francesco Mangiapane and Tiziana Migliore (eds), *Images of Europe*, 69–89. Cham: Springer.

Billig, Michael (1995). *Banal Nationalism*. London: Sage.

Blaazer, David (1999). 'Reading the notes: Thoughts on the meanings of British paper money'. *Humanities Research*, 1: 39–54.

Blaazer, David (2002). 'Sterling identities'. *History Today*, 52: 12–18.

Blaazer, David (2016). 'Mainstreaming money: Perspectives on currency in the history of the British Isles'. *History Australia*, 13(1): 52–66.

Broden, Thomas F. (2014). 'La sémiotique greimassiene et la sémiotique peirceinne: Visées, principes et théories su signe'. *Estudos Semióticos*, 10(2): 1–16.

Buarque de Holanda, Sérgio (1995). *Raízes do Brasil*. São Paulo: Companhia das Letras.

Buarque de Holanda, Sérgio (2000). *Visões do paraíso*. São Paulo: Brasiliense/Publifolha.

Caetano, Gerardo (2010). 'Ciudadanía y nación en el Uruguay del Centenario (1910–1930): La forja de una cultura estatista'. *Iberoamericana*, 39: 161–76.

Candido, Antônio (1970). 'Dialética da Malandragem (caracterização das Memórias de um sargento de milícias)'. *Revista do Instituto de Estudos Brasileiros*, 8: 67–89.

Cerulo, Karen A. (1995). *Identity Designs: The Sights and Sounds of a Nation*. New Brunswick: Rutgers University Press.

Cigena, Daniel (2022). 'Polémica por los billetes: historiadoras y escritoras opinan sobre las nuevas "heroínas"'. *La Nación*, 24 May. www.lanacion.com.ar/cultura/polemica-por-los-billetes-historiadoras-y-escritoras-opinan-sobre-las-nuevas-heroinas-nid24052022.

Coratelli, Giorgio, Galofaro, Francesco and Montanari, Federico (2015). 'Introduction: On semiotics of economic discourse'. *Ocula*, 16: 1–9.

Corrain, Lucia (ed.) (2004). *Semiotiche della pittura. I classici. Le ricerche*. Rome: Meltemi.

Costa, Guilherme Ribeiro Tardin (2011). *O design das cédulas brasileiras do cruzeiro ao real (1970–2010)*. Masters diss., Escola Superior de Desenho Industrial, Universidade do Estado do Rio de Janeiro.

Davies, Glyn (2002). *A History of Money. From Ancient Times to Present Day*. Cardiff: University of Wales Press.

de Gennaro, Faustina (2016). 'Los billetes cuentan'. *LIS. Letra. Imagen. Sonido*, 16: 213–30.

de Heij, Hans (2012). *Designing Banknote Identity*. Amsterdam: de Nederlandsche Bank.

de Saussure, Ferdinand (1959). *Course in General Linguistics*. New York: Columbia University Press.

Demaria, Cristina (2006). *Semiotica della memoria*. Rome: Carocci.

Demuru, Paolo (2015). 'Malandragem vs Arte di arrangiarsi: Stili di vita e forme dell'aggiustamento tra Brasile e Italia'. *Actes Sémiotiques*, 118.

Diez, Thomas (2004). 'Europe's others and the return of geopolitics'. *Cambridge Review of International Affairs*, 17(2): 319–35.

Dittmar, Jakob (2009). 'British coins: Minting a national pictorial programme', in Anton Kirchhofer and Jutta Schwarzkopf (eds), *The Workings of the Anglosphere. Contributions to the Study of British and US-American Cultures*, 193–201. Trier: Wissenschaftlicher Verlag Trier.

Dodd, Nigel (1994). *The Sociology of Money: Economics, Reason, and Contemporary Society*. Cambridge: Polity Press.

Dondero, Maria Giulia (2020). *The Language of Images*. Cham: Springer.

Eco, Umberto (1975). *A Theory of Semiotics*. Bloomington: Indiana University Press.

Edensor, Tim (2002). *National Identity, Popular Culture and Everyday Life*. Oxford: Berg.

Eich, Stefan (2022). *The Currency of Politics. The Political Theory of Money from Aristotle to Keynes*. Princeton: Princeton University Press.

Fabbri, Paolo (2019). 'Identidades colectivas'. *DeSignis*, 31: 285–9.

Ferguson, Nial (2019). *The Ascent of Money. A Financial History of the World*. London: Penguin.

Fernandes, Amaury (2008). *Uma etnografia do dinheiro. Os projetos gráficos de papel-moeda no Brasil após 1960*. PhD diss., Instituto de Filosofia e Ciências Humanas, Universidade do Estado do Rio de Janeiro.

Floch, Jean-Marie (1985). *Petites mythologies de l'œil et de l'esprit*. Paris: Hadis/ Benjamin.

Floch, Jean-Marie (1986). *Les formes de l'empreinte*. Périgueux: Fanlac.

Floch, Jean-Marie (1990). *Sémiotique, Marketing et Communication*. Paris: Presses Universitaires de France.

Floch, Jean-Marie (1995). *Identités visuelles*. Paris: Presses Universitaires de France.

Fontanille, Jacques (2008). *Pratiques sémiotiques*. Paris: Presses Universitaires de France.

Fontanille, Jacques (2015). *Formes de vie*. Liège: Presses Universitaires de Liege.

Fornäs, Johan (2012). *Signifying Europe*. London: Intellect Books.

Fornäs, Johan (2017). 'A cultural perspective on European borders', in Matts Andrén (ed.), *Cultural Borders and European Integration*, 7–20. Gothenburg: Center for European Research at the University of Gothenburg.

Francis, Daniel (1997). *National Dreams. Myth, Memory and Canadian History*. Vancouver: Arsenal Pulp Press.

Freyre, Gilberto (2001). *Brazil: An Interpretation*. New York: Knopf.

Gabriel, Gottfried (2016). 'Ästhetik und Rhetorik des Geldes', in Stephan Hartmann and Christian Thiel (eds), *Der schöne Schein. Symbolik und Ästhetik von Banknoten*. Augsburg: Battenberg Gietl Verlag.

Geertz, Clifford (1973). *The Interpretation of Cultures*. New York: Basic Books.

Gellner, Ernest (1983). *Nations and Nationalism*. Oxford: Blackwell.

Gilbert, Emily (1998). 'Ornamenting the façade of hell: Iconographies of 19th-century Canadian paper money'. *Environment and Planning D: Society and Space*, 16: 57–80.

Gilbert, Emily (1999). 'Forging a national currency: Money, state-making and nation-building in Canada', in Emily Gilbert and Eric Helleiner (eds), *Nation-States*

and Money: The Past, Present and Future of National Currencies, 23–44. New York: Routledge.
Gilbert, Emily, and Helleiner, Eric (eds) (1999). *National-States and Money: The Past, Present and Future of National Currencies*. London: Routledge.
Gimeno-Martínez, Javier (2016). *Design and National Identity*. London: Bloomsbury.
Gorin, Martin (1989). 'Présentation'. *Communications*, 50: 5–6.
Greimas, Algirdas J. (1983). *Du sens II*. Paris: Seuil.
Greimas, Algirdas J. (1986). *Sémantique structurale*. Paris: Presses Universitaires de France.
Greimas, Algirdas J. (1989). 'Figurative semiotics and the semiotics of the plastic arts'. *New Literary History*, 20(3): 627–49.
Grimson, Alejandro (2019). *¿Qué es el peronismo?* Buenos Aires: Siglo XXI.
Groupe μ (1992). *Traité du signe visuel*. Paris: du Seuil.
Hall, Edward T. (1966). *The Hidden Dimension*. New York: Anchor Books.
Hartmann, Stefan, and Thiel, Christian (eds) (2016). *Der schöne Schein. Symbolik und Ästhetik von Banknoten*. Augsburg: Battenberg Gietl Verlag.
Haver, Gianni (2013). 'Dame à l'antique avec lance et bouclier: Helvetia et ses déclinaisons', in M.-O. Gonseth, B. Knodel, Y. Laville and G. Mayor (eds), *Hors-champs. Eclats du patrimoine culturel immatériel*, 274–82. Neuchâtel: Musée d'ethnographie de Neuchâtel.
Helleiner, Eric (1998). 'Electronic money: A challenge to the sovereign state?' *Journal of International Affairs*, 51(2): 387–409.
Helleiner, Eric (2003). *The Making of National Money*. Ithaca: Cornell University Press.
Hentschke, Jens. R. (2012). 'Artiguista, white, cosmopolitan and educated: Constructions of nationhood in Uruguayan textbooks and related narratives: 1868–1915'. *Journal of Latin American Studies*, 44(4): 733–64.
Hewitt, Virginia (1994). *Beauty and the Banknote: Images of Women on Paper Money*. London: British Museum Press.
Hewitt, Virginia (1995). *The Banker's Art: Studies in Paper Money*. London: British Museum Press.
Hewitt, Virginia (1999). 'A distant view. Imagery and imagination in the paper currency of the British Empire, 1800–1960', in Emily Gilbert and Eric Helleiner (eds), Nation-States and Money: The Past, Present and Future of National Currencies, 97–116. New York: Routledge.
Hewitt, Virginia, and Keyworth, John M. (1987). *As Good as Gold. 300 Years of British Bank Note Design*. London: British Museum Press.
Hjelmslev, Louis (1947). *Prolegomena to a Theory of Language*. Madison: Wisconsin University Press.
Hobsbawm, Eric (1991). *Nations and Nationalism since 1780: Programme, Myth, Reality*. Cambridge: Cambridge University Press.
Hobsbawm, Eric, and Ranger, Terence (eds) (1983). *The Invention of Tradition*. Cambridge: Cambridge University Press.

Hodge, Robert, and Kress, Gunther (1989). *Social Semiotics*. London: Polity Press.

Hymans, Jacques E. C. (2004). 'The changing colour of money: European currency iconography and collective identity'. *European Journal of International Relations*, 10(1): 5–31.

Jürg, Willi, and Dubach, Margaretha (1998). *Das wahre Leben der Helvetia*. Zurich: Haffmans.

Kreis, Georg (1991). *Helvetia im Wandel der Zeiten. Die Geschichte einer nationalen Repräsentationsfigur*. Zurich: NZZ.

Kress, Gunther, and van Leeuwen, Theo (2001). *Reading Images. The Grammar of Visual Design*. London: Routledge.

Kumar, Krishan (2003). *The Making of English National Identity*. Cambridge: Cambridge University Press.

Lagopoulos, Alexandros, and Boklund-Lagopoulou, Karin (2021). *Theory and Methodology of Semiotics. The Tradition of Ferdinand de Saussure*. Berlin: De Gruyter.

Lagopoulos, Alexandros, Boklund-Lagopoulos, Karin, Dondero, Maria Giulia, Fontanille, Jacques, Katsaridou, Maria and Walldén, Rea (2025). *Semiotics of Images. The Analysis of Pictorial Texts*. Berlin: De Gruyter.

Le Jeune, François (2023). 'État des lieux de la recherche sur le multiculturalisme canadien'. *Études Canadiennes*, 95: 9–42.

Leone, Massimo (2019). 'Rostros populares, rostros populistas: para una semiótica de la efigie heroica (el caso de José Gervasio Artigas)'. *DeSignis*, 31: 171–9.

Lévi-Strauss, Claude (1958). *Anthropologie structurale*. Paris: PLON.

Levitsky, Stephen, and Ziblatt, Daniel (2018). *How Democracies Die*. London: Penguin.

Lorusso, Anna Maria (2010). *Semiotica della cultura*. Bari: Laterza.

Lorusso, Anna Maria (2015). *Cultural Semiotics*. Basingstoke: Palgrave Macmillan.

Lotman, Jurij (1998). 'La memoria de la cultura', in *La semiosfera, II*, 152–62. Madrid: Cátedra.

Lotman, Jurij (2005). 'On the semiosphere'. *Sign System Studies*, 33(1): 205–29.

Lusane, Clarence (2022). *Twenty Dollars and Change. Harriet Tubman and the Ongoing Fight for Racial Justice and democracy*. N.p.: City Lights.

Maissen, Thomas (2001). 'Die Schöpfung der Helvetia in der bildenden Kunst und in der Dichtung', in Stefan Hess and Tomas Lochman (eds), *Basilea. Ein Beispiel städtischer Repräsentation in weiblicher Gestalt*, 84–101. Basel: Schwabe.

Manchia, Valentina (2020). *Il discorso dei dati. Note semiotiche sulla visualizzazione delle informazioni*. Milano: Franco Angeli.

Mangano, Dario (2018). *Che cos'è la semiotica della fotografia*. Rome: Carocci.

Marrone, Gianfranco (ed.) (2012). *Semiotica della natura, natura della semiotica*. Milano: Mimesis.

Marrone, Gianfranco (2021). *Introduction to the Semiotics of the Text*. Berlin: DeGruyter.

McGinley, Christina L. (1993). 'Coining nationality: Woman as spectacle on 19th century currency'. *American Transcendental Quarterly*, 7(3): 247–69.

Migliore, Tiziana (2021). 'A proper name for a proper union. Europe's mythological model', in Francesco Mangiapane and Tiziana Migliore (eds), *Images of Europe*, 27–45. Cham: Springer.

Migliore, Tiziana, and Colas-Blaise, Marion (2022). *Semiotica del formato*. Milano: Mimesis.

Millard, Laura (1993). 'Images of Canada. Canadian bank notes'. *Border/Lines*, 28: 30–2.

Monestier, Martin (1982). *L'Art du papier monnaie*. Paris: Éditions du Pont Neuf.

Montoro, Juan Manuel, and Moreno Barreneche, Sebastián (2021). 'Towards a social semiotics of geo-cultural identities. Theoretical foundations and an initial semiotic square'. *Estudos Semióticos*, 17(2): 121–43.

Montoro, Juan Manuel, and Moreno Barreneche, Sebastián (2025). 'Identidades geoculturales: propuesta para el abordaje de la identificación con el espacio geográfico desde la semiótica sociocultural', in Sabine Pfleger and Eduardo Chávez Herrera (eds), *Identidades en la modernidad tardía*, 108–28. Ciudad de México: ENALT.

Moreno Barreneche, Sebastián (2021). 'Artiguismo, restauración y usos estratégicos del pasado. La construcción discursiva de la identidad colectiva asociada al partido Cabildo Abierto'. *Cuadernos del CLAEH*, 113: 11–34.

Moreno Barreneche, Sebastián (2023a). 'Is social semiotics a unitary research field? An introductory and comparative mapping of Argentinean, Brazilian, French, Italian and English-speaking semiotic approaches to social meaning-making'. *Estudos Semióticos*, 19(3): 56–79.

Moreno Barreneche, Sebastián (2023b). *The Social Semiotics of Populism*. London: Bloomsbury.

Moreno Barreneche, Sebastián (2023c). 'Values: A core component in the discursive construction of Europe and the EU'. *Social Semiotics*, 33(4): 686–93.

Moreno Barreneche, Sebastián (2025). 'Los (muy formales) rostros de la cultura. Sentidos de la identidad nacional en los billetes del peso uruguayo'. *Inmediaciones de la Comunicación*, 20(2).

Morris, Richard B. (1973). *Seven Who Shaped Our Destiny. The Founding Fathers as Revolutionaries*. New York: Harper and Row.

Mugnaini, Fabio (1994). 'Messages sur billets de banque: la monnaie comme mode d'échange et de communication'. *Terrain*, 23: 63–80.

Müller, Felix (2024). *Helvetia und die Helvetier. Eine Spurensuche*. Zurich: Chronos.

Murilo de Carvalho, José (1990). *A formação das almas*. São Paulo: Companhia das Letras.

Navarro, Marysa (ed.) (2013). *Evita. Mitos y representaciones*. Buenos Aires: Fondo de Cultura Económica.

North, Michael (2009). *Kleine Geschichte des Geldes. Von Mittelalter bis heute.* Munich: C. H. Beck.

Oakley, Todd, and Zlatev, Jordan (2024). 'Origins of money: A motivation & sedimentation model (MSM) analysis'. *Semiotica*, 257: 1–27.

Olaya, Marcos (2007). 'Civilización y barbarie. Dos interpretaciones del rol letrado frente al proyecto modernizador en América Latina: Sarmiento y Martí'. *Cuyo. Anuario de Filosofía Argentina y Americana*, 24: 187–204.

Palmer, Catherine (1998). 'From theory to practice. Experiencing the nation in everyday life'. *Journal of Material Culture*, 3(2): 175–9.

Paolucci, Claudio (2021a). *Cognitive Semiotics. Integrating Signs, Minds, Meaning and Cognition*. Cham: Springer.

Paolucci, Claudio (2021b). 'European identity and the sexual function of Erasmus program. Nomadism, bilingualism and "Swiss language"', in Francesco Mangiapane and Tiziana Migliore (eds), *Images of Europe*, 47–58. Cham: Springer.

Peirce, Charles S. (2020). *Selected Writings on Semiotics, 1894–1912*. Berlin: De Gruyter.

Penrose, Jan (2011). 'Designing the nation. Banknotes, banal nationalism and alternative conceptions of the state'. *Political Geography*, 30: 429–40.

Penrose, Jan, and Cumming, Craig (2011). 'Money talks: Banknote iconography and symbolic constructions of Scotland'. *Nations and Nationalism*, 17(4): 821–42.

Perusset, Alain (2020). *Sémiotique des formes de vie*. Louvain-la-Neuve: De Boeck.

Raento, Pauliina, Hämäläinen, Anna, Ikonen, Hanna and Mikkonen, Nella (2004). 'Striking stories: A political geography of Euro coinage'. *Political Geography*, 23: 929–56.

Raoulx, Benoit (2022). 'De la "région" au "territoire". Quelques repères pour penser la mise en mots de l'espace canadien'. *Études canadiennes/Canadian Studies*, 92: 9–39.

Rastier, François (2005). 'Deniers and the golden calf: From fetishes to idols'. *Semiotica*, 154: 95–126.

Ribeiro, Darcy (1995). *O povo brasileiro*. São Paulo: Global.

Risse, Thomas (2003). 'The Euro between national and European identity'. *Journal of European Public Policy*, 10(4): 487–505.

Risse, Thomas (2011). *A Community of Europeans? Transnational Identities and Public Spheres*. Ithaca: Cornell University Press.

Rosano, Susana (2006). *Rostros y máscaras de Eva Perón. Imaginario populista y representación*. Rosario: Beatriz Viterbo.

Rossi, Pietro (2007). *L'identità dell'Europa*. Bologna: Il Mulino.

Sachs-Hombach, Klaus (ed.) (2021). *Bildwissenschaft. Disziplinen, Themen, Methoden*. Frankfurt: Suhrkamp.

Santaella, Lucia (2002). 'Introduction: La mise en oeuvre de la sémiotique de Peirce. Difficultés et stratégies', in Anne Hénault (dir.), *Questions de sémiotique*, 433–44. Paris: Presses Universitaires de France.

Sassatelli, Monica (2017). '"Europe in your pocket": Narratives of identity in euro iconography'. *Journal of Contemporary European Studies*, 25(3): 354–66.

Sassattelli, Monica (2021). 'Europe's cosmopolitan identity: Images of unity in diversity in the euro', in Francesco Mangiapane and Tiziana Migliore (eds), *Images of Europe*, 195–208. Cham: Springer.
Scavino, Dardo (2020). 'El "nosotros" político: un "yo" caracterizado'. *DeSignis*, 33: 159–65.
Searle, John (1995). *The Construction of Social Reality*. London: Penguin.
Sebreli, Juan José (2008). *Comediantes y mártires*. Buenos Aires: Debate.
Sedda, Franciscu (2021). 'National self-determination and the limits of Europe', in Francesco Mangiapane and Tiziana Migliore (eds), *Images of Europe*, 123–40. Cham: Springer.
Simmel, George (1978). *The Philosophy of Money*. London: Routledge.
Skey, Michael (2013). *National Belonging and Everyday Life: The Significance of Nationhood in an Uncertain World*. Basingstoke: Palgrave Macmillan.
Skey, Michael, and Antonsich, Marco (2017). *Everyday Nationhood. Theorising Culture, Identity and Belonging after Banal Nationalism*. Basingstoke: Palgrave Macmillan.
Smith, Anthony D. (1991). *National Identity*. Reno: University of Nevada Press.
Smith, Anthony D. (2004). *The Antiquity of Nations*. London: Polity.
Spufford, Peter (1988). *Money and Its Use in Medieval Europe*. Cambridge: Cambridge University Press.
Standish, David, and Dunn, Joshua (2000). *The Art of Money: The History and Design of Paper Currency from around the World*. San Francisco: Chronicle Books.
Tajfel, Henri (1982). 'Social psychology of intergroup relations'. *Annual Review of Psychology*, 33: 1–39.
Thiesse, Anne-Marie (1999). *La création des identités nationales. Europe XVIIIe–XXe siècle*. Paris: du Seuil.
Thiesse, Anne-Marie (2000). 'Des fictions créatrices: les identités nationales'. *Romantisme*, 30(110): 51–62.
Tiercelin, Claudine (2002). 'La sémiotique philosophique de Charles Sanders Peirce', in Anne Hénault (dir.), *Questions de sémiotique*, 15–52. Paris: Presses Universitaires de France.
Traini, Stefano (2006). *Le due vie della semiotica*. Milano: Bompiani.
Tschachler, Heinz (2001). 'Dollar bill', in Dennis R. Hall and Susan Grove Hall (eds), *American Icons: An Encyclopedia of the People, Places, and Things that Have Shaped Our Culture*, vol. I, 205–12. Westport: Greenwood Press.
Tschachler, Heinz (2010). *The Greenback: Paper Money and American Culture*. Boston: McFarland.
Turri, Maria Grazia (2009). *La distinzione fra moneta e denaro*. Rome: Carocci.
Turri, Maria Grazia (2014). 'Dal denaro alla moneta. Oggetti sociali e linguaggio'. *Rivista Italiana di Filosofia del Linguaggio*. n.pag.
UNESCO (1972). 'Convention concerning the protection of the world cultural and natural heritage'. https://whc.unesco.org/en/conventiontext.

UNESCO (1982). 'Mexico City declaration on cultural policies'. www.lacult.unesco.org/docc/1982_MONDIACULT.pdf.
Unwin, Tim, and Hewitt, Virginia (2001). 'Banknotes and national identity in Central and Eastern Europe'. *Political Geography*, 20: 1005–28.
Urdapilleta-Muñoz, Marco, and Núñez-Villavicencio, Herminio (2014). 'Civilización y barbarie. Ideas acerca de la identidad latinoamericana'. *La Colmena*, 82: 31–40.
van Leeuwen, Theo (2005). *Introducing Social Semiotics*. London: Routledge.
Venegas Cienfuegos, Martín (2018). 'Identidad nacional en los billetes del bicentenario chileno'. *LIS. Letra, Imagen, Sonido*, 19: 40–54.
Verón, Eliseo (1987). 'La palabra adversativa. Observaciones sobre la enunciación política', in Eliseo Verón, Leonor Arfuch, María Magdalena Chirico, Emilio de Ipola, Noemí Goldman, M. Inés González Bombal and Oscar Landi (eds), *El discurso político. Lenguajes y acontecimientos*, 13–26. Buenos Aires: Hachette.
Verón, Eliseo (1988). *La semiosis social*. Barcelona: Gedisa.
Violi, Patrizia (2014). *Paesaggi della memoria*. Milano: Bompiani.
Volkova Americo, Ekaterina (2017). 'O conceito de fronteira na semiótica de Iúri Lotman'. *Bakhtiniana*, 12(1): 5–20.
Walkenhorst, Heiko (2009). 'The conceptual spectrum of European identity'. *Limerick Papers in Politics and Public Administration*, 3: 1–22.
Weatherford, Jack (1997). *The History of Money. From Sandstone to Cyberspace*. New York: Crown.
Wennerlind, Carl (2001). 'Money talks, but what is it saying? Semiotics of money and social control'. *Journal of Economic Issues*, 35(3): 557–74.
Williams, Raymond (1973). *The Country and the City*. New York: Oxford University Press.
Williams, Raymond (1976). *Keywords*. New York: Oxford University Press.
Zelizer, Viviana (2017). *The Social Meaning of Money*. New York: Basic Books.
Zielonka, Jan (ed.) (2002). *Europe Unbound. Enlarging and Reshaping the Boundaries of the European Union*. London: Routledge.

Index

www.ingramcontent.com/pod-product-compliance
Ingram Content Group UK Ltd.
Pitfield, Milton Keynes, MK11 3LW, UK
UKHW020247290926
15470UKWH00002B/783